Service-Learning and The First-Year Experience:

Preparing Students for Personal Success and Civic Responsibility

Edward Zlotkowski

Editor

NATIONAL RESOURCE CENTER
FOR THE FIRST-YEAR EXPERIENCE®
& STUDENTS IN TRANSITION
UNIVERSITY OF SOUTH CAROLINA, 2002

Campus Compact

Cite as:

      Zlotkowski, E. (Ed.). (2002). *Service-Learning and the First-Year Experience: Preparing Students for Personal Success and Civic Responsibility* (Monograph No. 34). Columbia, SC: University of South Carolina, National Resource Center for The First-Year Experience and Students in Transition.

Sample chapter citation:

      Duckenfield, M. (2002). Look who's coming to college: The impact of high school service-learning on new college students. In E. Zlotkowski (Ed.), *Service-Learning and the First-Year Experience: Preparing Students for Personal Success and Civic Responsibility* (Monograph No. 34) (pp. 39-50). Columbia, SC: University of South Carolina, National Resource Center for The First-Year Experience and Students in Transition.

The Freshman Year Experience® and The First-Year Experience® are service marks of the University of South Carolina. A license may be granted upon written request to use the terms The Freshman Year Experience and The First-Year Experience. This license is not transferrable without written approval of the University of South Carolina.

Additional copies of this monograph may be obtained from the National Resource Center for The First-Year Experience and Students in Transition, University of South Carolina, 1629 Pendleton Street, Columbia, SC 29208. Telephone (803) 777-6029. Telefax (803) 777-4699.

Special gratitude is expressed to Scott Slawinski, Editorial Assistant for copy editing, Sarah Huxford, Composition Assistant for layout and design; Lark Patterson and Amy Murray, Editorial Assistants for proofing; Holli Armstrong, Editorial Assistant for composition assistance, and Tracy Skipper, Editorial Projects Coordinator for project management and copy editing.

Service-learning and the first-year experience : preparing students for personal success and civic responsibility / Edward Zlotkowski, editor.

    p. cm. -- (The first-year experience monograph series ; no. 34)
    Includes bibliographic references.
    ISBN 1-889271-38-1 (alk. paper)
    1. Student service--United States--Case studies. 2. College freshmen--United States--Conduct of life. 3. College student development programs--United States--Case studies. I. Zlotkowski, Edward A., 1944- II. Series.

LC220.5 .S455 2002
361.3'7--dc21

                                                 2002012088

Contents

Section IV:
Summing Things Up

Preface

John N. Gardner

It has fallen to me, thanks to Edward Zlotkowski's invitation, to offer a preface for this volume. I requested that Zlotkowski develop this monograph, but I did not anticipate how much I was going to learn from the project. I thought I already knew a great deal about service-learning and its special application to the first year of college.

Zlotkowski's work over the decade of the '90s and beyond parallels my own, both of us building on our careers as teaching faculty and reaching beyond our own campuses to teach new pedagogues to faculty and student affairs colleagues alike. Both of us realized that we could improve student learning by forming strategic partnerships and alliances with other higher education colleagues. Our work exists in a culture where the greatest rewards flow to those who spend proportionately far more time on their own learning and its scholarly documentation than on the learning of their students. There are natural similarities in our respective initiatives and those of our colleagues interested in such areas as the development of first-year seminars and learning communities, improved partnerships between academic and student affairs colleagues, connecting campuses to their host communities through the performance of service, and using the first year of college as a more intentional foundation for desirable outcomes such as an enhanced emphasis on service and civic engagement.

As a result of my exposure to Zlotkowski's work in the early 1990s, as well as my direct involvement as a member of the Board of Trustees of The International Partnership for Service-Learning, I concluded that I could strengthen the University of South Carolina's first-year seminar, University 101, which I directed from 1974-1999, though the integration of service-learning. University 101 incorporated service-learning in 1995, but my reading of this monograph highlighted a number of ways in which that effort could have been enhanced. In retrospect, I believe that we could have given our faculty more assistance and support with designing service-learning initiatives. We could have articulated more clearly the potential connections between service-learning, the first-year seminar, and our institutional mission statement. And we were totally oblivious to the extent of prior service-learning in which our students might have been engaged and the implications of that experience for their continued service activities in college.

The Intersections Between Two Reform Movements

As you read this monograph, you will likely be struck by the many connections between service-learning and the first year-experience. I am particularly encouraged by how service-learning might address what I believe is the "unfinished reform agenda" of the first-year experience movement. In an address to the 2001 National Conference on The First-Year Experience, I argued that in spite of our successes, we still have an unfinished agenda composed of a number of key issues, the first of which is the continuing high level of failure and attrition in the first year.

In their chapter, based on their experiences at Indiana University-Purdue University at Indianapolis (IUPUI), Hatcher, Bringle, and Muthiah make a compelling case for the obvious linkages among (a) programs that seek to foster student retention, (b) campus environments focused on the success of first-year students, (c) efforts to focus students more intentionally on civic engagement and meaningful service experiences, and (d) the research related thereto. Similarly, in this monograph's important chapter on "Service-Learning and the First-Year Experience: Outcomes Related to Learning and Persistence," the authors/researchers from the University of California, Los Angeles, cite the finding that service, particularly on a general level, is positively correlated with retention. And they note that in a second-year pilot study, "Your First College Year," first-year students who participated in service reported higher levels of satisfaction with various levels of campus life and that the differences were greatest for students who participated in course-based service-learning (where, for example, they may have more contact with faculty outside of class).

A second issue in this unfinished agenda is that too many innovative first-year programs and educators are marginalized; the first-year reform movement is not one primarily of faculty, even though it is more than 20 years old. This disturbing fact is another reason I am excited about service-learning, which, by definition, is incorporated into credit-bearing courses and hence involves faculty who are perceived to be less marginalized than many non-faculty participants in first-year experience programs. Thus, service-learning is one way to move first-year initiatives from the periphery to the academic mainstream. Service-learning is a concept that proponents can employ significantly to broaden the conversation about the importance of the first college year, including a variety of individuals and groups in that conversation—the institution's president and chief academic officer, the faculty, as well as student affairs colleagues. This concept can also serve as a catalyst to mobilize a wide range of constituents concerned about the first year of college.

In my address, I also maintained that our unfinished agenda has failed to grapple with the fact that not all students see the need for some type of intentional first-year experience. Likewise, chapter authors in this monograph do not all agree that service-learning should be a mandatory component of the first college year, particularly in light of the challenges in delivering a quality service-learning experience to adult and part-time students. However, service-learning provides an alternative first-year experience that some might deem more worthwhile than a first-year orientation course and that may have many of the same positive outcomes.

Thus, I believe service-learning strengthens the chances that more campuses will come to a consensus on some type of desirable first-year learning experience using many similar pedagogies of engagement.

In a parallel vein, I observed that the first year continues to be conceptualized in terms of the archetypal 18-year-old, full time, residential male student, as opposed to the majority: female commuting students of all ages and hues. In addition to our colleagues at IUPUI, Tom O'Connell makes a compelling case in his chapter for how to bring service-learning to the adult learner (and how not to do so), thus addressing the needs of a growing population at many campuses. Without such initiatives, adult students might be neglected due to their absence from other, more widespread first-year programmatic interventions.

I also noted that the issue of assessment continues to need our attention. Assessment is not practiced throughout first-year experience activities, and even at those institutions where assessment is practiced, decisions are often made without considering assessment findings. Several chapters in this monograph note the role of assessment in designing, refining, and institutionalizing service-learning programs for first-year students. You will find that this work offers compelling testimony about the ways in which service-learning contributes to first-year student success.

Another issue in this unfinished agenda is that the first-year experience is often not intentional enough in promoting enhanced student learning. While service-learning is designed to promote a number of meritorious objectives, it is clear from a reading of this volume that service-learning's overriding intentional objective is the improvement of student learning in the formal curriculum. To the extent that service experiences can be a more intentional construct for the first year of college, the enhancement of first-year student learning will have been achieved.

Further, the first year on many campuses is still not explicitly linked to institutional mission statements and to desired outcomes of the senior year. This monograph provides multiple examples of how service-learning can make our campuses more mission-intentional in and through concrete practices. In this regard, Frankle and Ajanaku's chapter is especially interesting, for it illustrates compellingly how service-learning can bring to fruition the service traditions of many of our campuses. Regional accrediting bodies exercise considerable influence on institutions of higher learning to be more focused on delivering the promises inherent in their mission statements; service-learning offers a powerful way to achieve this.

In short, a major issue in our unfinished agenda is what happens beyond the first year. Currently, we still pull the plug too soon on first-year support and thus create a self-fulfilling prophecy that ensures a second-year slump. The chapters in this volume offer multiple examples of institutions with both first-year and senior-year seminars into which service can be incorporated. As our team of contributors from Portland State University cogently argues, one of the key roles of service-learning in the first-year curriculum is and must be to serve "as a gateway to other service-learning courses in the four-year curriculum." Now that many campuses have developed successful programs for first-year students, educators are asking how this effort can be taken beyond the first year. For example, the national conversation about the reality of the "sophomore slump," with its attendant high attrition, is growing. Service-learning is one promising answer to this call to enhance the second year of college.

As a final component of the unfinished agenda for the first year, I maintained that too few senior institutional leaders, including presidents and chief academic officers, empathize with the problems of contemporary students because when they went to college, they did not experience the benefits of first-year programs, probably were not on federal financial aid, and probably did not have the characteristics of the majority of today's first-year students. I am very hopeful that greater contact between service-learning proponents and those who advocate for enhanced first-year experience initiatives can and will increase the involvement of the presidents and chief academic officers whose support is so essential. The enormous success of Campus Compact as a presidents' organization and the connection of the Compact to so many service-learning initiatives makes me very hopeful that we can draw upon the base of leaders supporting service and civic engagement to include a focus on a service-rich first-year experience.

Reading this work truly connected me with broader issues of the first-year experience, and it has yielded many other insights, findings, and conclusions about service-learning. These I share in the volume's concluding chapter.

John N. Gardner,
Senior Fellow
National Resource Center for The First-Year Experience and Students in Transition
University of South Carolina

Executive Director
Policy Center on the First Year of College
Brevard College

April 2002

Introduction
Edward Zlotkowski

Service-Learning and the First-Year Experience

This monograph documents the congruence of two powerful educational concerns: the success of first-year students and the potential of service-learning as a teaching-learning strategy. Over the past 10 years in particular, both these concerns have gained an ever larger group of adherents. However, until recently, neither has fully realized how important each could be to the other or the degree to which many of their values, challenges, and even goals overlap.

In his essay "Toward Pragmatic Liberal Education," Bruce Kimball (1995), a historian of education at the University of Rochester, identifies seven concerns that he sees as "becoming prominent" in liberal education today: (a) multiculturalism, (b) values and service, (c) community and citizenship, (d) general education, (e) commonality and cooperation between college and other levels of the education system, (f) teaching interpreted as learning and inquiry, and (g) assessment (p. 97). Whether or not one subscribes to Kimball's overall thesis, it would be hard to deny the centrality of most of these concerns both to those seeking to develop effective first-year programs and to those seeking to establish effective service-learning programs.

One could, in fact, argue that the concerns of these two groups not only overlap but that, the better we understand the needs of first-year students and the conditions that make service-learning an effective learning strategy, the more the two concerns would seem to demand cooperation. Consider, for example, the following passage from Jewler's (1989) "Elements of an Effective Seminar: The University 101 Program":

> It occurred to the founder of University 101 that, if faculty could view students more positively, if they could experiment with interactive teaching methods that fostered the development of a community of learners, and if they could meet with other faculty and staff on common ground in this endeavor, the benefits to students, faculty, and the institu-

tion would be overwhelming. For freshmen and faculty alike, University 101 subscribes to the belief that development is not a one-dimensional affair but must reach far beyond the intellect and into emotional, spiritual, occupational, physical, and social areas. (p. 201)

The importance of developing through "interactive teaching" a faculty-student collaborative effort, teaching as something shared by an academic community, the necessity of transcending a narrowly intellectual approach to student development—all these positions are also fundamental to service-learning, both in theory and in quality practice. Indeed, when just prior to this passage Jewler identifies among the "philosophical underpinnings" of University 101 its belief that one of higher education's "most important missions is the development of people who will be the movers and shakers of the next generation" and its contention that education "should be exciting . . . fun . . . and provide learning for the instructor as well as the students" (p. 200), he is pointing precisely to that social efficacy and academic dynamism that service-learning seeks to bring to the undergraduate curriculum.

At this point, I should perhaps stress, especially for the benefit of those who approach this book from a non-service-learning perspective, that everything that follows is predicated on a fundamental distinction between service-learning *as an academic undertaking* and traditional community service or volunteerism. Unless one respects this distinction, some of the points made in the ensuing chapters may well be confusing. To be sure, the term "service-learning" is not always used elsewhere in such a specific, exclusive sense (though that is the direction in which usage is moving). Not only are there some who apply the term to any service activity with explicit learning objectives and a strategy to meet them, but there are also many others who use it as a kind of stylish synonym for "community service."

Indeed, although the contributors to this volume all reserve the term for curriculum-based, academically structured and facilitated service activities, this cannot be claimed for some of the research cited. For example, Duckenfield (Chapter 4) points to research indicating an increase from 27% in 1994 to 80% to 1999 in community service and volunteer activities of American high school students. At the same time, the level of service-learning programming grew from a mere 9% to approximately 46%. Since "service-learning" in this case is explicitly identified as a "major *educational reform initiative* in our public schools," one would like to assume that the term has been reserved only for classroom-related, grade-appropriate service (p. 39, emphasis added). However, we have no way of knowing whether those who reported a growth in service-learning, as opposed to community service, did indeed understand the term in this way. Nor can we determine if the service and the classroom-based work were linked in a truly substantive, significant way.

This being said, the reader should assume that, as much as possible, "service-learning" is used here to refer to fully legitimate academic undertakings, and that such an understanding presents those who design and facilitate first-year programs with several new opportunities and challenges. On the one hand, we now have a significant body of students who, thanks in part to service-learning experiences at the high school level, are already better prepared to learn and lead than many college faculty and staff imagine (see Furco, Chapter 1). Will such students be given the kinds of opportunity for intellectual and civic initiative they have come to expect? How can their skills be used to help their first-year peers become more motivated, engaged learners?

However, a very different set of opportunities and challenges arises in conjunction with that far larger number of high school students who have merely been required to jump through the hoop of a formal community service requirement. For such students, whose experience of community work is not associated with meaningful learning and formal leadership opportunities, the first college year may well turn out to be the death knell of all future civic engagement. Despite a definite increase in the number of first-year students who indicate they expect to be involved in some kind of service activity in college (23.8% in 2000 vs. 14.2% in 1990), the first-year experience remains the most significant time when students with service activities in their past (up to 81% in 2000) turn away from such activities as a part of their future (see Vogelgesang et al., Chapter 2). As several of the case studies presented in this book suggest, a failure to distinguish between the inclusion of "still another community service requirement" and an educationally resonant service-learning experience can readily contribute to this turn.

Volume Overview

Section 1 of the monograph consists of several chapters that make a case for service-learning in first-year programming. Andy Furco's chapter, "High School Service-Learning and the Preparation of Students for College: An Overview of Research," explores how our approach to the first college year may need to be recontextualized in light of the growing number of high school students who come to college with service-learning experiences. Furco's review of the research strongly suggests "the outcomes of service-learning for high school students reflect many of the academic, personal, and social adjustment issues faced by college students in their first year" (p. 6). This of, course, has important implications not just for first-year programs but also for high school teachers and counselors.

Chapter 2, "Service-Learning and the First-Year Experience: Outcomes Related to Learning and Persistence," by Lori Vogelgesang, Elaine Ikeda, Shannon Gilmartin, and Jennifer Keup not only reviews what the available research tells us about first-year students and service-learning; it also makes clear just how much additional research needs to be done if we are to understand service-learning's potential to enhance first-year student success and establish a strong foundation for future civic engagement. As the authors note, few studies of cognitive development over the first year have addressed service-learning directly. Instead they have focused on the impact of intercollegiate athletic participation, on- versus off-campus employment, organization and clarity of class presentations, Greek affiliation, first-generation status, remedial course enrollment, and women's perceptions of a "chilly" campus climate. Given what Furco and Duckenfield suggest about service-learning's developmental potential, one can only hope the gaps in the research record discussed in Chapter 2 will soon be addressed.

In the final chapter in this section, "Service-Learning and the Introductory Course: Lessons from Across the Disciplines," I examine some of the lessons we can learn about the introductory discipline-specific course from the essays included in the American Association for Higher Education's 19-volume series on service-learning in the disciplines (1997-2002). Here we begin to see some of the concrete consequences of a widespread tendency to regard the introductory course as little more than an opportunity to fill students' heads with disembodied information.

Introductory courses in disciplines as varied as biological engineering, history, and Spanish suggest an effective service-learning alternative.

A second section, consisting of two essays, introduces us directly to both traditional-aged students and the adult learners who are beginning to fill our college classrooms. First, Marty Duckenfield, in a chapter entitled "Look Who's Coming to College: The Impact of High School Service-Learning on New College Students" picks up on a number of the themes introduced in Chapter 1, delving into some of the factors behind the growth of K-12 service-learning and profiling some of the high school service-learning students she refers to in her title. Like Furco, Duckenfield stresses the impressive congruence between what high school service-learning students learn and what college will demand of them. Indeed, her chapter concludes with a set of recommendations by experienced pre-collegiate service-learning students on ways in which they themselves can contribute to the success of their fellow first-year students.

Chapter 5, "A Matter of Experience: Service-Learning and the Adult Student," by Tom O'Connell, shifts our attention to those "nontraditional" students who actually constitute a new educational majority. Drawing on years of experience in working with adult learners, O'Connell sketches out some of the concerns and values that should guide our work with those who have decided to continue their post-secondary education on a different timetable. His chapter helps us see the distinctive ways in which service-learning must be understood and implemented if it is to be of value to individuals who, unlike their younger colleagues, often bring with them a rich history of public and private work experiences.

Section 3, by far the book's longest section, offers a series of course models that explore a variety of issues related to implementation. Some of these models (that of the University of Rhode Island) make service-learning mandatory for all first-year students while others (that of Indiana University-Purdue University, Indianapolis) offer it as an elective feature of individual first-year seminars. In the final essay of this section, Tom Deans and Nora Bacon focus exclusively on the ways in which service-learning can be introduced into the introductory composition course. However, regardless of the differences among these varied approaches, they all share several key features, perhaps the most important of which is the recognition that the service activities must be carefully and substantively tied to legitimate course objectives. Simply inserting a community service experience into a first-year course accomplishes little unless that experience functions as a well-designed learning experience. As Jayne Richmond of the University of Rhode Island explicitly notes: "We soon realized that what we were doing was community service, even though what we wanted to do was service-learning. Thus, we began a process of assessing student learning, community partnerships, and faculty involvement" (p. 68).

In this regard, the profile from Cal State Fullerton raises an important related issue. Kathy O'Byrne and Sylvia Alva, the authors of this chapter, relate that most program participants registered gains in areas such as a sense of social responsibility and appreciation of the systemic nature of social disadvantage. However, their program assessment also suggested that service experiences need to be very carefully tied to the development of (a) a sense of civic responsibility and (b) career-related skills. Unless this is done, students may learn to appreciate the complexity of social issues but may not learn to see themselves as civic professionals with important public problem-solving skills.

The book's final section consists of a single chapter. In "What, So What, Now What: Reflections, Findings, Conclusions, and Recommendations," John Gardner, one of the true pioneers of the first-year experience, not only summarizes what for him are the volume's key points but also identifies a set of lessons and action steps that those wishing to link service-learning and the first-year experience will find invaluable. His remarks are followed by an appendix featuring four additional program summaries: a communication program related to the issues discussed by Deans and Bacon; an environmental program related to the issues I discuss in chapter three, and two programs that link academic service-learning with residence halls.

Conclusion

Few would deny that our understanding of what an effective contemporary education demands and what constitutes a truly inclusive approach to student development has changed over the last quarter century (Kimball, 1998). As the faculty advisory committee of the Lowell Benion Center of the University of Utah has noted, "Higher education is at a crossroads. At few moments in our country's history have so many questioned the importance and relevance of higher education to contemporary society" (Zlotkowski, 1999, p. J-1). Consequently, we must all recognize that, in addition to "foundational" and "professional" knowledge, our institutions are equally responsible for the creation and dissemination of "socially responsive" knowledge. As the committee goes on to point out, the many social challenges that now demand our attention

> force us as academicians to no longer assume that *we can perform our teaching role without playing close attention to the impact of that role on the communities that surround us . . .* simply providing opportunities for volunteer service will not enable universities to meet the social demands of the coming decades. [emphasis added] (p. J-5)

If one function of substantive first-year programs is to prepare new students to understand both the challenges and the opportunities of higher education at the beginning of the 21st century and to appropriate for themselves the identity of a truly educated person, it is hard to see how such programs can be true to themselves without developing some kind of socially engaged dimension.

Indeed, one can go even further. Given what we now know about the role of unstructured, "real-world" experiences in the design of effective pedagogical strategies and the development of lifelong learners (see, Abbott, 1996), it is hard to see how first-year programs can prepare new students to maximize their learning potential unless those programs abandon the often unexamined assumption that significant academic learning takes place only on campus—in classrooms, libraries, and residence halls. It is my hope that readers of this monograph will find in its essays a compelling rationale for rethinking where and how the learning that best serves our students and our communities takes place.

References

Abbott, J. (1996, March). The search for next-century learning. *AAHE Bulletin*, 3-6.

Jewler, J. (1989). Elements of an effective seminar: The university 101 program. In M. L. Upcraft & J. N. Gardner (Eds.), *The freshman year experience: Helping students survive and succeed in college* (pp. 189-215). San Francisco: Jossey-Bass.

Kimball, B. (1995). Toward pragmatic liberal education. In R. Orrill (Ed.), *The condition of American liberal education* (pp. 1-12). New York: The College Board.

Zlotkowski, E. (1999). *Successful service-learning programs: New models of excellence in higher education.* Boulton, MA: Anker.

Zlotkowski, E. (Ed.). (1997-2002). *AAHE's series on service-learning in the disciplines.* Washington, DC: American Association for Higher Education.

Section 1

Making the Case for Service-Learning in the First Year of College

High School Service-Learning and the Preparation of Students for College: An Overview of Research

Andrew Furco

Currently, a growing number of the nation's K-12 schools are encouraging students to participate in school-sponsored community service and service-learning activities. A recent survey conducted by the National Center for Education Statistics found that during the 1998-99 school year, 57% of all public schools organized community service activities for their students and 32% of all public schools organized service-learning activities as part of their curriculum (Skinner & Chapman, 1999). This survey, along with several other large-scale surveys, has found that most K-12 community service and service-learning activities take place at the high-school level (Maloy & Wohlleb, 1997; National Center for Education Statistics, 1997; Skinner & Chapman, 1999).

Over the years, the rise in community service and service-learning activity at the high-school level has been substantial. In 1984, it was estimated that 27% of the nation's high schools offered their students some type of community service activity (Newmann & Rutter, 1985). By 1999, the number had more than tripled to 83% of all high schools (Skinner & Chapman, 1999). Especially striking is the recent proliferation of high school service-learning programs, which connect community service activities to students' academic work. A 1999 National Center for Education Statistics survey found that during the 1998-99 school year, 46% of the nation's high schools offered service-learning to their students (Skinner & Chapman, 1999).

As more high school seniors graduate having had community service and service-learning experiences, what impact might such experience have on students' preparation for college? More specifically, in what ways might students' engagement in high school service-learning prepare them for a smoother transition to college life and ensure a more successful first-year experience? This chapter explores some possible answers to these questions.

The First-Year Experience

For most traditional-aged students, the first year of college brings with it a broad range of academic, social, and personal challenges. According to Cook (1997), the transition from high school to college is the "most dramatic normative, age-graded change" during the late adolescent years (p. 3). For many first-year students, the transition to college is fraught with isolation and bewilderment. Oftentimes, the successful transition to college must take place far removed from the comfort and support of family and longtime friends. To be successful, first-year students must gain membership in the new and unfamiliar academic and social communities of the campus (Lokitz & Sprandel, 1976; Tinto, 1985). According to Tinto, these two communities are linked; students' failure to become integrated and to establish competent membership in either of these spheres may result in their withdrawal from college. In essence, the first-year experience is "a test of social-psychological adjustment as much as an academic one" (University of California, 1989, p. 4).

Academic Adjustments

Immediately upon entering college, students must work to achieve membership in the college's academic community. Many first-year students are challenged by more stringent grading standards, heavier course loads, and less personalized teaching practices than those to which they have grown accustomed in high school. In comparison to high school classes, college courses require students to spend more time learning material directly from texts than from an instructor. In addition, college courses require students to think more analytically and address larger theoretical concepts, maintain a culture in which the student-teacher relationship is less personal, and demand that they do more academic work outside of class (Erickson & Strommer, 1991). Having to adjust quickly to these new academic pressures can deflate the self-confidence of an individual whose prior self-perception was one of being a competent student. Anderson (1985) argues that these pressures result in students' development of self-defeating perceptions, negative behavior patterns, confusion, and indecision—all of which are detrimental to their academic success.

The higher academic expectations that challenge traditional-aged first-year students produce a variety of responses. One common response is student withdrawal or disengagement from the learning process (Tinto, 1985). Recent national surveys show that students in their first year have become increasingly more academically and socially disengaged from college (Sax, Astin, Korn, & Mahoney, 1999). Erickson and Strommer (1991) have noted that first-year students are generally more difficult to reach and teach than their more senior classmates. They suggest that most high school graduates enter college without the analytical skills necessary to engage in college-level academic work and are in need of much remedial work. Moreover the structure of the high school curriculum and the way it is delivered do not prepare students to assume personal responsibility for managing their own schedules or academic programs (Erickson & Strommer, 1991).

As a result, students often disempower themselves from the academic enterprise by expecting others to set their academic agendas. One consequence of this is that they take courses and do their academic work without a full investment of their energies. Disengagement and disempowerment can reduce students' overall motivation to learn and ultimately can diminish their capacity to take full advantage of the academic experience (Boyer, 1987).

Social and Personal Adjustments

In addition to making academic adjustments, first-year students must also seek membership in their college's social community (Tinto, 1985). In their new environment, they must establish their sense of belonging by seeking out new peer groups and friendships. Much has been written about the role of peer influence and pressure in the retention and adjustment of college students (Heath, 1968; Billson & Terry, 1982; Upcraft, 1985). The fostering of collaborative peer groups plays a crucial role in helping students to feel less alienated.

Building alliances with other students who have similar interests and beliefs is one common social coping strategy found among first-year college students (Upcraft, 1985). Fostering collaborative peer groups through co-curricular and extracurricular activities often fulfills this need and helps students feel more connected to the college (Carnegie Foundation for the Advancement of Teaching, 1990; Upcraft, 1985). This sense of social connectedness is important not just for students' social adjustment, but also for their academic success and personal well-being (Simpson, Baker, & Mellinger, 1980; Upcraft, 1985). The reinstatement of a comfortable social environment through the establishment of new social circles can increase the likelihood of student retention; this is especially true if the social circles are formed within the first month of enrollment (Simpson, Baker, & Mellinger, 1980).

Feelings of insecurity and lowered self-esteem can become a cause for anxiety and stress, affecting the personal and social as well as the academic well-being of first-year students. For the at-risk student who enters college with an already low self-esteem and high sense of insecurity, the first year can be especially fraught with loneliness, a poor self-concept, unhappiness, powerlessness, and separation anxiety (Gardner & Jewler, 1989). The establishment of a social community helps boost the student's social and personal competence and can reduce the high levels of self-consciousness and the sense of alienation from the larger campus community frequently found among first-year students (Carnegie Foundation for the Advancement of Teaching, 1990).

Approaches to Enhancing Academic and Social Adjustment of First-Year Students

One way colleges and universities have sought to address incoming students' adjustment needs is by offering new student orientations and first-year experience programs. These efforts, which are often quite intensive and may last for an entire year, are designed to help students learn about the campus and reflect on their experiences as college students. Through these programs, new college students learn how to use the library, maneuver through the campus's academic programs and procedures, take advantage of the institution's support networks and programs, and interact effectively with faculty.

Evidence suggests that such programs are successful in helping students better acclimate themselves to their institutions, reduce their feelings of alienation, enhance their attitude toward learning, increase their interest in non-classroom activities, and gain a better understanding of academic expectations (Titley, 1985). On certain campuses, orientations for incoming students have been found to promote greater student satisfaction with school, greater intellectual growth, and greater persistence through to graduation (Forrest, 1985). For example, a study of the Provisional

Year (currently the Transition Year) at the University of South Carolina, a program in which all incoming students identified as at-risk must participate, found that the attrition rate of students who participate in the program is 7% lower than that of the first-year class as a whole (Spitzberg & Thorndike, 1992). The overarching goal of these efforts is to help students adjust not only academically, but personally and socially as well.

In a study of 87 first-year students at a mid-sized university, Smith (1994) investigated how the level of students' sense of separation and individuation influenced their adjustment to college. Smith's study revealed that students who engaged in problem-focused coping strategies reported higher college adjustment and greater persistence. Providing first-year students with the space to reflect on and address issues that have personal meaning to them can enhance their adjustment to college life.

Recently, there has been a growth in college programs that seek to reach out to prospective students before they arrive at college. This approach has spawned a number of outreach programs that aim to prepare high school students for college academically, personally, and socially—especially students from underrepresented and at-risk populations. These programs involve tutoring and mentoring efforts in which college students and college faculty work with high school students toward enhancing the latter's academic skills and assisting them with college applications and test preparation. There is currently a growing body of evidence on the success of these programs to prepare high school students for admission to college (University of California, 2001).

One area in particular that shows promise in helping to enhance students' academic and social preparation for college is their engagement in high school community service and service-learning activities.

High School Service-Learning Participation Outcomes

Findings from a number of research studies on high school service programs suggest that service-learning can have a positive effect on a variety of student development dimensions. The research on K-12 service-learning has found that high quality service-learning experiences can enhance high school students' academic, personal, social, civic, and career development (Billig, 2000; Andersen, 1999; Furco, 1994, 1997).

In many instances, the outcomes of service-learning for high school students reflect many of the academic, personal, and social adjustment issues faced by college students in their first year. Although there has been no formal study of the direct effects of students' high school service-learning experiences on students' adjustment to their first year of college, there is an interesting parallel between the issues first-year college students face and the types of outcomes high school community service and service-learning are purported to foster. This parallelism warrants some discussion.

Academic Outcomes

As mentioned earlier, as students move from high school to college, they must adjust to more stringent grading standards, heavier course loads, more analytical approaches to problem solving, additional personal responsibility, and more academic work outside of class. For some students, these adjustments can manifest themselves in lower self-confidence, a lessened sense of competence, self-defeating perceptions and negative behavior patterns, lower motivation to learn, and increased disengagement from the college academic community.

However, there is some evidence to suggest that these behaviors and feelings may actually manifest themselves before a student arrives at college. For example, evidence indicates that students become increasingly bored with their studies and more disengaged from school during the latter part of their high school years. A 1999 national survey conducted by UCLA found that 36% of first-year students reported being frequently bored during their senior year in high school. Moreover, a record number of these students reported that they overslept, missed classes, or did not make their appointments (Sax et al., 1999). The onset of high school "senioritis," a syndrome in which high school seniors turn their attention from the present to life after high school, might explain this disengagement (Sax et al, 1999). Zuker (1997) identifies "senioritis" as "the final two months of the senior year often thought of as anticlimactic by seniors" (p. 20). Some educators (e.g., Sax et al., 1999) attribute "senioritis" to the lack of a challenging curriculum, one that fails to involve maturing students actively in more independent and sophisticated learning activities. High school seniors frequently cope with "senioritis" by finding outlets in which they can engage in more socially and personally meaningful academic and nonacademic activities.

Boyer (1987) suggests that having academic experiences that are directly applicable to the students' lives is one way to retain seniors' engagement in school. Several studies have found that engagement in service-learning can enhance students' academic motivation in high school. Studies have revealed that high quality service-learning experiences can result in more regular class attendance, increased motivation to learn, and deeper engagement in their studies (Follman, 1998; Furco, 1997; Loesch-Griffin et al., 1995; Melchior, 1998; O'Bannon, 1999; Shumer, 1994; Supik, 1996). For high school seniors suffering from "senioritis," service-learning can be an effective way to invigorate the curriculum and to challenge students enough to keep them engaged in the learning process.

In addition to increasing students' motivation, service-learning can provide students with opportunities to develop academic skills they will need in college. When done well, service-learning requires students to apply academic work outside of class, to exercise their analytical problem-solving skills to address authentic and complex social issues, to move between working independently and collectively on issues, and to assume more personal responsibility for learning. Findings from several studies of service-learning have found that after participating in service-learning, high school students' grade point averages increased; math, reading, and language arts test scores were higher; and the students were less likely to drop out of school (Follman, 1999; Supik, 1996; Shumer, 1994). Such findings suggest that service-learning may increase high school students' academic persistence by allowing students to flex their academic skills in ways that keep them interested and engaged in learning.

Social and Personal Adjustments

Beyond the academic benefits of service-learning, studies of high school service-learning suggest that service-learning can be a powerful strategy for affecting students' social competencies and personal development. For example, studies conducted by Melchior (1998); Follman (1997); Allen, Kuperminc, Philliber, & Herre (1994); and Shaffer (1993) have found that high school students who have participated in service-learning show higher levels of self esteem and individuation, reduced levels of alienation, and less likelihood of engaging in high-risk behaviors. The benefits of service-learning seem to span all groups of students, regardless of their ability, ambition, or academic standing.

In line with Tinto's (1985) notion of linked academic and social communities, service-learning appears to be a means of engaging students in activities that bridge the two spheres. It provides opportunities for students to conduct personal reflection through which they can delve into complex issues and situations that are both academically enriching and personally relevant. When combined with the aforementioned academic outcomes, the personal and social benefits of service-learning may place some high school graduates in a better position to meet the challenges of the first year of college.

As mentioned earlier, first-year college students seek out collaborative peer groups to reduce their sense of alienation. These social groups help establish a comfortable social environment that can boost students' sense of self-esteem and social and personal competence.

At the high school level, service-learning provides a safe space for students to make individual and collective contributions to a situation and analyze how their efforts can make a difference for others. As Billig (2000), Morgan and Streb (1999), Melchior (1998), and others suggest, such experiences can promote their development of social competence, social responsibility, and interpersonal development.

Implications of High School Service-Learning for the First Year of College

The findings from these and other studies of K-12 school-sponsored service programs suggest that the engagement of high school students in community service or service-learning activities can provide space for students to begin their transition to college. Even though the college program and overall college experience may not be a central focus of the high school service-learning experience, service-learning can nonetheless provide an opportunity for high school students to assume more adult-like responsibilities and engage in activities that more closely resemble the responsibilities they will encounter in college. Specifically, through well-designed service-learning experiences, high school students who engage in service-learning have an opportunity to practice a host of important skills relevant to their success as college students.

This idea is supported by a study (Brown, 1996) comparing different types of orientation programs and their propensity to increase students' ($n = 277$) persistence in college and overall adjustment to the campus. The study examined three types of orientation programs offered at a university: a traditional classroom informational program, a seminar-based program (i.e., an extended orientation seminar), and an outdoor education orientation program. Students who participated in the outdoor orientation had the best adjustment scores in the academic, social, personal, and institution-attachment adjustment areas at the end of their second semester and second year. Brown suggests that these outcomes resulted from the challenge inherent in outdoor orientation programs, the investment of students' time and energy, and the opportunities for bonding among the faculty, staff, and students. The findings of Brown's study seem to suggest that engaging students in the application of their skills in authentic settings outside the classroom is one way to challenge them to develop the important problem-solving strategies and coping skills needed to adjust well to the first year of college. Service-learning may be an effective way to develop structured opportunities for students to have such experiences. Through service-learning, students can

- ♦ Assume and manage individual and collective responsibilities
- ♦ Develop their capacity for thinking and planning ahead
- ♦ Build social relationships with new and unfamiliar individuals and agencies
- ♦ Exercise self-esteem and work on developing self-confidence
- ♦ Apply and test leadership skills in a variety of settings and contexts
- ♦ Develop and employ analytic abilities
- ♦ Apply the concepts and theories of academic courses appropriately to meet authentic needs outside of the classroom
- ♦ Collect data and information through reading and research and make determinations based on their analysis of the data
- ♦ Practice various techniques for reflecting on learning
- ♦ Develop a belief in and a sense of commitment to a cause
- ♦ Learn to balance multiple tasks within time, resource, and energy constraints

Engaging students in service-learning experiences during high school can give them a head start in practicing and honing these essential college survival skills. As service-learning activities at the high school level continue to grow, their effect on first-year student readiness should be studied. And, as an increasing number of colleges and universities adopt service-learning as a means to promote the academic, personal, social, and civic engagement of students (Eyler & Giles, 1999), the effect of high school service-learning experiences on students' preparedness for collegiate service-learning courses also should be examined.

The Implication of High School Service-Learning for Collegiate Service-Learning Experiences

In a study of undergraduates who participated in service activities, Astin, Sax, and Avalos (1999) found that the involvement of college students in service activities is highest for students who, during high school, volunteered, helped others in times of need, participated in student government or leadership groups, served as peer tutors, or participated in after-school activities such as drama. This finding suggests that engagement in service programs during high school may not only better prepare students to confront some of the social, academic, and personal adjustment issues that are invariably part of the first year of college, but it may also increase students' propensity to engage in community service and service-learning during college.

A ramification of the increase in the number of high school service-learning programs is that more students are arriving at college knowing how to employ a variety of commonly used service-learning techniques such as reflection, journal writing, and conducting community needs assessments. College faculty who teach service-learning courses may need to give consideration to students' prior community experiences and design service-learning activities that appropriately challenge those students.

Surely, the kinds of service-learning experiences students have in high school are likely to differ from those they will have in college. The more closely supervised high school service-learning experiences are likely to give way to ones in college where students have much more responsibility for, independence in, and oversight of their projects. The projects' level of sophistication is also likely to be greater as students apply increasingly more advanced academic concepts to increasingly more complex social issues. Not only might the students' service-learning projects have a broader impact on the community, but the nature of their reflection, the depth of their discourse and analysis, and the particulars of their final products also are likely to become grander in scale.

Another ramification of the influence of high school service-learning on college service-learning is that as more high schools encourage students to volunteer and as more high schools engage students in academically meaningful service-learning activities, more students may purposely seek out admission to colleges and universities that will be able to offer them high-quality community service and service-learning opportunities. Students who have benefited from service-learning experiences during high school, especially those whose service-learning involvement helped boost their self-esteem, self-understanding, and sense of belonging, may want to ensure that they are able to secure similar experiences at the start of their college careers. There are already signs of such a trend. According to several recent articles and surveys (Astin, Sax, & Avalos, 1999), volunteerism among college freshman in the United States is at an all-time high. The 1999 CIRP Freshman Survey found that 38.4% of the more than 250,000 first-year students surveyed had volunteered one or more hours within the prior twelve-month period, the highest percentage since first-year students were first surveyed on this issue in 1987 (Sax et al., 1999).

Civic Development

One final area needs attention: the connection between service-learning and students' civic development. Although the issue of civic participation (e.g., voting, engaging in the political process) is not prevalent in the literature on the high school-college transition or the first-year experience, it is a central component of service-learning. Studies have found that high school service-learning can be an effective way to enhance students' civic participation and sense of social responsibility (Root, 1997). The development of these attributes may play an important role in getting older adolescents to become civic-minded and civically active adults.

Interestingly, although student volunteerism is at an all-time high, students' participation in the political process remains low. The 1996 CIRP Freshman Survey revealed that despite having been a presidential election year, only 16.2% of first-year college students discussed politics during 1996. In addition, the number of students who worked in a political campaign fell to 6.6% from 7.6% in 1995 and 16.4% in 1969 (Sax, Astin, Korn, & Mahoney, 1996). This drop in political participation is attributed to a growing sense of powerlessness to effect change and a lack of issues that interest first-year college students.

More recent analyses suggest that the situation has only gotten worse (Battistoni, 2002; Bennett, 2000; Sax, Astin, Korn, & Mahoney, 2000). For example, the 2000 CIRP Freshman Survey found that political engagement among first-year college students was at an all-time low (Sax, Astin, Korn, & Mahoney, 2000). Bennett (2000) suggests that political apathy among Americans develops at a young age, making it difficult to transform politically apathetic young people into civic-minded adults. According to Battistoni (2002), first-year students arrive on college campuses "with few experiences of lived democracy—let alone respect for their autonomy or voice—either in their schools or in their daily lives outside of schools" (p. 3). In this regard, higher education has a responsibility to prepare its students for active, civic participation and engagement (Battistoni, 2002).

Getting young people to develop a passion for and belief in a particular social cause may be one of the best ways service-learning can get young adults on the path to lifelong, active civic participation. Studies of high school students' involvement in service-learning show that the engagement of students in community service and service-learning activities helps students nurse their passion for particular causes (Furco, 2001). As students enter adulthood and become eligible to vote, they may begin to apply this mindset to active participation in the political process. In addition, by involving students in service-learning when they are younger, one may be able to help them develop a clearer sense of the causes in which they believe and the importance of their individual voices and efforts in making things happen.

Conclusion

The participation of high school students in service-learning may help prepare students not only for their first year of college, but also for their development into active, civic-minded adults. However, at this time, more research is needed to determine the direct effects of students' involvement in high school service-learning on their trajectories as college students and adult citizens.

Although it is not certain at this time to what extent engagement in high school service-learning will enhance students' adjustment to college and their first-year experience, there is some evidence to suggest that service-learning during the high school years fosters a number of outcomes that may be beneficial to first-year students' academic and social adjustment needs. Research studies that investigate the direct effect of high school service-learning on students' college adjustment would help us better understand any connection that might exist.

Specifically, studies that focus on the longitudinal effects of service-learning on students' personal, social, civic, and academic development could help provide a clearer understanding of the ways in which high school service-learning experiences promote development of those assets that place students in a better position to succeed in their first college year and beyond. In addition to focusing on the longer-term effects of service-learning, studies should explore the effect of service-learning on different types of students. For example, investigations of how service-learning affects high school students who are school leaders (i.e., who hold offices in student government and in other student organizations) versus students who are less involved in leadership activities could shed light on the added value service-learning has for those with limited leadership experience. It is, of course, these less experienced students who are most likely to face challenges in adjusting to college.

Beyond helping to prepare high school students for their first year in college, high school service-learning experiences may also help prepare them to be successful in more sophisticated service-learning experiences while in college. Having had an opportunity to participate in structured service activities connected to the curriculum, students may have a better sense of the kinds of social issues they are interested in, have a better idea of which types of reflection activities work best for them, and perhaps have more realistic expectations regarding what they can accomplish during a college service-learning course. Better articulation between the K-12 and higher education service-learning fields can help shed some light on the important ways in which the participation of students in service-learning throughout their educational experience can best be structured to maximize educational development.

And finally, using service-learning to put young people on a path towards active civic participation may begin to help address some of the falling rates of participation that have been identified in national surveys. Regardless, the engagement of high school students in service-learning activities seems to be a winning prospect that can enhance the academic, social, personal, and civic development of young people.

References

Allen, J. P., Kuperminc, G., Philliber, S. & Herre, K. (1994). Programmatic prevention of adolescent problem behaviors: The role of autonomy, relatedness, and volunteer service in the Teen Outreach Program. *Journal of Community Psychology, 22,* 617-38.

Andersen, S. (1999). *A review of school-based community service and service-learning.* Washington, DC: Corporation for National Service.

Anderson, E. C. (1985). Forces influencing student persistence and achievement. In E. Noel, R. Levitz, D. Saluri, & Associates (Eds.), *Increasing student retention,* (pp. 44-61). San Francisco: Jossey-Bass.

Astin, A. W., Sax, L. J., Avalos, J. (1999). The longterm effects of volunteerism during the undergraduate years. *Review of Higher Education, 22*(2), 187-202.

Battistoni, R. M. (2002). *Civic engagement across the curriculum: A resource book for service-learning faculty in all disciplines.* Providence: Campus Compact.

Bennett, S. E. (2000). Political apathy and avoidance of news media among generations X and Y: America's continuing problem. In S. Mann & J. Patrick, (Eds.). *Education for civic engagement in democracy.* Bloomington, ID: ERIC Clearinghouse for Social Studies.

Billig, S. H. (2000, May). Research on K-12 school based service-learning: The evidence builds. *Phi Delta Kappan, 81*(9), 658-664.

Billson, J. M., & Terry, M. B. (1982, Fall). In search of the silken purse: Factors in attrition among first generation students. *College and University, 58,* 57-75.

Boyer, E. L. (1987). *College: The undergraduate experience in America.* New York: Harper and Row, Publishers.

Brown, D. A. (1996). *Assessment of anticipated and actual college adjustment in freshman-oriented students.* University of Maryland, College Park. Unpublished dissertation.

Carnegie Foundation for the Advancement of Teaching. (1990). *Campus life: In search of community.* Princeton, NJ: Princeton University Press.

Cook, M. J. (1997). An exploratory study of learning styles as a predictor of college academic adjustment. Unpublished manuscript. Fairfield, CT: Fairfield University.

Erickson, B. L., & Strommer, D. W. (1991). *Teaching college freshmen.* San Francisco: Jossey-Bass.

Eyler, J., & Giles, D. (1999). *Where's the learning in service-learning.* San Francisco: Jossey-Bass.

Follman, J. (1998, August). *Florida learn and serve: 1996-97 outcomes and correlations with 1994-95 and 1995-96.* Center for Civic Education and Service. Tallahassee: Florida State University.

Forrest, A. (1985). Creating conditions for student and institutional success. In E. Noel, R. Levitz, D. Saluri, and Associates (Eds.), *Increasing student retention,* (pp. 62-77). San Francisco: Jossey-Bass.

Furco, A. (1994). A conceptual framework for the institutionalization of service programs in primary and secondary education. *Journal of Adolescence, 17*(4), 395-409.

Furco, A. (1997). *School-sponsored service programs and the educational development of high school students.* Berkeley: University of California.

Furco, A. (2001). Is service-learning really better than community service? A study of high school service programs. In A. Furco & S. H. Billig, (Eds.), *Service-learning: The essence of the pedagogy. Advances in service-learning research, Volume 1.* Mahwah, NJ: Lawrence Erlbaum.

Gardner, J. N., & Jewler, J. A. (1989). *College is only the beginning. A student guide to higher education* (2nd ed.). Belmont, CA: Wadsworth Publishing.

Heath, D. H. (1968). *Growing up in college: Liberal education and maturity.* San Francisco: Jossey-Bass.

Loesch-Griffin, D., Petrides, L. A., & Pratt, C. (1995). *Rethinking classrooms and community: Service-learning as educational reform.* Oakland, CA: East Bay Conservation Corps.

Lokitz, B. D. & Sprandel, H. Z. (1976, July). The first year: A look at the freshman experience. *Journal of College Student Personnel, 17*(4), 274-279.

Maloy, R., & Wohlleb, B. (1997). *Implementing community service in K-12 schools: A report on policies and practices in the eastern region.* Eastern Regional Information Center. Amherst, MA: University of Massachusetts.

Melchior, A. (1998). *National evaluation of learn and serve America school and community based programs.* Waltham, MA: Brandeis University.

Morgan, W., & Streb, M. (1999). *How quality service-learning develops civic values.* Unpublished paper. Bloomington, IN: Indiana University.

National Center for Education Statistics. (1997). *National household survey: student participation in community service activity.* Washington, DC: U.S. Department of Education.

Newmann, F. N., & Rutter, R. A. (1985-86, December-January). A profile of high school community service programs. *Educational Leadership, 86,* 64-71.

O'Bannon, F. (1999). Service-learning benefits our schools. *State Education Leader, 17,* 3-5.

Root, S. C. (1997). School-based service. A review of research for teacher educators. In J. A. Erickson & J. B. Anderson, (Eds.), *Learning with the community: Concepts and models for service-learning in teacher education,* (pp. 42-72). Washington, DC: American Association for Higher Education.

Sax, L. J., Astin, A. W., Korn, W. S., & Mahoney, K. M. (1996). *The American freshman: National norms for fall 1996.* Los Angeles: Higher Education Research Institute.

Sax, L. J., Astin, A. W., Korn, W. S., & Mahoney, K. M. (1999). *The American freshman: National norms for fall 1999.* Los Angeles: Higher Education Research Institute.

Sax, L. J., Astin, A. W., Korn, W. S., & Mahoney, K. M. (2000). *The American freshman: National norms for fall 1999.* Los Angeles: Higher Education Research Institute.

Shaffer, B. (1993). *Service-Learning: An academic methodology.* Unpublished paper. Stanford, CA: Stanford University.

Shumer, R. (1994). Community-based learning: Humanizing education. *Journal of Adolescence, 17*(4), 357-367.

Simpson, C., Baker, K., & Mellinger, G. (1980). Conventional failures and unconventional dropouts: Comparing different types of university withdrawals. *Sociology of Education, 53,* 203-214.

Skinner, R., & Chapman, C. (1999). *Service-Learning and community service in K-12 public schools.* National Center for Education Statistics. Washington, DC: U.S. Department of Education.

Smith, A. W. (1994). *Separation-individuation and coping: Contributions to freshman college adjustment.* Unpublished dissertation.

Spitzberg, I. J., & Thorndike, V. V. (1992). *Creating community on college campuses.* Albany: State University of New York.

Supik, J. (1996). *Valued youth partnerships: Programs in caring.* San Antonio, TX: Intercultural Research and Development Association.

Tinto, V. (1985). Dropping out and other forms of withdrawal from college. In E. Noel, R. Levitz, D. Saluri, & Associates (Eds.), *Increasing Student Retention,* (pp. 28-43). San Francisco: Jossey-Bass.

Titley, B. S. (1985). Orientation programs. In E. Noel, R. Levitz, D. Saluri, & Associates (Eds.), *Increasing student retention,* (pp. 221-243). San Francisco: Jossey-Bass.

University of California, (2001, Fall). *Expanding educational opportunity: A status report on the educational outreach and K-12 improvement programs of the University of California.* Office of the President.

University of California. (1989, July). *The forces influencing college student persistence: A review of the literature.* Office of the President.

Upcraft, M. L. (1985). Residence halls and student activities. In E. Noel, R. Levitz, D. Saluri, and Associates (Eds.), *Increasing student retention,* (pp. 319-344). San Francisco: Jossey-Bass.

Zuker, R. F. (1997, Fall). Stress points in the college transition: What to expect/How students cope. *College Board Review, 182,* 14-21.

Service-Learning and the First-Year Experience: Outcomes Related to Learning and Persistence

Lori J. Vogelgesang
Elaine K. Ikeda
Shannon K. Gilmartin
Jennifer R. Keup

During the past decade, research on college student involvement in community service and service-learning has grown exponentially. At the same time, there has been an increase in research on the first-year experience. In this chapter we review the ways in which service-learning research intersects with research on the first year of college and suggest outcomes that might be enhanced by incorporating a service-learning experience early in students' undergraduate careers. We close with suggestions for future research.

In the research we examine here, students were asked how often they performed community service or volunteer work, and then whether this service during the college years was done in connection with a course. For the purposes of this chapter, then, we define service-learning as participation in community service work in connection with an academic course. Thus, it is a form of experiential education, related to other experience-based approaches such as internships, active learning, participatory action research, and problem-based learning.

Trends Among First-Year College Students

Over the past 35 years, the Higher Education Research Institute (HERI) at UCLA has conducted an annual survey of first-year college students. From these data, we see that the 1990s witnessed a steady increase in the percentage of first-year students indicating they had frequently or occasionally performed volunteer work during their senior year of high school. In 1990, 63% reported participating in volunteer work, and the percentage increased each year, with a full 81% stating they had participated in 2000.

However, participating in service during the high school years does not appear to translate directly to service participation during college. While 81% of entering first-year students indicate they have participated in service during the past year, less than 24% think there is a "very good chance" they will participate in service during college. Even so, today's first-year students expect to be involved in service during college in greater numbers than ever before. In 1990,

14.2% of entering first-year students estimated that there was a "very good chance" that they would participate in volunteer work or community service during college; by 2000, the percentage had increased to 23.8% (Astin, Korn, & Berz, 1990; Sax, Astin, Korn, & Mahoney, 2000). Thus, although students are increasingly likely to have performed volunteer work in high school and are more likely to *expect* to participate in similar work in college, there remains a formidable gap between service participation in high school and service expectations for the college years. The reason for this gap is not clear but may be due in part to students' inaccurate perceptions of college life. Still, the recent increase in the popularity of service-learning on many campuses suggests that students are more likely than they were in the past to have the opportunity to perform service connected with a course.

How Service-Learning Affects Students

In 2000, HERI completed a quantitative and qualitative study comparing the effects of service-learning and community service on the cognitive and affective development of college undergraduates.[1] Briefly, this study found that undergraduate service participation shows significant positive effects on all 11 outcome measures: academic performance (GPA, writing skills, critical thinking skills), values (commitment to activism and to promoting racial understanding), self-efficacy, leadership (leadership activities, self-rated leadership ability, interpersonal skills), choice of a service career, and plans to participate in service after college (Astin, Vogelgesang, Ikeda, & Yee, 2000). These findings are similar to those of other recent studies using different samples and methodologies to assess similar—i.e., academic, affective, cognitive—outcomes (Batchelder & Root, 1994; Eyler & Giles, 1999; Eyler, Giles, & Braxton, 1997; Hesser, 1995; Kendrick, 1996; Myers-Lipton, 1996; Osborne, Hammerich, & Hensley, 1998; Strage, 2000).

The HERI study also found that performing service *as part of a course* (service-learning) adds significantly to the benefits associated with nonacademic service for all outcomes except interpersonal skills, self-efficacy, and leadership.[2] Not surprisingly, the additional benefits associated with course-based service are strongest for the academic outcomes, especially writing skills.

Particularly relevant when considering whether the first year is an appropriate time for a service experience is the finding that service participation appears to have its strongest effect on the student's decision to pursue a career in a service field.[3] This effect occurs regardless of whether the student's incoming career choice is in a service field, a non-service field, or "undecided." One explanation could be that placing service experiences early in students' college years encourages them to make career-choice decisions that incorporate service.

However, the HERI study not only examined *whether* service-learning has an effect on students' cognitive and affective development, but it also explored reasons *why* the service-learning experience might produce the observed effects. In this regard, both qualitative and quantitative results underscored the power of *reflection* to connect the service experience to the academic course material. The primary forms of reflection assessed among participants were discussions among students and with professors as well as written reflection in the form of journals and papers.

Service-learning is powerful in part precisely because it enhances the likelihood that students will, in fact, reflect on their service experience. Both the qualitative and quantitative findings of the HERI study provide strong support for the notion that service-learning courses should be specifically and carefully designed to help students make connections between their service experiences and the academic material. This is illustrated in the following statement in which a professor shares what happened in a service-learning course where she did not incorporate in-class reflection on the service experience:

> I really believe that the service needs to be facilitated by the instructor to make [the] connection. It's reflected in my [course] evaluations. When I have incorporated service learning [reflection] into the classroom, my evaluations have skyrocketed. When I didn't do that, likewise the evaluations reflected it as well, unfortunately in the other direction. A lot of [the students] would write "I thought this was a total waste of time, service learning. I didn't really like it at all." Some people liked it because they have a volunteer spirit within them, but a lot of students didn't see the usefulness; they didn't understand why they were doing it. I think sometimes as faculty we assume, "reflection is there." We assume the students are going to make the connections, because the reading is reflective. But we have to make it [the connection] for them. (Astin et al., 2000, p. 77)

In addition to underscoring the centrality of reflection to the learning process, the study's qualitative findings suggested that service-learning is effective because it facilitates four types of outcomes: an increased sense of personal efficacy, an increased awareness of the world, an increased awareness of one's personal values, and increased engagement in the classroom experience. Both faculty and students also develop a heightened sense of civic responsibility and personal effectiveness.

In sum, this study provides evidence that participation in service-learning has consistent, albeit moderate, positive outcomes for undergraduate students.[4] But if this is true in general, might not first-year students in particular benefit from participation in community-based work?

Service-Learning and the First-Year College Experience

Estimated rates of student attrition over the first year of college are cause for concern. According to ACT, for example, more than 25% of first-year students at four-year institutions and almost 50% of students at two-year institutions do not return to the same college for their second year (ACT, 2001). While research on the factors behind first-to-second year persistence is varied and extensive, common to the conceptual core of much of that work is Tinto's (1975, 1987, 1993) theory of student departure. Tinto sketches a sequential model of persistence that underscores the role of students' academic and social integration into the campus community. Put simply, first-year student departure is probable if the student is poorly integrated and weakly committed to the institution and to degree attainment.

As a participation- and reflection-intensive curricular component designed to facilitate student engagement, service-learning would seem to be a natural vehicle of integration and persistence. However, few retention studies have examined the link between service-learning and students' willingness to persist. Instead, studies have considered the impact of high school friends (Christie & Dinham, 1991), expectations for college (Braxton, Vesper, & Hossler, 1995), career self-efficacy (Peterson, 1993), precollege orientation programs (Pascarella, Terenzini, & Wolfle, 1986), and institutional attributes (Berger & Braxton, 1998) as well as place of residence (Pike, Schroeder, & Berry, 1997) and sense of community among students living in residence halls (Berger, 1997).

Studies of student adjustment to the first college year—an outcome closely related to persistence—also tend to overlook the implications of service-learning. Rather, adjustment research has explored the role of family structure (Arnstein, 1980; Fulmer, Medalie, & Lord, 1982; Hoffman & Weiss, 1987; Holmbeck & Wandrei, 1993; Kenny & Donaldson, 1991; Lopez, Campbell, & Watkins, 1988) and psychological separation from parents (Hoffman, 1984; Holmbeck & Wandrei, 1993; Lapsley, Rice, & Shadid, 1989; Lopez, Campbell, & Watkins, 1986; Rice, Cole, & Lapsley, 1990) in addition to minority status (Smedley, Myers, & Harrell, 1993), peer social networks (Kenny & Stryker, 1996), and disillusionment caused by unmet college expectations (Baker, McNeil, & Siryk, 1985).

Likewise, few studies of cognitive development over the first year address service-learning directly. These studies instead highlight the effect of intercollegiate athletic participation (Pascarella, Bohr, Nora, & Terenzini, 1995), place of residence (Inman & Pascarella, 1998), on- versus off-campus employment (Pascarella, Bohr, Nora, Dester, & Zusman, 1994), organization and clarity of class presentations (Pascarella, Edison, Nora, Hagedorn, & Braxton, 1996), Greek affiliation (Pascarella, Edison, Whitt, Nora, Hagedorn, & Terenzini, 1996), first-generation status (Terenzini, Springer, Yeager, Pascarella, & Nora, 1996), remedial course enrollment (Hagedorn, Siadat, Fogel, Nora, & Pascarella, 1999), and women's perceptions of a "chilly" campus climate (Pascarella, Whitt, Edison, Nora, Hagedorn, Yeager, & Terenzini, 1997). In sum, most research on the first college year has not assessed the effect of service-based curricula on key first-year outcomes.

Still, research suggests that pedagogy does matter with respect to first-year success and retention. Specifically, pedagogical techniques that encourage students to participate in discussions and critically assess course material seem likely to increase integration and persistence (Braxton, Milem, & Sullivan, 2000). This latter finding is thematically consistent with Tinto's (1997) observation that "learning communities"—programs that enable a smaller cohort of students to proceed through a series of interconnected courses—are conducive to persistence by enhancing students' connections both to scholarship and to one another.

Indeed, the positive relationship between certain pedagogical techniques and retention not only affirms Tinto's model (i.e., techniques that engage students also strengthen students' ties to their campus and, accordingly, their decision to persist) but also recalls Astin's (1984) theory of student involvement, with which Tinto's model dovetails nicely. Astin has suggested that the relationship between student involvement and student development is direct, linear, and positive. That is, the more time, physical energy, and psychological energy students devote to the learning process, the greater the developmental benefits they accrue. Invested, active students are more likely to flourish academically and personally and to persist toward graduation. Involvement, moreover, might be most advantageous toward the beginning of a student's career. For example, Milem and Berger (1997) note that involvement during the "first six to seven weeks of a semester" is significantly related to retention. In short, "involvement"—perhaps as a precursor to "integration"—encourages student success, particularly if present at the very onset of the learning process.

Although the HERI study does not focus specifically on first-year students, it does offer evidence to support the idea that service-learning might increase the likelihood of persistence because it facilitates greater student involvement and interaction with peers and with faculty. As one professor remarked in an interview, "The primary difference between those who performed service and those who did not is in excitement, commitment, interest in the readings, questioning . . . . They were just so alive in class . . . I could hardly contain them. They talked avidly. It was a very lively class." Another professor made a similar comment:

> . . . it turns into a bedlam. You walk in and everybody's talking and everybody's got a discussion going and everybody's trying to interchange information, and they're making arrangements to meet . . . and you kind of have to settle everybody down before you can get class started. But it is a really good sign of the fact that they've become involved in the class and that it's become important to them.

These comments provide only anecdotal support, and, as illustrated in this review of the research on the first-year experience, there is in general a scarcity of studies that consider the relationship between service-learning and students' first year in college. However, one recent pilot study does offer some preliminary insight into this relationship. The next section of this chapter describes this study's findings.

Findings from a Pilot Study

Sponsored by grants from The Atlantic Philanthropies and The Pew Charitable Trusts, HERI and the Policy Center on the First Year of College have developed "Your First College Year" (YFCY), a follow-up instrument to the Cooperative Institutional Research Program (CIRP) Freshman Survey that is specifically designed to assess student development over the first year of college.[5] This instrument includes a variety of items that examine aspects of first-year student behavior, beliefs, adjustment, academic achievement, and identity formation as well as first-year service participation and classroom experiences. Thus, YFCY is a tool helpful in assessing the effects of community service and service-learning on student involvement, integration, adjustment, and retention. Although the results described below are not generalizable to the national population of first-year students given the limited sample included in the YFCY pilot administration, they nonetheless provide an important perspective on the first year of college and suggest directions for future research.

Over half (59.4%) of the students in the YFCY sample reported that they performed service work during their first year of college, while just under a quarter (24.3%) reported that they participated in service linked to their coursework.

Both correlation and cross-tabulation analyses indicate that students who participated in service during the first year of college, both generally and as part of a course, reported higher levels of satisfaction with various aspects of campus life than students who did not. Differences in the level of satisfaction are greatest between students who participated in course-based service and students who did not participate in service at all. These differences hold for both academic aspects of involvement ("amount of contact with faculty") and personal development aspects ("leadership opportunities," "opportunities for community service," and "overall sense of community among students"). Somewhat surprising, then, is the finding that only generic service, rather than service-learning, can be related to students' feelings of satisfaction with their "overall college experience."

YFCY results also suggest that involvement in community service enhances feelings of personal success among first-year students. Students who did not participate in service tended to feel less successful after one year in college than did those who took part in service in any form. Specifically, those who did not participate in service were statistically less likely to feel successful in establishing meaningful connections with faculty or staff, establishing a network of friends on campus, or developing effective study skills. What is interesting here is that students who participated in service not linked to a course were also more likely to feel successful in all three areas (as well as in adjusting to academic demands, understanding academic expectations, and accessing campus services). Although below we explore issues such as the quality of the service-learning experience and other possible explanations for these findings, it is noteworthy that in this particular pilot study, course-based service does not appear to enhance satisfaction above and beyond "generic" community service. Nevertheless, service participation in general is related to a stronger feeling of connection with faculty members, and this pilot finding is consistent with previous work.

Also important to note is the relationship between service participation and first- to second-year persistence. Findings indicate that participation in service specifically as part of a course is not associated with second-year re-enrollment. However, service participation on a general level during the first college year is significantly and positively related to retention. Findings also support an indirect relationship between service participation and persistence as mediated by involvement and integration. In other words, volunteerism and service-learning appear to enhance involvement and facilitate integration (both social and academic) during the first year of college, and these, the research shows (Astin, 1984, 1993; Pascarella & Terenzini, 1991; Tinto, 1975, 1987, 1993), are critical to student retention.

Suggestions for Future Research and Conclusion

Clearly, further research ought to explore the relationship between service-learning and retention, and consider areas that were not explored in the YFCY pilot study. Not only must the quality of the service experience be carefully assessed but also whether it was required.

It is, moreover, possible that the benefits of service-learning and the positive effect of reflection require more than one year to accrue. Perhaps their effect surfaces at some distance from the actual service-learning experience and thus proves to be significant well after the end of the first college year. Another issue needing to be explored is the symbiotic relationship between students' sense of connection to an institution and their interest in enrolling in service-learning courses. It is easy to imagine that some students may be predisposed to choose a service-learning course, have a positive experience, and then choose other courses or experiences—even a major—where faculty employ similar pedagogical approaches. Such a "snowball effect" may explain why an effect is evident in the longer term follow up studies, such as the HERI service-learning study, but does not appear in YFCY, which examines change after only one year.

Hence, it will be important to explore directly service-learning's effect during the first year proper but also to understand better just how first-year service experiences shape the rest of a student's college career and his commitment to service beyond college. Is there reason to believe, as we have suggested, that experiences in the first year predispose students to continue to seek such experiences? Further work on student career choices and service participation might be one way of examining this. However, it also would be interesting to examine former students' post-college community service commitments, regardless of career choice. Surely someone in any field can choose to apply his or her professional expertise to improve the community. Alternatively, someone may choose to use an avocational skill for the community's benefit.

Notes

1. For a description of the study's methodology, see Appendix A.
2. Positive results for the latter two outcomes were borderline (i.e., $p < .05$).
3. For this study, service field included medical careers (clinical psychologist, dentist, nurse, optometrist, physician, and therapist), and nonmedical service careers (elementary, secondary, or college teacher; clergy; forester/conservationist; foreign service; law enforcement; school counselor; and principal).
4. It is possible that the actual benefits of service-learning participation are understated in the quantitative portion of this study, since we did not study merely what might be considered "ideal" service-learning courses, but rather incorporated all course-based service. Other research (e.g., Eyler & Giles, 1999) reinforces a rather obvious notion: The effect of a service-learning experience is greater when the experience is a high-quality one.
5. For a detailed description of the pilot study, see Appendix B.

References

ACT. (2001). *National college dropout and graduation rates*, 1999. Retrieved February 3, 2002 from http://www.act.org/news.

Arnstein, R. L. (1980). The student, the family, the university, and transition to adulthood. In S. C. Feinstein, P. L. Giovacchini, J. G. Looney, A. Z. Schwartzberg, & A. D. Sorosky (Eds.), *Adolescent psychiatry: Developmental and clinical studies* (Vol. 12, pp. 160-172). Chicago: University of Chicago Press.

Astin, A. W. (1984). Student involvement: A developmental theory for higher education. *Journal of College Student Personnel, 25*, 297-308.

Astin, A. W. (1993). *What matters in college? Four critical years revisited.* San Francisco: Jossey-Bass.

Astin, A. W., Korn, W. S., & Berz, E. R. (1990). *The American freshman: National norms for fall 1990.* Higher Education Research Institute, University of California, Los Angeles.

Astin, A. W., Vogelgesang, L. J., Ikeda, E. K., & Yee, J. A. (2000). *How service-learning affects students.* Higher Education Research Institute, University of California, Los Angeles.

Baker, R. W., McNeil, O. V., & Siryk, B. (1985). Expectation and reality in freshman adjustment to college. *Journal of Counseling Psychology, 32*, 94-103.

Batchelder, T. H., & Root, S. (1994). Effects of an undergraduate program to integrate academic learning and service: Cognitive, prosocial cognitive, and identity outcomes. *Journal of Adolescence 17*(4), 341-355.

Berger, J. B. (1997). Students' sense of community in residence halls, social integration, and first-year persistence. *Journal of College Student Development, 38,* 441-452.

Berger, J. B., & Braxton, J. M. (1998). Revisiting Tinto's interactionalist theory of student departure through theory elaboration: Examining the role of organizational attributes in the persistence process. *Research in Higher Education, 39,* 103-119.

Braxton, J. M., Milem, J. F., & Sullivan, A. S. (2000). The influence of active learning on the college student departure process: Toward a revision of Tinto's theory. *Journal of Higher Education, 71,* 569-590.

Braxton, J. M., Vesper, N., & Hossler, D. (1995). Expectations for college and student persistence. *Research in Higher Education, 36,* 595-612.

Christie, N. G., & Dinham, S. M. (1991). Institutional and external influences on social integration in the freshman year. *Journal of Higher Education, 62,* 412-436.

Eyler, J. & Giles Jr., D. E. (1999). *Where's the learning in service-learning?* San Francisco: Jossey-Bass.

Eyler, J., Giles Jr., D. E., & Braxton, J. (1997). The impact of service-learning on college students. *Michigan Journal of Community Service Learning 4,* 5-15.

Fulmer, R. H., Medalie, J., & Lord, D. A. (1982). Life cycles in transition: A family systems perspective on counseling the college student. *Journal of Adolescence, 5,* 195-217.

Hagedorn, L. S., Siadat, M. V., Fogel, S. F., Nora, A., & Pascarella, E. T. (1999). Success in college mathematics: Comparisons between remedial and nonremedial first-year college students. *Research in Higher Education, 40,* 261-284.

Hesser, G. (1995). Faculty assessment of student learning: Outcomes attributed to service-learning and evidence of changes in faculty attitudes about experiential education. *Michigan Journal of Community Service Learning, 2,* 33-42.

Hoffman, J. A. (1984). Psychological separation of late adolescents from their parents. *Journal of Counseling Psychology, 31,* 170-178.

Hoffman, J. A., & Weiss, B. (1987). Family dynamics and presenting problems in college students. *Journal of Counseling Psychology, 34,* 157-163.

Holmbeck, G. N., & Wandrei, M. L. (1993). Individual and relational predictors of adjustment in first-year college students. *Journal of Counseling Psychology, 40,* 73-78.

Inman, P., & Pascarella, E. (1998). The impact of college residence on the development of critical thinking skills in college freshmen. *Journal of College Student Development, 39,* 557-568.

Kendrick, J. R. Jr. (1996). Outcomes of service-learning in an introduction to sociology course. *Michigan Journal of Community Service Learning, 3,* 72-81

Kenny, M. E., & Donaldson, G. A. (1991). Contributions of parental attachment and family structure to the social and psychological functioning of first-year college students. *Journal of Counseling Psychology, 38,* 479-486.

Kenny, M. E., & Stryker, S. (1996). Social network characteristics and college adjustment among racially and ethnically diverse first-year students. *Journal of College Student Development, 37,* 649-658.

Lapsley, D. K., Rice, K. G., & Shadid, G. E. (1989). Psychological separation and adjustment to college. *Journal of Counseling Psychology, 36,* 286-294.

Lopez, F. G., Campbell, V. L., & Watkins, C. E. (1986). Depression, psychological separation, and college adjustment: An investigation of sex differences. *Journal of Counseling Psychology, 33*, 52-56.

Lopez, F. G., Campbell, V. L., & Watkins, C. E. (1988). Family structure, psychological separation, and college adjustment: A canonical analysis and cross-validation. *Journal of Counseling Psychology, 35*, 402-409.

Milem, J. F., & Berger, J. B. (1997). A modified model of college student persistence: Exploring the relationship between Astin's theory of involvement and Tinto's theory of student departure. *Journal of College Student Development 38*(4), 387-399.

Myers-Lipton, S. J. (1996). Effect of a comprehensive service-learning program on college students' level of modern racism. *Michigan Journal of Community Service Learning, 3*, 44-54.

Osborne, R. E., Hammerich, S., & Hensley, C. (1998). Student effects of service-learning: Tracking changes across a semester. *Michigan Journal of Community Service Learning, 5*, 5-13

Pascarella, E., Bohr, L., Nora, A., Dester, M., & Zusman, B. (1994). Impacts of on-campus and off-campus work on first year cognitive outcomes. *Journal of College Student Development, 35*, 364-370.

Pascarella, E. T., Bohr, L., Nora, A., & Terenzini, P. T. (1995). Intercollegiate athletic participation and freshman-year cognitive outcomes. *Journal of Higher Education, 66*, 369-387.

Pascarella, E., Edison, M., Nora, A., Hagedorn, L. S., & Braxton, J. (1996). Effects of teacher organization/preparation and teacher skill/clarity on general cognitive skills in college. *Journal of College Student Development, 37*, 7-19.

Pascarella, E., Edison, M., Whitt, E. J., Nora, A., Hagedorn, L. S., & Terenzini, P. (1996). Cognitive effects of Greek affiliation during the first year of college. *NASPA Journal, 33*, 242-259.

Pascarella, E. T., & Terenzini, P. T. (1991). *How college affects students*. San Francisco: Jossey-Bass.

Pascarella, E. T., Terenzini, P. T., & Wolfle, L. M. (1986). Orientation to college and freshman year persistence/withdrawal decisions. *Journal of Higher Education, 57*, 155-175.

Pascarella, E. T., Whitt, E. J., Edison, M. I., Nora, A., Hagedorn, L. S., Yeager, P. M., & Terenzini, P. T. (1997). Women's perceptions of a "chilly climate" and their cognitive outcomes during the first year of college. *Journal of College Student Development, 38*, 109-124.

Peterson, S. L. (1993). Career decision-making self-efficacy and institutional integration of underprepared college students. *Research in Higher Education, 34*, 659-685.

Pike, G. R., Schroeder, C. C., & Berry, T. R. (1997). Enhancing the educational impact of residence halls: The relationship between residential learning communities and first-year college experiences and persistence. *Journal of College Student Development, 38*, 609-621.

Rice, K. G., Cole, D. A., & Lapsley, D. K. (1990). Separation-individuation, family cohesion, and adjustment to college: Measurement validation and test of a theoretical model. *Journal of Counseling Psychology, 37*, 195-202.

Sax, L. J., Astin, A. W., Korn, W. S., & Mahoney, K. M. (1999). *The American Freshman: National Norms for Fall 1999*. Higher Education Research Institute, University of California, Los Angeles.

Smedley, B. D., Myers, H. F., & Harrell, S. P. (1993). Minority-status stresses and the college adjustment of ethnic minority freshmen. *Journal of Higher Education, 64,* 434-452.

Strage, A. A. (2000). Service-learning: Enhancing student learning outcomes in a college-level lecture course. *Michigan Journal of Community Service Learning, 7,* 5-13

Terenzini, P. T., Springer, L., Yeager, P. M., Pascarella, E. T., & Nora, A. (1996). First-generation college students: Characteristics, experiences, and cognitive development. *Research in Higher Education, 37,* 1-22.

Tinto, V. (1975). Dropout from higher education: A theoretical synthesis of recent research. *Review of Educational Research, 45,* 89-125.

Tinto, V. (1987). *Leaving college: Rethinking the causes and cures of student attrition* (1st ed.). Chicago: The University of Chicago Press.

Tinto, V. (1993). *Leaving college: Rethinking the causes and cures of student attrition* (2nd ed.). Chicago: The University of Chicago Press.

Tinto, V. (1997). Classrooms as communities: Exploring the educational character of student persistence. *Journal of Higher Education, 68,* 599-623.

Vogelgesang, L. J., & Astin, A. W. (2000). Comparing the effects of community service and service-learning. *Michigan Journal of Community Service Learning, 7,* 24-34.

Appendix A
How Service-Learning Affects Students: Methodology Notes

The data from this study were collected as part of the Cooperative Institutional Research Program (CIRP), with sponsorship from the American Council on Education. Conducted by the Higher Education Research Institute (HERI) at the University of California, Los Angeles, the CIRP annually collects data on entering first-year students using the Student Information Form (SIF), a questionnaire designed as a pretest for longitudinal assessments of the impact of college on students. The College Student Survey (CSS), which provides longitudinal follow-up data, is typically administered four years after college entry.

For this study, longitudinal data were collected from 22,236 college undergraduates attending a national sample of baccalaureate-granting colleges and universities; most of them were first-year students in the fall of 1994. These students were surveyed again in the fall of 1998. Thirty percent of the students participated in course-based community service (service-learning) during college, and an additional 46% participated in some other form of community service. The remaining 24% did not participate in any community service during college. The effect of service-learning and community service was assessed on 11 different dependent measures: academic outcomes (3 measures); values (two measures); self-efficacy and leadership (three measures); career plans; and plans to participate in further service after college. Most of these outcomes were pretested when the students were in their first year of college.

Multivariate controls were used for both first-year student characteristics and institutional characteristics (e.g., size, type, selectivity) before the comparative impact of service-learning and community service on the 11 student outcomes was assessed.

The qualitative portion of the study involved in-depth case studies of service-learning on three different campuses. Individual and group interviews with faculty and students, together with classroom observations, were conducted at each site.

For a more detailed description of the study, see *How Service-Learning Affects Students* (Astin, Vogelgesang, Ikeda & Yee, 2000). Detailed notes on methods for the quantitative portion of the study can also be found in "Comparing the Effects of Community Service and Service-Learning" (Vogelgesang & Astin, 2000).

Appendix B
Your First College Year: Methodology Notes

In Spring 2000, a total of 5,229 first-year, full-time students at 19 institutions who participated in the 1999 Cooperative Institutional Research Program (CIRP) Freshman Survey were included in the pilot administration of "Your First College Year" (YFCY). Year one pilot institutions were selected based on institutional type, control, and enrollment to ensure a diverse sample. Of the CIRP Freshman Survey respondents, the Higher Education Research Institute (HERI) randomly selected a given number of students per pilot school to receive the first wave of YFCY surveys in early spring.

Each survey packet contained a cover letter from HERI and the Policy Center on the First Year of College, a cover letter from the student's institution, a copy of the survey instrument, and a business reply envelope. Two weeks after the first mailing, all students received a reminder postcard, and four weeks after the first mailing first-wave non-respondents were sent a second copy of the survey. Data collection ended in early summer 2000. The response rate for each institution ranged from approximately 6% to 30%, with an overall response rate close to 20% (a total sample size of 992 students). To collect second-year re-enrollment data for every student included in the YFCY mail-out sample, HERI conducted a survey of registrars at the 19 pilot campuses in fall 2000.

The descriptive analyses (i.e., correlations and cross-tabulations) discussed in this chapter use this sample. Students were considered to have participated in general volunteer work if they responded that they had "frequently" or "occasionally" performed volunteer work since entering college. Students were included in the course-based service group if they responded that the courses at their current (or most recent) institution "frequently" or "occasionally" included "community service linked to coursework (service-learning)." To measure persistence, registrars indicated whether students did or did not return to their college for a second year. Adjustment variables were selected from various YFCY survey items assessing students' feelings of academic and personal success as well as measures of student satisfaction with various aspects of campus life.

Service-Learning and the Introductory Course:
Lessons From Across the Disciplines

Edward Zlotkowski

Of the more than 100 courses profiled in the American Association for Higher Education's (AAHE) series on service-learning across the disciplines, approximately one tenth are introductory courses, largely or exclusively elected by first-year students. Unlike the first-year seminar, these courses represent standard departmental offerings with a traditional disciplinary focus. However, very much like the first-year seminar, they must carefully take into account the special needs of first-year students. Indeed the failure of traditional introductory courses to do so is, in many disciplines, a matter of growing concern. For example, Fox and Ronkowski (1997) recently looked at the preferred learning styles of political science students. They concluded that

> . . . in lower level introductory courses, a greater emphasis should be placed on activities that provide concrete and active experiences for students, since lower division students indicated a greater preference for these styles than upper-class students. If one of the aims of lower division classes is to interest as many students as possible, particularly women and traditionally underrepresented students, in choosing political science as a major . . . then this strategy could be beneficial toward meeting this goal. (p. 736)

Sociologists, biologists, and historians have articulated a similar concern with the traditional introductory course in their disciplines (Association of American Colleges, 1991).

Such a concern is well-founded. Like political science, many disciplines are experiencing a disturbing decline in the number of students who elect to continue studying them. For example, a joint task force (Association of American Colleges, 1991) convened by the Mathematical Association of America (MAA) and the Association of American Colleges (AAC, now the Association of American Colleges and Universities [AAC&U]) noted that,

27

> Data from many sources show that women and members of certain minority groups often discontinue their study of mathematics before they are prepared for jobs or further school. Black and Hispanic students drop out of mathematics at very high rates throughout high school and college, and only a tiny fraction complete an undergraduate mathematics major. (p. 87)

Not surprisingly, the failure of students to pursue degrees in the traditional arts and sciences helps to limit their academic role. The same MAA-AAC report (1991) also points out that

> Today mathematics is the second largest discipline in higher education. Indeed, more than 10 percent of college and university faculty members and student enrollments are in departments of mathematics. More than half of this enrollment, however, is in high school-level courses, and most of the rest is devoted to elementary service courses. (p. 77)

It is not difficult to imagine the deleterious effect a shortage of arts and sciences majors could have on a range of social sectors from education itself to nonprofit and public administration.

Clearly, the solution to declining student interest in many of the arts and sciences is not simply a function of what happens in the introductory course, nor is the solution to the design of an effective introductory course simply a matter of incorporating a service-learning component. Nonetheless, it is worth pausing to look at some of what we know not only about today's students but also about effective teaching and learning, and their relationship to work outside the traditional classroom.

In a piece entitled "Essential Demographics of Today's College Students," Edmund Hansen (1998) reviews a number of statistics that should be of interest to any course designer likely to encounter first-year students. He notes, for example, that "just 34% of freshmen report having spent six or more hours per week studying during their senior year in high school," that 36% of them "report having been frequently 'bored in class' during their last year of high school," and that "the average adolescent" views approximately 35 hours of television programming per week" (pp. 4-5). Meanwhile, almost three out of every five students identified "the chief benefit of a college education" as "increasing earning power" (p. 4), while those who recognized "developing a meaningful philosophy of life" as an important objective shrank to just a little over two out of five.

In other words, many of the students filling the seats in introductory courses have already developed habits and attitudes that represent a barrier to sustained attention and meaningful intellectual engagement. Confronted by courses that aggravate rather than challenge their sense of the irrelevance of non-vocational knowledge, the students vote with their feet, making their first college-level political science, sociology, history, biology course also their last. According to a task force chaired by the American Sociology Association's Carla Howery (1991), "90 percent of students in introductory sociology never take another sociology course" (p. 195).

Exacerbating this situation still further is the fact that, as the joint MAA-AAC task force put it (Association of American Colleges, 1991), "Too often [instructors] assume with little reflection that what was good for their own education is good enough for their students, not realizing that most of their students . . . have very different styles of learning" (p. 84). Indeed, Charles Schroeder (1995), in a study of student versus faculty learning styles, came to precisely the same conclusion:

> As faculty, we have generally espoused the common belief that students learn and develop through exposure—that the *content* is all-important. We have been accustomed to a traditional learning process where one who knows (the teacher) presents ideas to one who does not (the student). Many of us prospered under the traditional lecture system, where the focus is on coverage of material through teaching by telling. This approach may work for us but it may not work for the majority of today's students. (p. 22)

He then goes on to discuss the results of research that indicate that while "over 75% of faculty prefer [an] intuitive learning pattern" — i.e., "the realm of concepts, ideas, and abstractions" (p. 25) —"approximately 60% of entering students prefer [a] sensing mode— i.e., "the concrete, the practical, and the immediate" (p. 22).

Statement after statement by discipline-related groups bears out Schroeder's identification of "content" as the unexamined but nonetheless "all-important" focus of introductory courses. According to a task force of the American Institute of Biological Sciences (Association of American Colleges, 1991), many of the more than 300 biology majors who participated in a survey

> . . . felt compelled to comment on their experiences in the beginning biology course. They appeared to feel some sorrow for the non science majors enrolled in this first biology course as well as for the students planning to major in biology.

> Statements such as "yearlong rat race," "course in memorization," and "waste of time" were used by majors to describe their experiences in the beginning biology courses" (p. 13)

A group of historians (Association of American Colleges, 1991) has come to a similar conclusion. Decrying what they see as prevalent practice, they suggest that "building on the precollegiate experiences of the entering college students, the foundation course should eschew the 'one-damn-fact-after-another' approach to history" (p. 47). After all, the "purposes of foundation courses are to excite as well as to inform, to engage the minds and imagination of those who may be indifferent to history or even antagonistic to it" (p. 52). It is indeed sobering to see the degree to which the observations of disciplinary groups clearly confirm the observations and critiques of higher education researchers.

One final problem with the traditional introductory course deserves to be mentioned. In his book *Intellect and Public Life: Essays on the Social History of Academic Intellectuals in the United States*, Bender (1993) warns that current threats to academic integrity do not stem from contamination by modes of discourse outside the academy:

> The risk now is precisely the opposite. Academe is threatened by the twin dangers of fossilization and scholasticism (of three types: tedium, high tech, and radical chic). The agenda for the next decade, at least as I see it, ought to be the opening up of the disciplines, the ventilating of

professional communities that have come to share too much and that have become too self-referential. (p. 143)

Many of the disciplinary statements referred to above share this concern. The biology group laments that "little attention is given to making the connections among science, technology, and society in most introductory courses" (Association of American Colleges, 1991, p. 13). The mathematicians complain that most mathematics courses "pay no more than superficial attention to the historical, cultural, or contemporary context in which mathematics is practiced" (Association of American Colleges, 1991, p. 89). The historians suggest that more attention needs to be paid to questions like "How do historians deal with questions of citizenship—their own and their students—in the courses they teach?" (Association of American Colleges, 1991, p. 59).

In other words, another function of the introductory course should involve locating the discipline and its concerns in a broader historical and intellectual context, making clear its potential role in addressing problems of the contemporary world and exploring its links to other areas of study. Failure to address such concerns may result in graduates who are technically competent professionals; it will not result in graduates who are also civically competent. As a report sanctioned by the American Psychological Association (1991) suggests, the study of psychology is not a self-contained undertaking. Rather, it "is a preparation for lifelong learning, thinking, and action; it emphasizes specialized and general knowledge and skills. The skills required to be a successful student do not always match those required to be a good citizen" (p. 155).

It is precisely this recognition of the necessity of attending to more than technical competence that Sullivan (1995) addresses in his book *Work and Integrity: The Crisis and Promise of Professionalism in America*:

> Resolving the problems of education, health care, and the effectiveness of American business . . . involves more than the selection of competencies necessary for achievement. It requires that academic professionals and their students develop new capacities beyond technical skills through communication with a far broader range of groups and issues in the society. (p. 164)

Nowhere does such an exploration of a discipline's broader, public dimension deserve more attention than in courses that introduce that discipline to new students. Social significance and personal interest are related if not identical concepts, and inattention to both cannot help but reduce the effectiveness of the introductory course as an experience with positive educational consequences.

Strategies to promote engagement—the engagement of students in their academic work and of disciplinary expertise in a wide range of public concerns—can take many forms. Foregrounding the ways in which course concepts relate to contemporary events as reported in the press, guest speakers, and interactive in-class activities can help achieve one or both of these objectives. However, given the magnitude of both engagement problems, it may be that classroom-based activities are not in and of themselves enough to offset habits of intellectual inertia developed during the high school years. As the MAA-ACC group (Association of American Colleges, 1991) notes in another context,

> Research shows that formal learning by itself rarely influences real-world behavior; many students continue to use their flawed intuitions instead of the concepts learned in the artificial classroom environment. . . . Students whose minds and eyes become engaged in the challenge of true discovery are frequently transformed by the experience. (pp. 83-84)

Designers and instructors of introductory courses would do well to pay special attention to the phrase "transformed by the experience."

As Fox and Ronkowski's (1997) study illustrates, the failure of some introductory courses to capture the lasting interest of first-year students can be especially acute when the students in question are female or minority. In discussing the effect of service-learning on Biology in Engineering, a first-year, second-semester core course at Louisiana State University, Lima (2000) notes,

> Emphasizing the social component of engineering could enhance the attractiveness of the engineering discipline, particularly for women and minorities. Indeed, the retention rate for women and minorities in the three years that SL projects have been implemented in this course has been substantially higher than the national average. (pp. 114-15)

The reason for this, according to Lima, is that experiencing "a tangible purpose and framework for the fundamental courses" motivates students by helping them to "understand why they are learning the required material" (p. 112).

Another instructor in a related area makes a similar point. John Kinnell, a biologist at Southern Methodist University, works with service-learning projects via an introductory course for non-majors. He found

> such projects are particularly meaningful for students whose primary field of study lies outside the sciences. Specifically, service projects help engage these students in biological issues that they often have little interest in understanding or to which they have had little exposure. SL projects add a human dimension to issues that often seem irrelevant to the life of the average college student. In addition, such projects help students gain an appreciation for the methods, complexity, and goals of scientific research. In many instances, having a positive experience outside the classroom can invigorate a student who does not have an aptitude for science and can stimulate his or her interest in the course content. (Kinnell, 2000, p. 9)

Kinnell's second point is particularly worth noting: Not only has integrating a service-learning option into his course stimulated greater overall student interest but that interest has, in turn, led to an increase in "the general quality of the [participating students'] reports. . ." (p. 13). More than 75% of these students "thought that their projects made the research more interesting and hence led them to dig a little deeper into the literature" (p. 13). Such an observation runs counter to the not infrequently held faculty assumption that service necessarily comes at the expense of scholarship. Indeed, as Astin and Sax (1998) report, the argument that service in general consumes time and energy that might otherwise go to academic work "has effectively been laid to rest by the results of our longitudinal analyses, which reveal significant positive effects [of student service involvement] on all 10 [measured] academic outcomes" (p. 255).

But it is not just faculty in science and technology who report that the inclusion of a service component improves the introductory course in multiple ways. In the history volume of the AAHE series, co-editor Bill Donovan (2000) reports on his first-year history survey. In showing slides of the Great Depression, Donovan found that many of his students simply could not relate to what the slides depicted and made comments based on clearly flawed assumptions. This experience framed for him a critically important task:

> In Alfred Lord Whitehead's words, how could I as a teacher bring to my students' notice, "some fundamental assumptions which . . . appear so obvious that people do not know what they are assuming because no other way of putting things have [sic] ever occurred to them." (p. 152)

Initially Donovan attempted to demonstrate the fallacy of student assumptions through in-class discussion. Still, he found himself wondering just "how many students had been actually convinced that their initial arguments contained problematic assumptions" (p. 152). It was only a matter of time before he decided in-class learning could be more effectively facilitated through off-campus experiences.

This was also the conclusion of Jonathan Arries, a professor of Spanish at the College of William and Mary. Unlike Donovan, Arries (1999) stumbled upon the efficacy of service experiences in the first-year course quite by accident. Spanish 151: Cultural Perspectives of U.S. Hispanics was designed to accommodate that "small number of freshmen who have studied Spanish for four or five years and have traveled or lived in a Spanish-speaking country" (p. 33). For this relatively advanced, already motivated first-year group, Arries designed a "course syllabus that, if not exactly driven by critical pedagogy, would at least permit students to write in a variety of ways about literature and films by Latino artists" (p. 39). When he casually mentioned to his students the possibility of "basing their research paper on a service experience" (p. 38) like the one he himself had the previous summer at a migrant workers' clinic, two of his students wound up going with him back to the clinic. What unfolded next was completely unanticipated:

> Even more surprising than [the students'] successful "reading of a myth" [i.e., some promotional/informational brochures produced by the clinic] without the benefit of my stock presentation on semiological systems was the fact that our roles had changed from "expert" professor and "non-expert" students to co-workers . . . . Our collaborative engagement in a problem-solving effort to help real people had carried us across a . . . pedagogical boundary which would have been much more difficult to cross in our regular classroom. (pp. 39-40)

In short, the experience wound up being transformative for both teacher and students, redefining the former's very understanding of "context":

> I now see it [context] as a personally lived event that gives a learner sudden insight or a discovery that therefore becomes a memorable schema or "subtext" she or he can use to make sense out of experiences in different settings, like an internal guidebook or map. Second, I learned that

"context" created by service can empower students, enabling them to demystify complex aspects of language and society. I learned that the "borders" imposed by institutional forms can and therefore must be crossed. The pleasure I myself experienced while crossing the borders of pedagogy, culture and language *with* my students made the hard work we did on the Eastern Shore (and subsequently in the classroom) like no other experience I have had as a teacher or a student. (p. 41)

Having himself entered into the learning process in a new way—solving problems *with* his students rather than providing them with "stock" explanations—Arries personally experienced the truth of Schroeder's (1993) warning about the limited effectiveness of "teaching by telling."

Thus, it would seem to make little difference whether one is teaching in the sciences or the humanities, at a research university or a liberal arts college, whether one's students are relatively unmotivated to begin with or members of a well-prepared first-year group. Appropriate, academically framed service experiences can help students develop unexpected levels of personal and intellectual engagement—an engagement in some cases critical to further involvement.

Even when further involvement by way of a declared major is not much in doubt, service-learning in the introductory course can play still other valuable educational roles. Take, for example, Montana State University's undergraduate business major, a program that aims at the "systematic integration of a developmental service-learning agenda into the business curriculum" (2000, p. 167). Here service-learning informs both "(1) the first course taken by first-year business students, the Freshman Seminar; and (2) the last course taken by undergraduate business students, the Senior Seminar, which also constitutes the capstone course" (p. 169). In the former, service-learning

> . . . is introduced in the context of the stakeholder model that emphasizes the interconnectedness of businesses and legal, regulatory, sociological and competitive environments. Students are asked to personalize the stakeholder model by identifying their primary and secondary stakeholders. Discussion focuses on students' roles as stakeholders in the college, university and community. They examine businesses that have been recognized as doing well by doing good, and discuss the role of business in promoting healthy communities. (p. 170)

In this way, the students' first-year service experience not only serves as preparation for the business core courses but also grounds that core in an awareness of business's public responsibilities.

It is this same civic dimension that both Lima (2000) and Kinnell (2000) identify as additional benefits of their first-year courses. As Kinnell (2000) notes,

> The uncertainty and range of students' responses [to their service projects] enable their instructors to emphasize the value of providing educational opportunities for all members of our society and the need to increase our nation's level of scientific literacy. An additional benefit of these projects is that they can increase the students' sense of civic responsibility and often serve as a catalyst for additional community service. (p. 9)

Lima (2000) makes a similar point in discussing how her project "was chosen to give students the opportunity to see beyond themselves and their education into the community at large" (p. 113). In facilitating such expanded vision, she hopes to help them see that "engineering must truly address social issues and fully interface with society [if it is] to be a vital, positive influence" (p. 116).

In an interview with AAHE, Edmund Tsang (1996), director of The Education 2000 Trust, has suggested that "higher-order thinking and problem-solving skills grow out of direct experience, not simply teaching; they require more than a classroom activity" (pp. 3-4). Student responses to the kinds of courses referenced in this chapter would seem to bear this out. Commenting on her experience in "Integrating Service-Learning into Introduction to Mechanical Engineering," one student noted that she was "really impressed with the complexity of this freshman-level course. Students are introduced to the design process, required to write reports, and communication is emphasized" (Tsang, 2000, p. 128). Nonetheless, it is clear that service-learning in any introductory course must be designed in ways that stretch but do not break the first-year student's sense of competence.

For this reason, many—though by no means all—first-year service-learning projects are of relatively limited scope (i.e., a single multi-hour off-campus service activity or a single event that is prepared for over a multi-week period). While even such limited community-based work must, of necessity, be carefully linked to course objectives, introductory course objectives may include—or even stress—such non-content-specific skills as team building, interpersonal communication, sensitivity to diversity, practical problem solving, and personal empowerment. In some cases, projects that require technical competency or conceptual sophistication may even be inappropriate.

Limited service projects that require little technical competency usually do not pose problems for community partners, at least not if they are thoroughly discussed and planned. Nevertheless, even a community partner aware of the difference between community service and service-learning, as described in the introduction to this monograph, may need help in making sure more generic, short-term projects do not inadvertently slide into simple community service. For this reason, first-year service projects may require more detailed guidelines and monitoring than would otherwise be the case. Failure to articulate, prepare, and process the learning-related dimensions of the experience clearly and deliberately may well result in students' assuming the learning agenda that underlies and justifies the service activity is of minimal importance.

However, in the end, it may not be special logistical or design considerations that pose the greatest challenge to effective use of service-learning in the introductory course. As several of the statements cited in the first part of this chapter serve to indicate, the educational model that informs many such courses can be accurately characterized as a kind of "grand tour," whereby the first course is seen as a way of mapping out the broad features of the discipline that electives will later explore in depth. Even when the course is intended for non-majors, this same coverage-driven approach prevails, perhaps in a somewhat "dumbed down" form, on the assumption that if students are to take only one course in the discipline, it should introduce them to a wide variety of its concerns. A "'one-damn-fact-after-another' approach" (Association of American Colleges, 1991, p. 47) is often the inevitable result.

Such an approach reflects what Sullivan (n.d.) has called a "default program of instrumental individualism" (p. 2), itself a corollary of an essentially positivistic epistemology that places its ultimate faith in the assembling and communication of "objective" facts. Whatever distracts attention or diverts time and energy from coverage of these facts must be rejected as intellectually fuzzy and academically suspect. That this approach is driving an increasing number of students to "elect" to put pre-professional how-to courses—courses whose "facts" at least seem to promise a comfortable financial future—at the center of their educational agenda is unfortunate but also someone else's fault.

Even farther back, somewhat obscured by this positivistic legacy, lies still another set of largely unexamined assumptions; namely, that the realm of practical doing is a but a pale shadow of the realm of pure knowing. As Harkavy and Benson (1998) have argued, this Platonic perspective, "uncompromisingly aristocratic and antidemocratic, . . . has had perhaps its greatest (and most pernicious) impact on Western education":

> For Plato, learning occurred through contemplative thought, not through action and reflection. Dividing the world into ideal and material universes, Plato viewed knowledge as deriving from the ideal spiritual universe of permanent and fixed ideas. He conceptualized the material world of objects and actions as merely "a shadowy, fleeting world" of imperfect imitations. (p. 12)

The contradictions between this position and the positivist focus on facts need not detain us here. Suffice it to say, the ways in which these two legacies complement each other have helped to make the introductory course an educationally dangerous undertaking. Not only must students navigate a sea of what is to them largely meaningless facts, but they must also eschew the assistance of useful applications and non-academic experiences that would, perforce, impede their progress toward the life of the mind and the touchstone of pure or basic research. Woe to that 60% of first-year students (Schroeder, 1993) who find utility, concrete particulars, and personal relevance an effective way to enter the educational arena!

Several years ago at an AAHE national conference (1996), then Chancellor of the University of Massachusetts David Scott made an observation to the effect that putting internships at the end of the academic career really made little sense. Internships should come at the beginning, so that students' remaining semesters could be used to unpack their experiences. The same logic applies to the introductory discipline-based course. If we want our first-year students to become truly liberally educated—regardless of their eventual major—we need to give them more reasons to take seriously all the academic disciplines to which they are exposed. The incorporation of service-learning into the introductory course is one promising way to achieve that end.

References

Arries, J. F. (1999). Critical pedagogy and service-learning in Spanish: Crossing borders in the freshman seminar. In J. Hellebrandt & L.T. Verona (Eds.), *Construyendo puentes (building bridges): Concepts and models for service-learning in Spanish,* (pp. 33-47). Washington, DC: American Association for Higher Education.

Association of American Colleges. (1991). *Reports from the field.* Washington, DC: Author.

Astin, A. W., & Sax, L. J. (1998). How undergraduates are affected by service participation. *Journal of College Student Development, 39*(3), 251-263.

Bender, T. (1993). *Intellect and public life: Essays on the social history of academic intellectuals in the United States.* Baltimore: Johns Hopkins.

Donovan, B. M. (2000). Service-learning as a tool of engagement: From Thomas Aquinas to Che Guevara. In I. Harkavy & B.M. Donovan (Eds.), *Connecting past and present: Concepts and models for service-learning in history,* (pp. 149-158). Washington, DC: American Association for Higher Education.

Fox, R. L., & Ronkowski, S. A. (1997). Learning styles of political science students. *PS: Political Science & Politics, 30*(4), 732-737.

Hansen, E. J. (1998). Essential demographics of today's college students. *AAHE Bulletin, 51*(3), 3-5.

Harkavy, I., & Benson, L. (1998). De-platinizing and democratizing education as the bases of service learning. In R. A. Rhoads & J. P. F. Howard (Eds.), *Academic service learning: A pedagogy of action and reflection,* (pp. 11-20). San Francisco: Jossey-Bass.

Kinnell, J. C. (2000). Educational benefits associated with service-learning projects in biology curricula. In D. C. Brubaker & J. H. Ostroff (Eds.), *Life, learning, and community: Concepts and models for service learning in biology,* (pp. 7-23). Washington DC: American Association for Higher Education.

Lamb, C. H., Lee, J. B., Swinth, R. L., & Vinton, K. L. (2000). Learning well by doing good: Service-learning in management education. In P. C. Godfrey & E. T. Grasso (Eds.), *Working for the common good: Concepts and models for service-learning in management,* (pp. 167-178). Washington, D. C.: American Association for Higher Education.

Lima, M. (2000). Service-learning: A unique perspective on engineering education. In E. Tsang (Ed.), *Projects that matter: Concepts and models for service-learning in engineering,* (pp. 109-117). Washington D. C.: American Association for Higher Education.

Schroeder, C. C. (1993). New students-new learning styles. *Change, 25*(5), 21-26.

Sullivan, W. M. (n.d.). The university as citizen: Institutional identity and social responsibility. Washington, D. C.: Council on Public Policy Education.

Sullivan, W. M. (1995). *Work and integrity: The crisis and promise of professionalism in America.* New York: HarperBusiness.

Tsang, E. (2000). Projects that matter: Concepts and models for service-learning in engineering. In E. Tsang (Ed.), *Integrating service-learning into introduction to mechanical engineering* (pp. 119-134). Washington, DC: AAHE.

Section 2

Looking at Today's Students

Look Who's Coming to College: The Impact of High School Service-Learning on New College Students

Marty Duckenfield

It is an exciting time to be a college professor if one believes in service-learning. The reason? Just look who is coming to college!

As Furco notes elsewhere in this monograph, a greater number of newly arriving college students already have multiple service-learning experiences under their belts and consequently bring with them an array of knowledge, skills, and attitudes that can only enhance the potential for the success of service-learning instruction in college. This chapter expands that discussion by providing an in-depth exploration of the practice of service-learning in grades K-12. By examining models of precollege service-learning programs and listening to the students involved in those programs, we enrich our understanding of the effect of prior service-learning experiences on incoming college students.

In fact, service-learning has been increasingly adopted over the past several years. What is the evidence of this sudden growth? The data described by Kleiner and Chapman (1999) indicate that, although the level of community service and volunteer activities of American high school students remained relatively stable from the mid-1970s to the early 1990s, it grew from 27% to over 80% between 1984 and 1999. In addition, school involvement through service-learning has significantly increased. In 1984, one would have found just 9% of all high schools with some form of service-learning, while in 1999, approximately 46% of high schools had some form of service-learning (Kleiner & Chapman, 1999). This amazing increase is due to several major efforts over the past decade that have combined in synergy to make service-learning a major educational reform initiative in our public schools.

In 1993, the original federal Commission on National and Community Service became the Corporation for National Service (CNS), and under its umbrella (which also includes AmeriCorps and Senior Corps) functions the Learn and Serve America program, which supports service-learning. State education agencies (SEAs) wrote proposals for funds to support the implementation of service-learning in local schools and school districts, and successful proposals—whether small planning grants or district-wide implementation grants—fostered the widespread growth of service-learning. As districts used some of their funds to send teachers and students to conferences and workshops, a network of enthusiasts formed, and early practice increased in quality as a result of professional development.

Private foundations also provided a significant boost to the growth of service-learning. The National Youth Leadership Council (NYLC), based in St. Paul, Minnesota, has been a key player in this area since its inception in the mid-1980s. NYLC has worked to train teachers, raise awareness, and develop policy, in part, through its annual conference. With the support of several foundations, NYLC established a network of 38 schools, called Generator Schools, that became laboratories for achieving excellence in service-learning practice. Many practical resources for schools across the country came out of this project.

With funding from CNS, NYLC reached out to over a dozen partners to establish the National Service-Learning Cooperative Clearinghouse in 1993. The Clearinghouse, located at the University of Minnesota, collects and disseminates information on service-learning. A cluster of training and technical assistance providers was also established. Regional conferences have provided high-quality professional development and enabled an increasing number of new service-learning practitioners to augment their pedagogical skills.

This coalition of educational organizations then developed a practitioner-based network of service-learning peer consultants. Funded by the Kellogg Foundation, this network assisted in the creation of a cadre of teachers skilled in service-learning who became trainers capable of addressing the needs of overburdened SEAs. In fact, thanks to their own hands-on experiences in the classroom, these advocates brought a crucial element of truth and validity to their training and consulting efforts. The NYLC-led and CNS-funded National Service-Learning Exchange now coordinates all of these efforts.

The students of peer consultants, known as youth consultants, assisted in these efforts and were given extraordinary opportunities to spread the word about service-learning and to teach its elements in chambers of commerce, college teacher education classes, national and regional workshops, and by hosting visiting teachers in their own schools. They were tapped for leadership positions in grant-making and advisory councils and began to produce their own resources for the service-learning field (Follman, 1997; Kelley, Specter, & Young, 2000; Wren Middle School Students, 1997).

Over this period, many educational organizations have adopted service-learning as central to their missions, and a number have provided schools with curricular materials that represent an excellent foundation for the successful implementation of high-quality service-learning. For example, the Los Angeles-based Constitutional Rights Foundation (CRF) joined forces with the Washington, DC-based CloseUp Foundation in order to forward their common goal of developing a nation of involved and informed citizens. Their *Active Citizenship Today* (ACT) curriculum has provided a resource that has gotten thousands of educators started on the service-learning highway. Lions-Quest International's *Skills for Action* curriculum, with its focus on developing personal and social responsibility through service-learning, has been another valuable entry point for teachers new to this approach.

In many local school districts throughout the country, community service or service-learning has become mandatory for graduation. For instance, the Maryland Student Service Alliance has provided teachers with a wealth of supporting resources and training to ensure that the requirement is met through service-learning rather than just hours of service. These resource tools (e.g., "The Courage to Care, the Strength to Serve" video and curriculum guides for all grade levels and special education) have gained acceptance throughout the nation. Again, community service was the starting point for many schools in developing service-learning programs.

The positive impact of service-learning on fostering good educational experiences and preventing dropouts is supported by much of the research on resiliency (Benard, 1991). This research strongly supported the contention that effective prevention strategies are built on methodologies that set high expectations for youth, provide caring and supportive adults, and give youth opportunities for meaningful experiences—all of which are found in well-designed service-learning programs. The National Dropout Prevention Center (NDPC), whose involvement in service-learning began in the early 1990s, makes available to K-12 educators professional development opportunities and has developed an array of resources that foster high quality service-learning in the public schools. Its *Pocket Guide to Service Learning* and its *Linking Learning With Life* series of service-learning guidebooks have been disseminated widely.

At the same time, other initiatives in the K-12 world—school-to-work, character education, intergenerational service-learning, and environmental service-learning—have helped bring still other new participants to the service-learning field. For example, states such as Minnesota and South Carolina have understood the connection between the workplace skills expected by the business community (e.g., communicating, interpreting, decision making, organizing, working in teams, and following schedules) and service-learning, and have provided opportunities for K-12 students to gain those skills by integrating service-learning into their state's school-to-work laws. Each state has developed supportive programs and resources for education practitioners.

Intergenerational service-learning, where young and old serve together, has been advocated by organizations such as Generations United and Generations Together. The South Carolina Department of Education's LINC project has supported the development of this approach to service-learning in the public schools and has produced several resources including a guide for developing such projects and linking the learning to the curriculum (Brandes & Green, 1999).

At the same time, connecting service-learning to environmental education has become a popular approach for public school science teachers. Many organizations exist in individual states to help schools form partnerships around specific environmental issues, and many of these organizations have excellent educational materials to supplement the school's curriculum. Earth Force is one national organization that is working to develop specific curricula for grades five through nine. Through environmental service-learning, students involved in Earth Force help to shape policy and community practice. The program is an exemplar of quality service-learning with training and materials emphasizing such principles as "academic integrity, school-community partnerships, civic action, student direction, performance assessment, and continuous reflection" (Richardson, 2000, p. 7).

Thus, the explosive growth of K-12 service-learning has not occurred in a vacuum. Its development has been bolstered by the development of teacher-friendly resources, an army of trained and experienced peer trainers and consultants, sufficient funds to support professional development opportunities at the state, regional, and national levels, as well as connections to a wide variety of educational initiatives.

Portraits of Service-Learning During the K-12 Years

In all areas of the curriculum—from math and the natural sciences to English, the social sciences, music, art, foreign languages, and physical education—educators are integrating service-learning into the academic programs of public schools. Some examples will illustrate both the breadth and depth of these initiatives.

Social Science—Civic Education

Like many American high schools, Iowa City High School has developed a course through its social studies department that is specifically designed to give students a greater sense of civic empowerment and responsibility. The course, called Global Portraits of Change, affords students an opportunity to see the effect of federal government policies at the local level, experience personal growth, understand that solutions to social problems are not simple, and finally see that they can make a difference.

A strong academic component focuses on student research on contemporary world problems as well as learning about power structures and strategies used to implement change. Then students become agents of change themselves in their local communities by "choosing a local problem, designing a way to solve the problem, completing a service-learning project, and writing reflectively about their experiences. Students . . . measure their learning through authentic assessments—photo essays, journals, posters, presentations, and papers—to show what they learned" (Finken, 1996, p. 111).

English—Writing

Hill and Pope (1997) describe a high school writing lab in Springfield Central High School in Springfield, Massachusetts. One group of students there decided to create a class project that involved writing for the environment and resulted in an "unexpected spin-off":

> The students started a schoolwide "Earth Action" club that involved special-needs students in all of its activities. Writing for class became writing to create Earth Action programs and document activities that included launching a recycling program, contacting elementary schools to work with Springfield students, planning and advertising Earth Day activities, and writing editorials and letters to promote different kinds of environmental awareness. (p. 190)

Science

In the fall of 1993, the author visited Rutherford High School in Panama City, Florida. Teachers, administrators, and students took a group of visiting educators to the site of their new school service project at Tyndall Air Force Base where, as part of an ongoing partnership, Rutherford students were turning two acres formally used as a dumping ground for old airport runway materials into a restored natural habitat. The project included the replanting of pine trees, the building of a nature trail (a 2,400-foot boardwalk), and the construction of an outdoor classroom.

Watkins and Wilkes (1993) describe a project where students get hands-on experience applying concepts learned in the science classroom:

> Teachers and students began their environmental research by identifying and studying the four main ecosystems in the area: wetland, grassy knoll, pine forest, and saltwater shoreline. Students worked in pairs on two-meter square plot studies to count and identify plant and animal species. Participants took soil core samples, which they then illustrated and described in reports on soil composition. Students studied soil types and textures, made visual field identification of animal species, and conducted laboratory observation of microorganisms. They also evaluated the area's soil porosity, or absorption capacity, and examined the interaction of soil porosity and pollution. Students collected and tested water samples from the inlet beach shoreline, fresh water wetlands, open bay shoreline, asphalt pile runoff, and ground water for salinity, pH balance, and clarity. (pp. 50-51)

Interdisciplinary Work

Another large-scale project can be found in rural South Carolina, in the School District of Marion Four, the smallest in the state. There, the service-learning program at Britton's Neck High School has received state, national, and international notice and is a demonstration site for the Kellogg Learning In Deed project.

Britton's Neck High School is best known for the construction of a rural fire substation, a project that has taken several years to complete. A visit to Britton's Neck always includes a stop at the substation, completely built by students, and where current students as well as recent graduates now serve as volunteer fire fighters. A needs assessment conducted by agriculture students at the school revealed inadequate fire service—the nearest fire station was nearly 15 miles away. Students brought the community together to begin planning the building of a new station and played leadership roles throughout the building process. Following the donation of a piece of land by a community member, agriculture students surveyed the land. Math students were able to make an estimate of the number of cinder blocks and the amount of concrete needed, and science students were able to analyze the potential environmental impact of the new substation. Economics students were able to determine the new fire insurance rates for local residents (which declined). All students worked to build the station, block by block.

Youth Leadership Experience

Throughout the nation, young people are frequently given a chance to take on unusually demanding leadership roles. One of the most interesting initiatives in this arena is the youth consultant program, originally developed under the auspices of a Kellogg-funded project of the National Service-Learning Cooperative Clearinghouse and the National Youth Leadership Council.

In this program, youth experienced in service-learning are partnered with experienced service-learning adult peer consultants to support new practitioners developing service-learning projects. The manual created by the project makes clear that the youth role is valued: "True youth-adult partnerships emerge when both are treated as important contributors to a program" (Liebl-Kamenov & Carle, 1999,

p. 32). Indeed, the youth consultants (YCs) at a National Service-Learning Leader School, Spring Valley High School in Columbia, South Carolina, have articulated an extensive list of roles they have played outside the classroom:

♦ Helping to plan, implement, and evaluate service-learning activities, projects, and programs
♦ Advocating meaningful student involvement by demonstrating the role of youths in developing service-learning programs
♦ Consulting with teachers, community members, and other youths in person and/or by mail, fax, e-mail, and phone
♦ Making site visits and attending meetings to represent the student perspective and to share service-learning experiences
♦ Serving on panels that further the cause of youth development and service-learning
♦ Making presentations to educators, community members, and/or other youth interested in service-learning
♦ Creating videos, multimedia productions, brochures, and other publications that document and share service-learning information and experiences
♦ Contributing articles for publications supporting youth development and service-learning
♦ Collaborating with other youth and adult Peer Consultant teams on presentations and special projects
♦ Providing leadership training for youth interested in school/community development (Kelley, Specter, & Young, 2000, p. 3)

Wren Middle School Youth Consultants (1997) describe similar duties for their YCs, even at the middle school level. It seems clear students who have been involved as youth consultants have a strong grasp of what service-learning is and a first-hand understanding of how one implements it in a school setting.

The Impact of Service-Learning on K-12 Students

Service-learning's attraction to educators in the public schools is based on several expected benefits to students. To be specific, many educators believe that this approach will enhance their students' personal growth by developing self-confidence and self-esteem, self-understanding, a sense of identity, independence and autonomy, openness to new experiences and roles, ability to take risks and accept challenges, a sense of usefulness and purpose, personal values and beliefs, a sense of responsibility for one's actions, and self-respect (Duckenfield & Swanson, 1992).

They also envision social growth as evidenced by enhanced communication and leadership skills, the ability to work cooperatively with others, a sense of caring for others, a sense of belonging, acceptance and awareness of others from diverse and multicultural backgrounds, and peer group affiliation. Finally—and quite critically in an educational milieu where meeting academic standards and scoring well on statewide tests are high on the agenda—they believe service-learning enhances intellectual growth by linking theory to practice and by developing problem-solving and decision-making skills, critical thinking skills, skills in learning from experience, and an overall positive attitude toward learning.

Because an especially important role for public education is the preparation of students for citizenship in a democratic society, service-learning is viewed as a way to provide opportunities that develop a sense of social responsibility; awareness of community needs; organizational skills; social action skills such as persuasion, policy research, and petitioning; and belief in one's ability to make a difference. At the same time, it apparently prepares students equally well for the workforce by helping them to develop human service skills; realistic ideas about the world of work; professionalism in dress, grooming, and manners; the ability to follow directions; the ability to function as a team member; and patterns such as punctuality, consistent work habits, and regular attendance.

Expectations like these clearly show that service-learning's supporters consider it a most powerful educational tool, one vital for reforming our public schools, but does the research show that these expectations are realistic? Billig (2000) has synthesized the research relevant to many of these areas. Her findings, summarized below, are very encouraging.

Many studies support the claim that service-learning affects both personal and social development. Evidence reveals increases in personal and social responsibility, communication abilities, social competence, self-esteem, self-efficacy, and a sense of treating others with kindness. Students have also been shown to develop bonds with more adults and a greater acceptance of cultural diversity. An increase in mutual, demonstrable respect between teachers and students is another result.

With regard to academic outcomes, service-learning has been correlated with higher state test scores and higher grades, reflecting more substantive academic engagement. Enhanced problem-solving skills and an increased interest in academics have also been documented. The same holds for citizenship skills, evidenced by greater awareness of community needs and the belief that one can personally make a difference. Moreover, high school students from strong service-learning programs have been shown to have a greater understanding of socio-historical contexts and to be more prepared to effect social change. Indeed, service-learning students have demonstrated an increased understanding of how government works. Longterm studies have suggested that such students are also more likely to be engaged in community organizations and, in the future, to vote. Research related to career awareness and readiness for the world of work has shown student gains in career skills, attitudes, and awareness—not to mention, awareness of career options (Billig, 2000).

In short, the research strongly supports the belief held by service-learning educators that the benefits of a service-learning approach are both wide-ranging and transformative.

Meet the Students

Let us now put some faces on the data cited here by meeting real students whose lives have been transformed by their service-learning experiences in the public schools. The author interviewed many young people, a group representative of those who will be coming to college with a service-learning background. The qualities they bring with them thanks to their service-learning experience mirror the research findings just referred to and are even more impressive in the flesh.

Amanda

Amanda is an outgoing and friendly 16-year-old junior in high school. As a middle school student, Amanda was very involved in service-learning experiences in her classes, for she was fortunate to have been a student at an NYLC Generator School. In addition, Amanda became one of a team of youth consultants, so her experience base is rich. She describes herself as having been very shy as a young girl but maintains that her service-learning experiences gave her an opportunity to develop her social skills, particularly her communication skills. Amanda has "taught" pre-service teachers about service-learning, has co-authored a book on youth consultants, and has helped create a video on the topic. She has been able to explore her ideas about her future career and, knows herself well enough to have begun choosing her college major with some confidence. "Service-learning has helped me with career decisions and has given me more options for my future," says this poised young woman. She credits service-learning with helping her work well with others in a team and with knowing how to listen well to others' ideas and accept constructive criticism. Now attending the Governor's School of Math and Science, Amanda has discovered that the time management skills she needed to develop as part of her service-learning work are helping her face the college-like atmosphere of her new school. She is also looking forward to *many* service-learning experiences when she goes to college.

Ron

Ron is a first-year college student whose prior service-learning experience was a key component of his high school English class. Ron clearly understood how the curriculum—a study of *Beowulf*—related to the senior class Hero Project. Skilled in reflection, Ron becomes thoughtful as he analyzes the changes in his own maturity during his service-learning experiences. Ron was fortunate to have a teacher and other adults as mentors who guided his growth in all areas during high school as he and they worked together to address community needs. These relationships of mutual respect and trust have left Ron with a desire to find more such associations in college. He understands what it takes to work in a group to achieve a common goal—and he is used to having adults from both his school and community be a part of that group. Ron states that "with service-learning, you need to work together as a team towards the same goal, not so much as teacher and student, but as co-workers." Ron believes that students today have many great ideas to offer, and just as he learned to listen to these ideas when he participated in high school service-learning projects, so he is hopeful that college professors will be willing to listen to his and his classmates' ideas.

Franklin

Franklin is also a first-year student. In his high school years, he was a Youth Consultant, and he is eager to see service-learning in as many of his college classes as possible. His face lights up as he talks about the many different projects in which he has been involved over the years. Like all well-trained youth consultants, Franklin can identify all the academic applications of his myriad service-learning projects, yet to him the most important component of service-learning is the emotional connection it forges among participants. Reflecting on his school's total involvement in service-learning, Franklin recalls, "you see kids *wanting to learn* with service-learning." Franklin's portfolio of leadership activities includes substantial contributions to his community, state, and nation, all a direct outgrowth of his experiences in the service-learning arena. In addition, his relationships with the adult leaders associated with his various activities are strong and reciprocal.

Qualities Gained Through Service-Learning

These students, like thousands of others involved in service-learning, show a level of maturity that will be most welcome to their future college professors. Their skills in teamwork, as both leaders and good listeners, and their ability to work with a variety of individuals, will help their fellow students as they work together to solve problems. They are, moreover, very self-confident and are well-prepared to take on the responsibilities frequently required in college-level service-learning. Their ability to manage their time well is another strength, and their willingness to help others proceed toward a common goal should not be underrated.

In short, students with a history of K-12 service-learning are more likely to be motivated from the start: motivated to do service as part of their coursework and motivated in general since they are more likely to have chosen their career paths. In the case of many fields, particularly in education and health, students find their career goals identified or strengthened by high school service-learning experiences. Consequently, their academic work becomes more relevant to them, and they already know the answer to "why do I have to learn this?"

Also of major significance is the fact that these students have had prior experience in reflection. Some students, having their first college-level service-learning experience, do not even know what the term means. Nor do they know how to analyze an experience—the "what," "so what," "now what" reflection cycle is totally foreign to them. However, many high school service-learning students have already developed skills in this area. Professors interviewed have noted a distinct difference in the quality of the reflections of the two groups, the more experienced students showing greater depth in their thinking and in the connections they are able to make among the curriculum, the service, and the larger issues involved. Students with previous exposure to service-learning also seem to show a greater awareness of the very existence of issues. Coming from a strong service-learning program, one student informally observed that students who had not been involved in service-learning were frequently surprised by the existence of some social issues.

Most of these students have had unique relationships with adults who have served in the dual capacities of mentor and colleague. These relationships have played an important part in the development of the self-confidence and maturity levels of these students, and they openly seek to replicate these associations with adults they respect at the college level. In addition, since they are accustomed to having adults value and treat their ideas with consideration and respect, they look forward to having this experience at the college level.

These future college students are experienced problem solvers, and they absolutely relish the opportunity to meet new challenges in college with what they consider will be greater knowledge and skills. And, very importantly, these students truly understand how real learning happens. They have experienced a variety of pedagogies during their years in public school, and service-learning is the one that puts excitement into their whole being when they talk about it. Intuitively, students know that when people care about something, their learning is enhanced. These students know that applying new skills to a real situation reinforces their learning. And they know that intrinsic motivation is a key to academic success.

Harnessing the Energy: Recommendations

One of the major thrusts of the K-12 service-learning movement has been to find consistent and authentic ways for youth to play more meaningful roles in the entire service-learning experience. The Youth Consultant program is certainly premised on that belief. A new Learning In Deed report, *Integrating Youth Voice in Service-Learning* (Fredericks, Kaplan, & Zeisler, 2001), cites an observation by Billig that outcomes of service-learning reach their highest levels when students are primarily responsible for planning, making decisions, solving problems, and assessing their learning. The lessons in this research are relevant to college-age youth as well.

The students interviewed for this chapter had many excellent suggestions for educators at the college level. Understanding that they have had important service-learning experiences both in high school and before, they believe there are ways in which they themselves can help facilitate the successful integration of service-learning into the college curriculum.

Experienced first-year students might:

♦ *Encourage classmates to become excited about service as part of a class.* Their enthusiasm for participation in service related to coursework could be tapped and become contagious, thus helping even reluctant students to approach this new experience with a more positive attitude.

♦ *Teach what service-learning is to their classmates.* One professor believed that his course's introductory session, conducted by an experienced service-learning student, on what service-learning is and why it is an effective way to learn, was crucial in introducing this teaching method to his first-year students.

♦ *Work with adults, including their professors, in a spirit of mutual respect and trust.* Why wait for these students to become graduate students? The opportunities exist *now* to establish a valuable, reciprocal relationship with them.

♦ *Be co-workers in solving community problems.* Service-learning students hope their college professors will join them as much as possible at their service sites, and, as one student put it, "put their PhD's in their pockets" and roll up their sleeves as they work alongside their students.

♦ *Be more involved in problem solving.* Service-learning students have a broad range of experience in coming up with solutions to community problems. Professors could build on this experience, thus bringing into their classes innovative and fresh approaches.

♦ *Help in group work.* Already skilled in teamwork, service-learning students could play a major leadership role in making service-learning more successful in the course.

♦ *Be used to lift their classmates to a higher level of reflective analysis.* The insights of service-learning students could be used to prod their classmates to probe issues to a greater depth. This, in turn, would raise the overall level of reflection and the overall quality of course learning.

Conclusion

Educators in colleges and universities will soon reap the benefits of the strong service-learning movement in the public schools. With the support of significant ongoing professional development opportunities, classroom teachers at all levels are constantly showing gains in their service-learning expertise. Their students have more and more opportunities to become engaged learners, to be aware of the world around them, to confront issues, and to work to solve problems. These students are developing the knowledge, skills, and attitudes that will serve them well throughout their college years.

References

Benard, B. (1991). *Fostering resiliency in kids: Protective factors in the family, school, and community.* Portland, OR: Northwest Regional Educational Laboratory.

Billig, S. (2000, July). The effects of service-learning. *The School Administrator, 57*(7), 14-18.

Brandes, B., & Green, R. (1999). *Off their rockers: Connecting the generations through service learning.* Clemson, SC: National Dropout Prevention Center.

Duckenfield, M., & Swanson, L. (1992). *Service-learning: Meeting the needs of youth at risk.* Clemson, SC: National Dropout Prevention Center.

Finken, H. (1996). Under construction: Knowledgeable, committed, and active citizens. In G. Gulati-Partee, & W. R. Finger (Eds.), *Critical issues in K-12 service-learning: Case studies and reflections.* Raleigh, NC: National Society for Experiential Education.

Follman, J. (1997). *Giving youth the power and the money: A guide to establishing youth service-learning councils.* Clemson, SC: National Dropout Prevention Center.

Fredericks, L., Kaplan, E., & Zeisler, J. (2001). *Integrating youth voice in service-learning.* Denver, CO: Education Commission of the States' Initiative, Compact for Learning and Citizenship.

Hill, D., & Pope, D. C. (1997). High school programs. In R. C. Wade (Ed.), *Community service-learning: A guide to including service in the public school curriculum.* Albany, NY: State University of New York Press.

Kelley, J., Specter, J., & Young, J. (2000). *Route to success: A leader school's youth consultant program.* Clemson, SC: National Dropout Prevention Center.

Kleiner, B., & Chapman, C. (November 1999). *Youth service-learning and community service among 6th through 12th grade students in the United States: 1996 and 1999.* Washington, DC: National Center for Educational Statistics.

Liebl-Kamenov, M., & Carle, P. (Eds.). (1999). *Youth consultant handbook.* St. Paul, MN: National Service-Learning Cooperative Clearinghouse.

Richardson, S. (2000). Active citizenship before high school. *Learning & Serving, 7*(1), 7.

Watkins, J., & Wilkes, D. (1993). *Sharing success in the southeast: Promising service-learning programs.* Greensboro, NC: SERVE Laboratory.

Wren Middle School Youth Consultants. (1997). *Youth consultants: Putting it all toge*ther. Clemson, SC: National Dropout Prevention Center.

Acknowledgments

Interviews with the following students and faculty were extremely helpful in developing the content of this chapter: Amanda Davis, Ron Wilson, Franklin Davis, Bethany Stubbs, Ginger Bishop, Derrell Dean, Courtney DeShields, and Jamaal Young. In addition, public school teachers Erin Darnell and Jerry Pace, and university faculty Dale Layfield and Carol Weatherford also provided great insights.

A Matter of Experience:
Service-Learning and the Adult Student

Tom O'Connell

There is a common narrative for service-learning at the college level. It goes like this. Young, mostly white, middle-class students leave the comfort of their college campus to engage with people often different than themselves in socially important work. In the process they learn civic skills and civic responsibility. In the best of worlds this "real world" experience has the added advantage of enriching the learning process itself. Discipline-based material comes alive as abstract theoretical perspectives are enhanced through the medium of direct and often powerful experience.

This storyline, of course, is over-generalized. For one thing, full-time students who begin and complete their college education between the ages of 18 and 22 are a distinct minority. As the distinguished demographer of higher education, Hodgins (as cited in Arenson, 2001) notes that of the almost 15 million students in college only 20% fit this description. In fact, almost half of today's college students are adults with children and jobs. Universities, while overwhelmingly middle class, are nevertheless surprisingly diverse places. State by state, the percentage of college students who are ethnic minorities is virtually the same as the percent of high school minority graduates. In California, for example, 54% of high school graduates are students of color compared to 53% of college students. In my own state of Minnesota, the figures are 10% and 9% respectively.

What is the purpose of service-learning, then, in educational environments where part-time adult students from a variety of class and cultural backgrounds are the norm? If there is an important role for service-learning as an educational strategy, what elements of program design are specifically relevant for older working students? Finally, in relation to the focus of this volume, is there a specific role for "first-year" community-based experiences when considering the more varied backgrounds and academic trajectories of the adult student?

Characteristics of the Adult Learner

Who exactly are adult students, and to what extent are they really different from "traditional" (18- to 22-year-old) students? One typology developed by Campbell, Wilson, and Hanson (1980) identified eight different categories of adult students based on the varied roles they assumed—from full-time worker and part-time student with heavy family responsibilities to full-time student with no work obligations and few family responsibilities. Neugarten (1979) points out that there is far more diversity among adults than, say, six-year-olds. Adults tend to "fan out," as their lives grow longer, the choices they make accumulate, and their lives follow unique paths (p. 89). At Metropolitan State University, where I teach, it is not unusual to have students ranging in age from 18 to 55. And with that diversity in age comes a wide range of cultural, class, and economic backgrounds: nurses, business people, service employees, computer technicians, social service providers. First-generation college students from the broad working and middle class—often women—mingle with recent immigrants and refugees from Laos, Somalia, Latin America. For almost everyone, college represents a transition: one that was sought out and eagerly embraced, or one that was forced by life circumstances (e.g., a divorce, a workplace injury, the need for a new credential).

To these differences in social roles and background one must add variations in aptitude, ability, and learning style. It should not be a surprise, but nevertheless bears emphasis, that not all adults learn alike. As the authors of one influential study put it, "we know that some are bright, others dull; some are knowledgeable, others ignorant; some are anxious, others self-confident; some process information in a rigid manner, others are able to digest complex, ambiguous material" (Chickering, Lynch, & Schlossberg 1989, p. 14).

Given this diversity, are there unique qualities that differentiate adults as learners? Scholars of adult education insist there are while cautioning against overgeneralization. Lynch and Chickering (1984) cite the following characteristics:

- A wider range of more sharply etched individual differences
- Multiple demands and responsibilities in terms of time, energy, emotions, and roles
- More—and more varied—past experiences
- A rich array of ongoing experiences and responsibilities
- More concern for practical application, less patience with pre-theory and abstractions
- Greater self-determination and acceptance of responsibility
- Greater need to cope with life transitions and with existential issues of competence, affect, autonomy, identity, relationships, purpose, and integrity (p. 49)

Brookfield (1986) adds the important observation that adult students are more likely to have developed the capacity for critical reflection. Through interplay of learned values and lived experience, adults often develop the ability to identify their own underlying assumptions and consider alternative ways to act and learn.

Adult Students, Service-Learning, and Experiential Education

When thinking about service-learning as a strategy specifically for adult students, it is helpful to consider two broad dimensions: the relationship between the adult student's accumulated experience and higher education and the relationship between service-learning and the diversity of interests and backgrounds that characterize adult students. Dewey reminds us that experience is an essential aspect of the learning process but is only truly educational when it leads to new learning. Experience can educate, and it can mis-educate. He also cautions against an either/or approach to the relationship between experiential and class-based learning (Dewey, 1963).

Adult students already have considerable experience. And it is this experience as workers, parents, taxpayers, neighbors, volunteers, former adolescents, and much more that they bring with such enthusiasm (and occasional impatience) to the classroom. Conversations with colleagues who have taught both traditional-aged and adult students confirm what the research suggests. Adult students, while differing in academic ability and level of scholarly commitment, are generally more likely to exhibit genuine interest in a wide range of academic subjects, including those that may not be relevant to their immediate vocational goals, as long as the teacher shows respect and leaves ample room for genuine discussion. The same students who slept through a history, political science, or literature class when they tried college right after high school often surprise themselves with just how interested they are in those subjects after 10 years raising kids and paying the mortgage (or rent). Professionally motivated as many of them are, they are equally engaged in classes that supplement their concrete work experience with a level of "intermediate theory" that helps them make sense of that experience and apply that theory either to their current work or to a new profession they are hoping to enter.

In Dewey's formulation, the opportunity for adult students to integrate and expand the knowledge they have gained through life experience with the background and theory they have learned in the classroom might seem to suggest that service-learning, as a form of experiential education, would be irrelevant for them. In fact, what the adult student might seem to need is a mirror image of what the less experienced student needs. In the theory/experience relationship, the traditional student, lacking experience, can benefit from direct and compelling engagement in specific social and vocational settings. If one turns this on its head, one might well suppose that the experience-rich adult student might benefit most from extended engagement in classroom study.

Of course, formulating the issue this way is an oversimplification. Dewey also points out that education is a continuing process, that there never is—or at least never should be—a point when the dialogue between experience and theory ends. The task for educators is to recognize the variety of experiences adult students have and to create learning strategies that will help students build on those experiences. This is as true for the pedagogy that has come to be known as service-learning as it is for other approaches.

When I use the term "service-learning" I am referring to an approach that has both civic/social and broader educational dimensions, a distinction that is made elsewhere in this volume. Service-learning, in the first sense, engages students in what Boyte and Kari (1996) refer to as "public work." Whether that work involves tutoring inner-city students or helping an inner-city business with a market analysis, students are moving beyond their own purely private pursuits and contributing to a larger, common good. At their best, however, service-learning opportunities provide both a genuine service to the community and powerful learning experiences for the student. Not only are the student tutors contributing to the education of the students they are helping, but they may also develop contextual knowledge about urban education and effective techniques for teaching reading. Likewise, the focus on inner-city business development teaches business students the practical dimensions of business planning and allows them to explore, in an immediate and often powerful way, the connection between business planning and social context.

Is the experience of the tutor/mentor or business planner similarly relevant for a 20 or a 35 year-old? Probably not. All learning is contextual, a product of the relationship between what the learner brings to a situation at a given time and the situation itself. If a business student has 10 years experience in business, she may not have learned how to do a market study in the formal sense, but unlike a 20 year-old, has already had significant experience delivering a service or a product in a business environment. Neither student, however, may have had experience with or background knowledge of business development in an inner-city context—unless, of course, one or both of the students themselves are from the inner city. Likewise, what the tutor/mentor brings to and learns from the experience of tutoring/mentoring varies radically based on a whole range of background factors including age, social class, and ethnic or cultural identity. A Hmong-speaking college student will bring valuable language skills and cultural understanding as a tutor of Hmong children in elementary school. Depending on what the intended outcomes of the learning experience are, the tutor may also improve her own English reading and writing skills, learn something about the theory and techniques of reading instruction, and, if working with African-American children as well, expand her own cultural understanding.

In short, service-learning programs are useful when they are designed to meet learning outcomes that are important to the student within the context of his or her life experience. This is as true for adult students as it is for younger students. But what kinds of outcomes are most relevant in the case of service-learning? We should be clear about the classic distinction between cognitive and affective outcomes and design service-learning opportunities with a clear eye toward exactly what outcomes we hope to achieve (Chazdon, 1997). The distinction between the cognitive domain (thinking skills and knowledge acquisition) and the affective domain (feeling and valuing) can be overdrawn but is nonetheless essential when designing service-learning experiences. Referring to the examples above, designing a service-learning experience with the affective goal of instilling positive attitudes toward community service may not be as appropriate say, for a Hmong student who is already deeply engaged in his community, as a learning experience designed to teach cognitive skills related to program planning or resource development or cross-cultural communication skills. Similarly, designing a community service experience to interest younger students in the political process (affective) may not be as necessary for a 35 year-old who has attended a precinct caucus and has voted in the last 10 elections.

Service-Learning, the Adult Student, and the First-Year Experience

When designing first-year service-learning programs that include adults, it is important to base them on both a clear understanding of the adult learner and a clear-headed notion of the relationship between adult students (both individually and as a group) and the learning outcomes one hopes to achieve through service-learning. As noted above, adult students are diverse and at the same time share some unique characteristics. What follows is a brief review of some effective practices that can either be incorporated into a first-year experience specifically or integrated more broadly into an adult student's college education.

Supporting and Challenging Students to Develop Individualized Approaches to Civic Learning

All students are, of course, unique, but adults come to higher education with a much more developed set of skills and experiences than many younger students. Some come with very focused educational goals, often professional in nature. They are often (but by no means always) long on "applied" skills and a little short on theory. Many have been active in their community, union, church, political party, or professional association. Many have had prior post-secondary training in a vocational school, the military, or professional development programs and (often) have had a brief and unsatisfying encounter with college right after high school. In other words, their "first year" on campus may not be their first experience with higher education.

An effective first-year program should engage students in a structured educational planning process. This process helps them identify the skills and knowledge they have already developed and those they want to further develop. Furthermore, it should acquaint them with the variety of ways they can meet their needs within the framework of the institution they are attending. At Metropolitan State University, for example, all students with fewer than 16 credits are required to attend a three-credit class, Metro 101—The First Year Experience, in which students do an inventory of knowledge gained through past experience, clarify their educational goals, and learn about the variety of learning options they have to meet those goals—including internships, assessment of prior learning, independent study, and classes.

This approach to individualized educational planning is as important when considering the goal of civic education as it is with other aspects of a liberal education. As noted above, some adult students come to higher education with a history of deep engagement in civic and community life. Others have had little or no experience. For the former, focused educational planning can help identify elements of civic knowledge that a student would like to—or, from a civic education perspective, "ought to"—develop further. Adult students with significant experience in volunteer service programs often bring a culturally nurtured distaste for (and lack of knowledge about) the political process. For them, the affective goal of "getting involved" is not the issue. What may be called for is a combination of cognitive knowledge (how the political system works) and affective change (getting over the reflexive notion that all politics is bad and ought to be avoided by well-meaning people). For the adult who has never ventured beyond strictly private concerns into broader public ones, effective individualized planning can help identify both appropriate learning outcomes and the best learning strategy. Often, providing a carefully structured experience of public involvement through service-learning is an appropriate way to accomplish both a specific affective goal (e.g., valuing, feeling comfortable about, becoming committed to) and the specific cognitive goals attached to an experience. Well-designed and effectively taught units within a first-year experience can provide adult students with forward momentum in their development as reflective and effective citizens.

Developing a Clear Understanding of the Meaning and Content of Civic Knowledge

If it is important to link service-learning activities to specific civic outcomes, it follows that it is equally important to identify just what those outcomes should be. What do we mean by civic education? What knowledge, skills, and perspectives do our respective institutions hope to develop in our students? Ideally, our institutions would develop their own clear and widely embraced answers to this question. But given the culture of academia, few institutions are likely to come up with answers that satisfy everyone. It is possible, however, for broad sectors of a university to engage in ongoing discussion and debate about the meaning of civic education. After all, defining concepts like citizenship, democracy, community, and justice is part of the ongoing work of our imperfect society and ought to have a central role in our curriculum as well.

Though it is difficult to arrive at consensus about the goals of civic education, there does need to be a clear understanding among those most involved in first-year programs about the relationship between specific civic learning outcomes and service-learning strategies. In an attempt to establish guidelines for a "citizenship requirement" at Metropolitan State University, we identified four dimensions of civic learning that could be addressed through a combination of experiential learning and structured analysis and reflection. In the end, the faculty decided not to implement this requirement, but the discussion helped move us forward in articulating a philosophy that informs the variety of *voluntary* approaches to civic engagement we offer students.

> *Political and Social Action*—Citizenship is about participating in the democratic process and participating with others to influence public policy and institutions.
>
> *Associational Life*—Citizenship is about association, the ability to participate in communities, workplaces, and institutions that shape the quality of our lives.
>
> *Service*—Citizenship is about service, about giving back to the communities that nurture us, and about taking responsibility for each other.
>
> *Morality*—underlying all is a moral and ethical dimension; it is through participation in the wider spheres of our lives that we develop ourselves as social beings with a capacity to judge and act for the common good. (Metropolitan State University, 1996)

Ideally, a first-year program would engage all students in dialogue about these (or other) dimensions of civic engagement and offer them a variety of opportunities to explore one or more of them further. One of the most powerful characteristics of experiential education is the opportunity it offers students of all ages and backgrounds to cross social boundaries, to "try out" new settings and contexts. "Gloria" (not her real name) came to Metro State with an impressive resume as a volunteer leader of a state-wide coalition to improve public education in Minnesota. She had chaired task forces, issued white papers, lobbied the legislature, and worked on political campaigns. From the comfort of her upper-middle class neighborhood she fought for educational reforms that she believed would benefit inner-city children. Yet she had little direct experience with inner-city schools. She had never entered into a relationship with inner-city children or their families. Highly competent in the political and public policy dimensions of civic learning, she decided to deepen her understanding of how educational policy plays out in the lives of inner-city children and the schools they attend. She became active in a tutoring program with one of Metro State's partner elementary schools, thereby increasing her understanding of both education policy and herself. In the process of reflecting on her experience as a tutor, she was able to identify the relationship between the *service* dimension of citizenship and the *political action* dimension that had been her forte.

Again, each student brings her own experience, aptitude, and interests to campus. What the designers of first-year experience programs can do is to provide a framework for reflection on the civic dimensions of those experiences and a road map for incorporating new dimensions of civic education into the adult student's educational program. But that framework must be a flexible one, allowing for the unique needs of adult and non-traditional first-year learners.

Assessing Prior Civic Learning

Although not all adult students enter or re-enter college with a deep store of civic experience, many of them have had experiences that can, when carefully nurtured and evaluated, constitute genuine college-level learning. Such students turn the traditional service-learning paradigm on its head. Rather than going *out* of the university to engage with society, they *come in* to the university to reflect on, theorize about, and articulate what they have learned from their community experience. As instructors in first-year programs work with these students to develop their educational plans, they can direct them to learning strategies that validate prior knowledge.

At Metropolitan State University, we have developed theory seminars that provide a structured group context for students to deepen their understanding of their experiences in specific knowledge areas. In my role as professor of political studies, I teach two theory seminars: *Community Leadership* and *Political Action*. Both meet for two Friday evenings and all day Saturday over the course of a semester. Participants range in background from state legislators to professional lobbyists, members of boards and commissions to leaders of neighborhood groups, social action organizations, church groups, nonprofit agencies, and service organizations. All bring rich experience to the table and many have developed a clear understanding of the operational principles of what they do. All benefit from the focused reading and writing exercises and the rich interaction they have with each other.

Exactly how can first-year programs support the recognition and validation of prior experience? First, as noted above, they can engage students in a careful inventory of their own civic engagement and point out mechanisms for drawing upon that engagement where possible. At Metro State, this is done in both the Metro 101 course and through a freestanding one-credit course entitled *Getting Credit for What You Know*. Second, in some cases theory seminars can themselves become part of a student's first-year experience. In this way, they can serve as an effective bridge for students seeking to integrate college learning into their often-busy lives. For example, if students already possess college-level writing and reading skills, they may well find a theory seminar a validating academic experience that moves them closer to their ultimate goal of achieving a college degree.

Creating Community-based Learning Opportunities That Honor Adult Needs

When planning community-based approaches to civic learning, whether specifically as part of the first-year experience or as part of an adult student's overall education plan, one must be especially mindful of the scheduling and logistical challenges faced by working students. As has already been pointed out, most adult students have multiple commitments. Full-time workers with children in school often have a day job and take classes on nights and weekends—with studying sandwiched in between household duties and time with the children. Given such restrictions, how can educators design community-based approaches to civic education?

To begin with, it is essential that the hours required for a service-learning course not exceed those of a traditional course. When students are engaged in service-learning, that work should be an integral part of their academic program rather than a required "add on." Furthermore, if a service-learning project is required as part of a first-year program, program leaders must make sure there are service opportunities available on evenings and weekends. Although both of these points may seem self-evident, they can necessitate a paradigm shift for colleges and universities that serve primarily younger students. On many campuses, service-learning is coordinated through student affairs, and community engagement is seen primarily as an extra-curricular activity—a form of volunteerism or, at best, as a "service option" within classes. The hidden assumption here is that students have flexible time. To be sure, adult learners are also free to join service organizations on campus. However, many will not do so because they already have active community lives or because they are temporarily trading time for academic credit. If those of us who promote civic learning do our jobs well, these adults will participate in civic life with renewed vigor and insight once they have completed their degrees.

How, then, does one deal concretely with adult time constraints while at the same time developing strong approaches to service-learning and other forms of community engagement? At Metro State, we have found that academic internships represent one flexible approach. Students receive credits just as they would for a traditional class but do the bulk of their learning in community settings. To be sure, even here students with full-time "day jobs" have far fewer options than those with part-time or flexible work schedules, but civic life does not shut down at five o'clock. My own social science department, for example, requires an internship for all our majors that combines 120 hours of field experience with three seminar sessions, several written exercises, and a final paper. To add flexibility, we allow 20 rather than the standard 15 weeks for completion of the internship. In this way, even those with the least flexible work schedules have been placed. One very busy businessman, who was particularly concerned about integrating an internship into his schedule, ended up serving on the campaign team of an acquaintance who was running for election to the Minnesota Supreme Court. Another student called in a panic with the announcement that she just had triplets! Since she was a solid writer with good research skills, we developed an applied research internship that she could do mostly from home.

Once again, a key goal of a first-year experience ought to be to introduce students to learning options that allow them to incorporate service-learning into their academic program. But should some form of community-based service-learning be *required* as part of a first-year seminar or an overall first-year program? Only if it is carefully planned with time and scheduling restraints of the adult student in mind.

Linking Civic Engagement with Professional Education

If scholars of adult education are correct in their claim that adult students tend to link their educational and career goals, it follows that advocates of civic learning would do well to understand and communicate clearly the connection between civic education and students' current or future roles as professionals. For less experienced, younger students, service on a resume can indeed be an important supplement to what is necessarily a rather limited work history. For adult students, the relationship between service-learning, civic education, and the development of a vocation is more varied and complex. But the relationship is real and can be discussed either as a matter of immediate self-interest or as a larger question of meaning. The fact that adult students are concerned with the pragmatics of a career does not mean that they are uninterested in questions of value and meaning as they relate to a career.

Service-learning can be an effective approach for students who are (a) exploring a career transition, (b) developing the practical or "applied" dimensions of a career, or (c) exploring the civic dimensions of their chosen professional field. For example, Metropolitan State University has just inaugurated a new teacher education program with the specific mission of preparing effective teachers for culturally diverse urban schools. Most of the students are adults who have strong life experiences in a variety of fields and want—or think they want—to make a difference in the lives of children. Rather than find out at the end of their teacher training that teaching in inner-city schools is not for them, students are placed in one-on-one and small group relationships with inner-city school children during the introductory seminar on urban education. This program-specific approach to exploring career transition mirrors dozens of experiences I have had with students over the years: the office manager who became the director of an issue-advocacy group after a service-learning project on the issue of campaign finance reform, the health care professional who became a community organizer after an internship with a community development corporation, and the cashier for a major retail chain who became a staff person in the governor's citizen information office after participating in a public service internship with state government.

At first glance, the "fit" between service-learning and vocational exploration appears strongest in education, the human services, and public service careers, but the possibilities are actually much broader. Service-learning projects offer great opportunities for students in a variety of majors and professional programs to develop relevant knowledge and skills further through direct work with community-based, nonprofit, and public organizations. At Metro State, as well as at colleges and universities across the nation, accounting majors staff tax preparation clinics in senior citizen complexes and low-income communities; communication majors offer document design services for nonprofit organizations; and undergraduate and graduate business majors provide marketing, business planning, and strategic planning for inner-city businesses and institutions. These projects (often organized as a service-learning component within a class) provide an opportunity for adult students to refine further, in a context that includes both "real world" activities and disciplined reflection, what they are learning in the classroom or may have already learned from prior experiences.

Finally, service-learning offers powerful opportunities for students to reflect on the civic and moral dimensions of their professions. What does it mean to be a professional? Is it all about the bottom line? What is the relationship between a given career and the larger public good? As Sullivan (1995) points out in his exploration of the possibilities of a renewed civic professionalism, "An authentic profession can provide a strong sense of identity because beyond providing a livelihood, it is a way of life with public value 'the kind of thing one can build a life around'" (p. 6).

It is common in these times for professional programs to offer courses in ethics: business ethics, the ethics of the health care profession, legal and ethical issues in law enforcement. Service-learning projects offer students in these professions an analogous opportunity to experience and reflect on the public dimensions of their work. It provides an opportunity for them to explore ways to put the skills they are developing to strong ethical and public use. Especially for adult students who have experienced jobs that lack deep, intrinsic meaning, such an exploration of broader public purpose can provide a strong motive for participating in service-learning projects.

A Final Word

In this chapter I have emphasized the importance of designing programs that integrate a clear conception of the adult learner with a broad understanding of the multiple goals and outcomes of service-learning. In an ideal world we would work with adult students as individuals with specific histories, life circumstances, goals, and aptitudes. First-year programs would challenge and guide students to reflect on and develop the civic dimensions of their college education. A variety of compelling service-learning opportunities would be available to help students develop cognitive and affective knowledge as individually appropriate. If students were *required* to participate in a service-learning project, the experience would be appropriate for the specific life experiences and educational path of each student.

This is a tall order. The challenge of creating a truly *individualized* approach to the development of civic knowledge through service-learning is daunting. In fact, implementing a Dewey-like approach to student learning in what are necessarily bureaucratic educational institutions has bedeviled progressive educators throughout the past century and will likely continue to present a challenge in the next. But understanding the adult learner and being clear about the goals and purposes of service-learning are necessary prerequisites to designing effective programs. First-year programs, when designed consciously and implemented reflectively, can play an important role in making the link between the experiences adults bring to campus and the wider civic goals that ought to inform every student's college education.

References

Arenson, K. (2001, August 5). Reading statistical tea leaves, who we are, where we are, and what it all means [Interview with Harry Hodgins]. *New York Times*, Education Supplement, p. 14.

Boyte, H. & Kari, N. (1996). *Building America: The democratic promise of public work.* Pittsburgh: Temple University Press.

Brookfield, S. D. (1986). *Understanding and facilitating adult learning.* San Francisco: Jossey-Bass.

Campbell, M. D., Wilson, L. G., & Hanson, G. R. (1980). *The invisible minority: A study of adult university students.* Final report submitted to the Hogg Foundation for Mental Health, Austin: Office of the Dean of Students, University of Texas.

Chazdon, S. (1997). *The seventh Q: A resource notebook for civic learning objectives.* Unpublished document available through Metropolitan State University, Center for Community-Based Learning: St. Paul.

Chickering, A., Lynch, A., & Schlossberg, N. (1989). *Improving higher education environments for adults.* San Francisco: Jossey-Bass.

Dewey, J. (1963). *Experience and education.* New York: Macmillan.

Lynch, A. Q. & Chickering, A. W. (1984). Comprehensive counseling and support programs for adult learners: Challenge to higher education. In G. W. Walz & L. Benjamin (Eds.), *New Perspectives on Counseling Adult Learners.* Ann Harbor: ERIC/CAPS.

Metropolitan State University. (1996). Dimensions of citizenship. Unpublished document, available through the Center for Community-Based Learning, Metropolitan State University: St. Paul.

Neugarten, B.C. (1979). Time, age, and the life cycle. *The American Journal of Psychology, 136*(7), 887-894.

Sullivan, W. (1995). *Work and integrity.* New York: Harper Collins.

Section 3

Learning From Practice

The University of Rhode Island's New Culture for Learning

Jayne Richmond

Ten years ago our president provided the blueprint for what he called "a new culture for learning." Some of the major premises of this blueprint were borrowed from Chickering and Gamson's (1999) "Seven Principles for Good Practice in Undergraduate Education," which emphasize the importance of active and collaborative learning, along with high expectations for faculty-student relationships. Our university community assumed the challenge of designing curricular and co-curricular programs that would incorporate these principles. We came to understand that success in this endeavor would mean that each of us would be increasingly responsible for student learning, that we would accomplish much of our work in teams, and that high expectations for ourselves in our own work would lead to high expectations for students.

The president's vision had practical implications. This new culture for learning would address the need for improvement in retention rates, in responsible use of limited resources, and in funding priorities. The president made it clear that since we could not be all things to all people, we would invest in our priorities and concentrate our resources in fields of study and research that engaged learners, improved community, and met the mission of the university. He created four focus areas: marine and environmental studies; health services; children, families, and communities; and enterprise and technology along with a liberal arts core. Each of these would provide a lens through which we would test and develop our programs and curriculum. Each area would be interdisciplinary in nature, and each would involve undergraduate students in active learning.

Motivating the university community to make these fundamental changes required understanding how engaging students in active learning would actually change the way we do things. We needed to articulate this value for faculty to function in a more collaborative and perhaps interdisciplinary way. What benefits for both faculty and students would be derived from creating a greater sense of community? What would be gained by designing an "engaged" university?

Guided by our mission as a land-grant, sea-grant, and urban-grant institution with responsibilities in teaching, service, and research for the benefit of all the citizens of Rhode Island, we recognized that the principles of service-learning provided an effective model for addressing both our historic mission and our new culture for learning. The benefits of service-learning to students and to institutions have been well documented in the literature and elsewhere in this monograph. The work of Astin and Sax (1998) demonstrates how participation in community service enhances students' development in academics, life skills, and civic responsibility. The Knight Higher Education Collaborative (Wegner, 2000) declares civic involvement through service-learning as the very foundation of an "engaged" university. And community building as defined by Boyer (1994) provides an inspiring description of a "new American college" that incorporates cross-disciplinary study around social issues, where undergraduates do field projects that matter outside the university, where learning happens in places like community clinics, and where faculty function as partners with community members.

And we know, based on the work of Eyler and Giles (1999) and Zlotkowski (2001) among others, that engaging students through service-learning is an effective means to stimulate student intellectual curiosity and motivation. Such an approach is supported as well by the work of David Kolb (1984), whose model of experiential learning implicitly makes clear the pedagogical strengths of service-learning. Kolb describes the learning process as creating a "transformational experience" informed by critical reflection, abstract conceptualization, and active experimentation. By combining a high-quality experience with opportunities for structured reflection, educators can improve problem-solving skills and successfully challenge students' cognitive beliefs, the basis for developing critical thinking.

This analysis is especially useful, considering what we know about today's college students. In their report on first-year college students, Sax, Astin, Korn, and Mahoney (2000) remind us that today's students are particularly desperate to find meaning in what they are learning and to make connections between the classroom and their lives. We know that students today want to be active learners but that they also self-report a sense of academic disengagement. They report that they feel very stressed and disconnected both from their peers and their faculty. Students express a greater sense of loneliness, and they seem less skilled in making the connections that would have them feel like members of a community. In fact, in the fall 1999 freshman norms study, only 21% of incoming students indicated that they had any interest in community action programs, and a declining number of students over the last 15 years believe they can or even want to influence social values.

These data sounded the warning bell for us, causing us to consider how we could better engage students—especially first-year students—in their learning and in this academic community. Our first step was to talk to faculty about who new students are and to identify how our current educational environment can sometimes work against our goals of connecting students to each other, to the faculty, and to their discipline. In other words, we needed to examine the effectiveness of our pedagogy and curriculum delivery models in capturing students' attention and making their college learning meaningful. What follows is the process we used to provide service-integrated learning communities to 75% of the incoming class.

First Steps

As we talked with our faculty about the above disconnects—between our desire to engage undergraduate students in active learning, to encourage interdisciplinary study, and to create a greater sense of community verses our traditional way of selecting courses absent a unifying aspect or theme—we readily captured their attention. With both the theoretical and practical evidence in hand, we began to come together as a community to design models of engaged learning that would help us to reach today's students and, we hoped, improve their retention and success in school. Service-learning, widely supported by the work of leaders in higher education research and policy development, provided a new paradigm for us to consider. And we liked it. Still, we found that actually making the shift in the way we do the "work of learning" remained a challenge. In other words, knowing the benefits did not necessarily translate into a mandate for change.

Not unlike other mandates for change on a college campus, this initiative required the commitment of faculty and administrators across the university community. The real mandate for change, we quickly learned, would come only with true faculty buy-in. We had the support and vision of the president to get us started. We also had a division of undergraduate studies called University College (UC) that is charged with aiding students in their transition to college and in providing special academic support services to assist their progression through college. Thus, University College assumed a leadership role in designing a model of experiential learning that integrated service and the first-year seminar within a loosely coupled learning community model. We began with what we had.

In 1995 we developed a new first-year seminar, URI 101: Transitions and Transformations. URI 101 is a one-credit course that introduces students to college life, including topics such as academic integrity, values formation, diversity, drugs and alcohol, library skills, advising, career planning, and time management. The purpose of the course was to improve retention by helping students develop academic skills, increase their awareness of support services on campus, involve them in the campus community, and provide an opportunity for them to talk with each other about the many social and academic issues that challenged them. In addition to using this new seminar as a vehicle for initiating students to the university and a major, we required that all new students participate in service as a component of this one-credit class.

Around the country, many change initiatives such as this one have depended on significant funds to support faculty development or release time for designing curricular innovations incorporating service-learning. In a difficult Rhode Island economy, we had no such funds. At this same time, however, Rhode Island Philanthropist Alan Shawn Feinstein was seeking to endow institutions that were committed to including service as part of the college experience. We decided to tie his agenda into our newly required first-year seminar. By incorporating community service into the URI 101 experience, we secured a one million dollar endowment and renamed the program The Feinstein Enriching America Program.

The Feinstein Enriching America Program required each student to perform 8 to 10 hours of community service as a class one Saturday during the fall semester. Our next significant challenge, then, was to design service experiences for over 2,400 first-year students within the URI 101 course. This one-credit class most often lasted only six weeks, so the majority of students would have to complete a service experience within the first few weeks of the semester. With approximately 100 sections of the course being offered, the staff faced the challenge of finding enough community placements. Nonprofit agencies, school districts, and service organizations collaboratively joined forces with the university to attempt to create meaningful service opportunities for students throughout Rhode Island.

We also had the challenge of supporting one full-time staff person to manage the logistics of these service experiences and of paying for buses, food, and a variety of other necessities. Our endowment was wonderful, but we still had only about $60,000 a year with which to work! We had to look hard at the strategy we had chosen. The three primary goals of the service unit were to help students see the importance of their role in the community, to examine the value of service, and to encourage a nurturing relationship among the class members.

We soon realized that what we were doing was community service, even though what we wanted to do was service-learning. Thus, we began a process of assessing student learning, community partnerships, and faculty involvement. The initial assessment process entailed interviewing all the stakeholders. Students from various disciplines participated in several focus groups. They discussed the positive and negative aspects of URI 101 and in particular the service component. Many students told us that the requirement had very little meaning for them. There was no connection to their course work, or to their career goals. Much of their concern came from doing service projects that seemed to them trivial or insignificant.

We then conducted site visits to the agencies and organizations with which we worked. These community partners shared many stories of success, as well as some of their concerns. Although grateful for the amount of work students had done in the community, some felt that the students had not been sufficiently prepared and that this was reflected in their attitudes and work ethic. Since the community partners clearly valued their relationship with the university, they were more than willing to work with us to strengthen and redesign the service projects to create more meaningful experiences for students.

The final assessment task required us to get input from the faculty. We asked for feedback in a variety of ways, including questionnaires and dialogues in departmental meetings. We were gratified to hear that most faculty felt the service component of URI 101 was an enriching experience that helped the class bond as a group and encouraged students to continue their work in the community. However, the faculty were unanimous in their assessment that service had to become a more meaningful part of the curriculum rather than just an "add-on" and that they needed the support of the URI 101 program to put the service projects into a learning context.

From Community Service to Service-Learning

Now we felt we had a mandate from all of our stakeholders to develop the community component of the course and to create real service-learning experiences. We undertook several steps to accomplish this. Cognizant that the service aspect of URI 101 would be for many students an introduction to service-learning, we had to be realistic in our expectations as to what we could accomplish. We revised our goals and established the following priorities:

- Students will gain a better understanding of themselves and their importance to the community.
- Students will become more aware of issues in the community and develop a sense of responsibility for addressing those issues.

♦ Students will be exposed to diverse communities and dialogue about pre-conceived notions regarding diversity.
♦ Students will develop cohesiveness as a class.
♦ Students will discuss their own sense of civic responsibility and plan for future involvement.

These very specific goals provided the faculty and students with a much better understanding of what their service project was meant to accomplish. Once again we viewed the available projects through the lens of the president's specified focus areas. On this basis, the URI 101 program identified 10 areas around which to develop community service experiences: (a) children and families, (b) education, (c) the elderly, (d) environment, (e) domestic violence, (f) health care, (g) homelessness, (h) housing, (i) hunger, and (j) literacy. More than 100 projects were designed, each intended to address one of these areas. In each case, students were given the materials needed to create a context in which they could process their service experience. For example, students working at the local food bank would not only learn about the agency's services but more importantly about issues of hunger in Rhode Island, the United States, and throughout the world.

We had come to the conclusion, then, that unless we created service-learning experiences, as opposed to community service exposure, we would not accomplish our goals of engaging students in active learning, encouraging interdisciplinary study, and creating a greater sense of community. We wanted to change the undergraduate experience at URI, to make experiential learning with a focus on service-learning the foundation on which we stood. Understanding that, we made the decision that our precious endowment should be used to establish the Feinstein Center for Service-Learning. This Center then became a part of University College, with a mission to support service-learning and experiential education across all units of the University of Rhode Island.

It was the right decision. Over the past five years, the Center has led to the growth of the following service-learning programs:

♦ *Feinstein Enriching America Program.* As part of URI 101: Traditions and Transformations, all new students participate in a one-day service-learning experience. The program is designed to ensure that each student is involved in a meaningful community service activity, reflects on this experience, and shares related thoughts and feelings with other students.
♦ *Faculty Fellows.* Each year 10 to 12 faculty members from across the disciplines are selected to receive a grant to help them implement service-learning in their courses. In addition, the Faculty Fellows meet monthly to share their experiences and receive additional training in service-learning. Each year, fellows from previous years meet to maintain support and communication with each other. Some of the fellows' curricular initiatives have included work in the state prison, with local elementary schools around nutrition, with local nonprofits around web site development, and with food banks and soup kitchens.
♦ *Curricular Integration.* Faculty are polled as to their knowledge about and incorporation of service-learning in their courses. Courses that do include service-learning have a special designation in the catalogue. Faculty who are interested in learning how to incorporate service-learning are identified and assisted.

♦ *Community Service to the University (CSV).* An instructor and an upper-class student who is called a mentor teach URI 101. The student mentors enroll in the CSV course for three credits. Their participation helps them learn the skills needed to facilitate a class like URI 101 and trains them in the fundamentals of service-learning. Mentors are responsible for helping the class choose and carry out the designated service experience.

♦ *Academic Minors in Leadership and Hunger Studies.* These are two examples of interdisciplinary minors in which service-learning is pivotal. Students are directed to courses that introduce a breadth of issues associated with their topic of interest and then focus their internship and service experiences on specific areas. For example, students in the hunger minor may study public policy, nutrition, child development, economic development, political science, community planning, or health and human sciences. These minors serve as models for a more comprehensive integration of service (i.e., beyond a single course).

Establishing a Three-Step Plan for Service-Learning in the First-Year Seminar

Based on feedback from our stakeholders, we designed a framework to guide classroom integration of three key service-learning concerns. Because we were designing a one-credit course with a service-learning component, and not a full-semester service-learning course, we were careful to keep our instructional modules simple and clear. Our model included (a) pre-reflection, (b) the service experience itself, and (c) post-reflection components designed specifically for each of the 10 topic areas.

Reflection is, of course, the key component in service-learning and provides the critical connection between service work and academic inquiry. Hence, we consciously created a reflection "envelope" around the actual service experience. By building reflection into the training for all faculty and mentors in all sections of URI 101, we were able to implement it more or less consistently across all course sections. We further structured our model by deliberately focusing on three themes: (a) the self, (b) the community, and (c) the service experience.

Focus on the Self

Students in URI 101 are given the pre-service questionnaire below (Figure 1). It asks them to consider the views they have held on service to others, on the community in which they live, and on their sense of values and expectations. This tool helps encourage group discussion and begins to prepare students for the service project they will undertake.

Focus on the Community

Students and community partners alike commented on the need to help students become better informed about the issues and the communities with which they would work. To accomplish this, fact sheets were developed for each of the 10 focus areas. Agency literature was provided, and specific pre-reflection exercises were created for each topic area. This helped to place the agencies within the framework of the larger issue they represented. Figure 2 (see following page) provides

Figure 1.
Sample Pre-Service Questionnaire

♦ Have you ever participated in community service? If so, what kind of activities did you do? How did you feel about your efforts in this activity?

♦ What issues in the community concern you? How do you imagine yourself contributing to solving these issues while in college? In ten years?

♦ In what ways do you think community service can enhance your education? For example, how can it broaden your knowledge of diversity, career choices, or social awareness?

♦ Ideally, what do you think is the most important aspect of doing a community service project?

---

a grid of sample topic areas and projects designed in each area. (See the Appendix for sample reflection questions for a single topic area.)

Focus on the Experience

A post-service questionnaire (Figure 3) was used to help the class process the service experience once it was completed. Post-service reflection is particularly important to encourage group discussion, explore the potential for future service, and connect the service experience to broader social issues, thereby increasing students' sense of civic awareness. Instructors also received a list of other community agencies working on similar problems so they could facilitate further student involvement, and many instructors gave their students post-service writing assignments.

Figure 3.
Sample Post-Service Questionnaire

♦ Describe your service project experience. On a scale from 1-10 (10 being the highest) what would you rate the experience? Why? Please note what you liked best and what you would do differently.

♦ How would you rate your involvement? Why?

♦ What new information did you learn about your service topic? In what way did the new information change your opinions of the issue or change your desire to be involved?

♦ How did engaging in the service project impact you both individually and as part of the group?

♦ Now that you have been involved in the community, would you participate in volunteer work in the future? Why or why not?

Figure 2.
Sample Grid of Service Experiences

Children and Families	Domestic Violence	Education	Elderly	Environment
American Red Cross. Students are trained on fire safety and prevention. They work in teams in at-risk areas to disseminate information about fire safety and prevention.	*Women's Resource Center.* Students work in teams to first do research on local and national domestic violence. They then launch a poster and marketing campaign to raise awareness about domestic violence.	*Shadow Day.* At-risk high school students are invited to spend the day with URI students to expose them to college life. Shadow day participants go to classes, eat lunch in the cafeteria, and attend organizational meetings with their matched students.	*Westerly Health Center.* Students interact with residents, organize games and activities, and help the non-profit agency (designed to help adults who can no longer manage on their own) with maintenance and outside work.	*Southside Community Landtrust.* Students do garden work and learn about food provision with a non-profit agency providing community gardens, education, and nutritional support to urban communities.
West Kingston Elementary School's PTO / Autumn Festival. Students in a theater-focused URI 101 organize activities and help facilitate programs to raise funds and further develop a nurturing environment at the school.	*Women's Resource Center.* Students in several classes come together with local children and community leaders to create awareness about Domestic Violence. They also take part in a silent march to end domestic violence.	*URI Discover Day.* Middle school students are invited to campus to spend the day with URI students. The program is designed to expose the younger students to higher education by having them take part in various educational activities.	*West Bay Manor.* Students in a music-focused URI 101 perform various eclectic musical performances for a local assisted-living center for the elderly. The students and participants then spend time talking about musical influences across generations.	*Audubon Society.* Students majoring in marine biology take part in the annual National Coastal Clean-up by working to rid local beaches and waterways of pollutants. The students document the debris they collect and send the data off for analysis.

Figure 2. (cont.)

Health Care	Homelessness	Housing	Hunger	Literacy
Leukemia & Lymphoma. "Light the Night" is an illuminated charity event that takes place in Providence to help raise awareness and funds for Leukemia. Students collect donations, help set up for the event and take part in a 2-mile walk.	*Transitional Housing.* A social service agency providing crisis intervention, counseling, case management, and advocacy services for families who are in transition or homeless. Students help clean and repair apartments for families on waiting lists.	*Habitat for Humanity.* Students help with new construction and renovation with a community organization dedicated to building and renovating homes for low-income families.	*Amos House.* Students interact with children and facilitate small group games such as face painting, story telling, and coloring in a soup kitchen that provides numerous social services for the needy.	*URI Book Buddy Program.* Elementary school students are invited to campus each Saturday afternoon to do a series of literacy activities with URI 101 students. Activities include reading, drawing, book making, and story telling.
URI Breast Cancer Awareness. Students register to be part of Lee Denim Day and prepare a marketing campaign to raise awareness and funds for breast cancer research.	*St. Patrick's Soup Kitchen.* Students work at a local soup kitchen preparing a daily meal and eating with the clients. They also collect clothing and supplies for the organization.	*Smith Hill Community Development Corporation.* Students help to renovate abandoned homes as part of a neighborhood rehabilitation program aimed at providing housing for low-income families.	*Rhode Island Food Bank.* Students help with salvage sorting, inspection of dry goods, and repackaging of food. Students receive a hunger presentation on issues that families in need face daily.	*Rhode Island READS Program.* This literacy volunteer program serves K-12 students throughout Rhode Island. URI students facilitate literacy-based outreach programs at local schools and libraries.

To help the diverse group of faculty who teach this course manage the entire process effectively, all of the materials described above are compiled into an instructor's service-learning packet. During the URI 101 faculty orientation, instructors select a specific service area and receive a corresponding version of the packet. Each packet includes a cover sheet describing how to use the enclosed materials, the pre-service questionnaire, information about the service topic, information about the participating community agency, reflection exercises, the post-service questionnaire, and a list of other agencies working in that particular service area. As a result of this faculty support, students acquire a better understanding of their role in the community and what their service work means for their own development as community members. The community partners can now work with students who are more engaged from the beginning and are able to provide more meaningful service because of the foundation established for students in the classroom.

Learning Communities—Connecting Service to Course Content Areas

A very important initiative we have designed that moves our program toward service-learning as an effective pedagogy is the incorporation of learning communities into the first-year experience. These consist of the URI 101 seminar plus a skills course with 25 or fewer students (either writing, communications, or math) and one or two more general education courses. A cohort of 25 students shares these courses, and the faculty who teach them are put into contact with each other to facilitate curriculum sharing.

Learning communities have proven to be a powerful tool for addressing student concerns about a sense of disconnection from their peers and instructors. By sharing common courses, students find that they work more in groups, focusing on academic issues outside of class (additional time on task), and feel better "known" by their teachers and peers. Now when a service project is chosen in URI 101, the implications of this project can be reviewed and discussed in the "content" courses these same students share in common.

For example, students who are interested in issues of social justice have several URI 101 sections from which to choose, including ones focused on hunger, nonviolence and peace studies, diversity, and leadership. Each of these students co-registers for a large section of Sociology 100 exploring issues of social justice. These students also register together in a writing or communications course that incorporates the focus on social justice into its class activities and assignments. The themes that tie the learning communities together, along with specially chosen service activities, are models of this approach.

Another example of a learning community at the University of Rhode Island can be found in our College of the Environment and Life Sciences. This diverse college requires that all new students take specific sections of URI 101. After the first six weeks of the semester, all first-year students and faculty in the college participate together in a service experience that focuses on environmental issues. (For example, two years ago a group of about 100 students worked to build an educational nature walk.) After their service experience, the students spend the next six weeks of the semester in an "introduction to the major" course taught by the same instructor who taught their URI 101 class. Such continuity helps them to connect with each other, their faculty, and their major.

Another example is provided by those students in the College of Business whose task it was to work with the Breast Cancer Association on "National Lee Denim Day" events. The class worked for several weeks in small groups selling pink ribbon pins and handing out flyers and information. It designed a strategy for advertising the day and maximizing fund-raising efforts. In the end, the students not only raised money for the association and became more informed about breast cancer, but they also used this experience to learn about teamwork, management, and marketing.

Marine biology is a very popular major at URI, attracting about 150 new students each year. For the past several years, these students have teamed up with the Audubon Society of Rhode Island to participate in an International Coastal Clean-up. On one Saturday in the fall, all Marine Biology students spend the day with their instructors learning about pollution and how it affects the environment while they help to clean Rhode Island's beaches and waterways. As debris is collected, it is tallied on a special sheet provided by the Audubon Society, and the data are then sent to Washington to be analyzed along with other data from around the country. Students are able to put their studies into practice within their first few weeks of college and feel like they are making a difference in an area about which they are concerned.

Finally, we have two sections of URI 101 intended for music majors. This group has participated in a music appreciation project for the last several years. Students have spent part of the semester coordinating a music appreciation workshop for seniors at a local retirement home. As part of their presentation, they have performed musical pieces and then spent time with the seniors talking about the seniors' favorite kinds of music and how music has changed over time. This project helps students to see how their work as future musicians and caring individuals can impact the community. They explore this experience through their special URI 101 seminar, but also in the concomitant learning community courses for music majors.

The Future of the Feinstein Enriching America Program

URI 101 and its related learning communities have been well received by both faculty and students. Instructors see the students bond as a group early in the semester. Students build a support network from the onset and use this network as a resource. Because the students naturally form a more cohesive group, and because instructors are encouraged to work with each other in the learning community cluster, course assignments are often shared and interdisciplinary learning occurs.

However, true reform requires more than the kinds of curricular innovations described above. Innovation must also involve faculty development and changes in resource allocation. We mentioned earlier the Faculty Fellows program provides funds to help faculty integrate community concerns and community involvement into their disciplinary work. We also mentioned the minors for students in areas such as leadership studies and hunger studies, both of which incorporate service-learning. Such minors provide an exemplary model for moving students from their introductory service-learning experience to service-learning within the context of an issue or a course.

We are tremendously proud of what we have accomplished with relatively little money. With the Feinstein endowment we have established the Center for Service-Learning, which has been the impetus for awareness of this approach to learning across the campus. We have assumed a mandate to engage all first year students in service and are moving steadily toward service-learning and curriculum integration. By concentrating on student learning, faculty involvement, and community partnerships, we have been able to marshal our limited resources to accomplish the greatest good.

Still, our current model is not without problems. While we can support all 100 sections of URI 101 with our training materials, we cannot guarantee the effectiveness of each course experience. Community agencies are often unable to communicate clear goals and needs, making it hard to achieve a good match. The commitment on the part of instructors to prepare students for their service experience is uneven, as is the commitment on the students' part. In fact, the nature of the service experience itself is variable. Each year, however, we use assessment tools to improve the effective partnerships we have formed, and eliminate those that do not meet the needs of either party. We carefully consider feedback from faculty who are on the front lines supporting the work of the Center and helping students have meaningful service-learning experiences within a context of other course learning. In fact, faculty often create service experiences based on their own research or professional affiliations, facilitating the service-learning component in their courses rather than relying on pre-designed service experiences facilitated by the Center.

Using limited resources wisely, we have provided essential support (logistically and programmatically) to a very large program. We carefully train student mentors and design in-class materials to assist faculty in integrating service with class content. We now have all support materials, including reflection activities and all service packets, online (www.uri.edu/volunteer/). Finally, we carefully assess the process and the activity with an eye toward improving the meaning of the activity for students and faculty alike. We know well that projects that are seen as trivial or simply irrelevant to student learning will often do more harm than good. Students and faculty will be turned away from community involvement.

While our program can boast many inspiring stories of success, we must continue to be vigilant in our efforts to improve this experience for students, faculty, and the community partners with whom we work. Such continuous improvement means that, in the final analysis, we have truly put the principles of service-learning to work for all of us.

References

Astin, A., & Sax, L. (1998). How undergraduates are affected by service participation. *Journal of College Student Development, 39*(3), 251-263.

Boyer, E. (1994, March 9). Creating the new American college." *The Chronicle of Higher Education*, p. 2.

Chickering, A., & Gamson, Z. (1999, Winter). Development and adaptations of the Seven Principles for Good Practice in Undergraduate Education. *New Directions for Teaching and Learning*, 75-81.

Eyler, J., & Giles, D. E. (1999). *Where's the learning in service-learning?* San Francisco: Jossey-Bass.

Kolb, D. (1984). *Experiential learning: Experience as the source of learning and development.* Englewood Cliffs, NJ: Prentice-Hall.

Sax, L. J., Astin, A. W., Korn, W. S, & Mahoney, K. M. (2000). *The American freshman: National norms for fall 2000.* Los Angeles: University of California, Los Angeles, Higher Education Research Institute.

Wegner, G. (Ed.). (2000). Knight collaborative. *Exemplars, Policy Perspectives, 9*(4).

Zlotkowski, E. Service-learning across disciplines. *Change, 33*(1), 24-33.

Appendix
Sample Reflection Exercise

Below is an example of an in-class exercise intended to facilitate awareness of a project area.

Housing: Budget Exercise

1. Divide your class into 4 small groups.

2. Give each small group
    ◆ Family description sheet
    ◆ Cost of living sheet
    ◆ Income sheet
    ◆ Questions to ask sheet
    ◆ Budget worksheet

3. Have the small groups fill out the budget worksheet based on the information received. If a family is unable to live within their means, have the students brainstorm alternatives for the family (i.e. get a second job, go back to school, etc.)

4. When the small groups have completed the exercise have each small group share the description of the family, the budget they came up with, and the changes made to allow the family to live within their means.

5. Process the activity with the students and connect it back to how important the work of agency they will work with really is and the impact it has on the clients it serves.

Note: The family descriptions and the cost of living information are based on real-life cases. Information was received from Transitional Housing in North Kingstown, RI.

Institutional Strategies to Involve First-Year Students in Service

Julie A. Hatcher
Robert G. Bringle
Richard Muthiah

Providing entering students with an educational culture that promotes academic success is a high priority for campus administrators and faculty. It is estimated that one third of all first-year students drop out of the college they first enter (Levitz & Noel, 1998). Although this national average has remained fairly consistent over the past 20 years, retention has become a more important issue for higher education because of the pressure of increased public accountability and an ever-competitive allocation of shrinking public resources. Furthermore, colleges and universities have an internal imperative—for both ethical reasons and institutional health—to exert their best effort to retain students (Bean, 1986). Improving retention is ethically demanded because students who do not persist to graduation receive fewer benefits from their truncated educational experiences. They may exit the system having made a significant financial investment and accruing debt with little return. At the institutional level, tuition income is lost when students drop out, and recruiting new students to replace those who have left adds to the cost of attrition. Additionally, institutional reputation is diminished if retention rates are low, potentially contributing to lower faculty and staff morale (Bean, 1986).

A campus environment that strategically focuses on first-year success, and at the same time takes seriously the importance of civic engagement, holds great potential for providing meaningful educational experiences that can improve retention. As Tinto (1999) suggests, students who are active learners, both in and out of the classroom, are more likely to persist:

> Students who are actively involved in learning activities and spend more time on task, especially with others, are more likely to learn and, in turn, more likely to stay. Unfortunately, most first-year students experience education as isolated learners. (p 6)

This chapter represents a case study of how Indiana University-Purdue University Indianapolis (IUPUI) strategically involves first-year students in service-learning and co-curricular service experiences as one of many institutional strategies to support retention. These are initial steps in developing a campus-wide culture that values the community engagement of faculty, staff, and students.

Indiana University-Purdue University Indianapolis

IUPUI is a commuter campus that offers undergraduate and graduate degrees through 21 different schools of Indiana University and Purdue University. With an enrollment of 27,000, IUPUI attracts a high percentage of first-generation college students and adult learners working towards professional advancement. Over the past decade, the institution's student profile has become more traditional, with the average age of entering students now at 18.7 and the percentage of full-time students exceeding that of part-time students. Yet IUPUI still reflects the trend in higher education where

> despite public impressions to the contrary, most students commute to college and work while taking classes. Many attend part-time and have significant obligations outside the college that limit the time they can spend on campus. For these students, indeed for most students, the classroom may be the only place where they meet faculty members and student peers, the one place where they engage the curriculum. (Tinto, 1999, p. 6)

University College

University College was created in 1997 to provide academic support to entering students prior to their formal admission to a degree-granting school (e.g., business, education, engineering and technology, liberal arts, social work). University College develops curricular and co-curricular initiatives to promote academic excellence and enhance first-year persistence. The faculty of University College come from every school on campus and are dedicated to improving undergraduate education. Together with professional staff (e.g., academic advisors, academic support staff, student affairs personnel) and campus administrators, the faculty provide academic leadership for University College. University College also coordinates the Peer Mentoring Learning Assistance Program, the Math Assistance Center, the Campus Orientation Program, Student Support Services, and the Honors Program. Hence, this unit is consistent with Tinto's recommendation of having an "organizational environment within which collaborative partnerships between academic and student affairs professionals are valued and creative responses to the questions of the first year are encouraged" (Tinto, 1999, p. 9).

Learning Communities

A cornerstone of University College is participation in Learning Communities (LC), a required one-credit class for all entering students. Unlike the common structure of a "learning community" in which students co-register for two or more classes with block scheduling (Gabelnick, MacGregor, Matthews, & Smith, 1990), the one-credit LC class at IUPUI has more in common with a first-year seminar (Jewler, 1989). It provides students, in a small class setting, with an introduction to academic culture, campus resources, and study skills that promote academic success. The template for learner outcomes includes increasing students' understanding of the culture and context of the university, critical thinking and communication skills, technology and library skills, knowledge of campus resources, and familiarity with the academic advising process. A unique aspect of the IUPUI LC model is the use and nature of its instructional teams, which consist of a faculty member, an academic advisor, a librarian, and a student mentor who work together to design and conduct the class. The strength of such an instructional team is that it creates "learning environments that actively involve students, faculty members, and staff in shared learning activities" (Tinto, 1999, p. 5). LCs can stand alone as one-credit courses offered either through University College or individual departments; they can also be linked to a three-credit class, thus involving a cohort of students in a four-credit combination of two courses. University College staff consult with faculty from each of the schools on campus to design discipline-specific LCs based on the template of learner outcomes; however, each class is unique, because the curriculum and curricular strategies used by the instructional team vary.

Gateway Courses

Gateway courses (e.g., English Composition, Psychology as a Social Science, Introduction to Sociology) have high first-year enrollment and typically serve as prerequisites for upper-level courses or graduation. A collaborative project between University College and the Center for Teaching and Learning in fall 2000 has allocated campus curriculum development resources for the improvement of 45 gateway courses. Faculty colloquia and curriculum development stipends provide instructors with resources to redesign their teaching and learning strategies in gateway courses so that first-year students are more actively involved in the learning process and, ultimately, more successful in their academic career at IUPUI. In Spring 2001, the campus received the Hesburgh Certificate of Excellence Award, a national award given by TIAA-CREF, in recognition of the Gateway Program to Enhance Student Retention.

Service-Learning at IUPUI

As a metropolitan university, IUPUI joins other colleges and universities that take seriously their role as active citizens in their local communities (Bringle, Games, & Malloy, 1999). With this goal in mind, since 1993, campus resources have supported the Office of Service Learning in its efforts to integrate service into academic study. The Office of Service Learning is now one of three programs within the Center for Service and Learning (CSL), a centralized campus unit that involves students, faculty, and staff in service activities that mutually benefit the campus and community. The CSL (a) supports the development and implementation of service-learning classes, (b) increases campus participation in community service activities, (c) strengthens campus-community partnerships, (d) advances the scholarship of service, and (e) promotes civic engagement in higher education. From the onset, these campus units have reported to the chief academic officer. Having a centralized unit situated in academic affairs increases the likelihood that service-learning will be institutionalized as an enduring curricular expression of the campus's commitment to civic engagement (Bringle & Hatcher, 2000).

IUPUI values service-learning as a curricular strategy that supports student success and contributes to the campus mission of building campus-community partnerships. The school defines service-learning as a credit-bearing educational experience in which students (a) participate in an organized service activity that meets identified community needs, and (b) reflect on the service activity in such a way as to gain further understanding of course content, a broader appreciation of the discipline, and an enhanced sense of civic responsibility. (Bringle & Hatcher, 1996, p. 222; Zlotkowski, 1998)

Service-learning, then, is a course-based experience. Service in the community is a structured part of the course design and course expectations. This aspect of service-learning is especially important for commuter students who have competing demands on their time and limited interest in co-curricular activities. They do, however, want to be a part of the campus community, and for a sense of community to grow on a commuter campus requires nurturing first and foremost in the classroom (Kuh, 1991; Tinto, 1999). The collaborative nature of service-learning contributes to community building. Learning through service is also inherently active. Through structured reflection, students are asked to derive educational and personal lessons from their service to the community. In this way, service-learning contributes to new understanding and clarification of personal and educational goals.

Research on service-learning identifies learning outcomes that are important for all students, particularly first-year students. Research confirms that students who participate in service-learning tend to be actively engaged in the learning process, develop peer relationships, communicate more frequently with faculty both in and out of class, clarify career and educational options, clarify personal values, and see themselves as active contributors to the community (Eyler & Giles, 1999; Gray, Ondaatje, & Zakaras, 1999; Osborne, Hammerich, & Hensley, 1998; Sax & Astin, 1997). First-year participation in service-learning "increases the likelihood that students will discuss their experiences with each other, . . . that students will receive emotional support from faculty," and that they will benefit from "an increased sense of personal efficacy, an increased awareness of the world around them, an increased awareness of . . . personal values, and increased engagement in the classroom experience" (Astin, Vogelgesang, Ikeda, & Yee, 2000, p. iii-iv). These outcomes are consistent with such dimensions of "first-year success" as developing academic and intellectual competence, establishing and maintaining interpersonal relationships, developing personal identity, deciding on a career and lifestyle, maintaining personal health and wellness, and developing an integrated philosophy of life (Upcraft & Gardner, 1989). Additionally, the retention literature is clear that interpersonal relationships with peers and faculty are critical to persistence (Pascarella & Terenzini, 1991; Tinto, 1987).

Service-Learning in Learning Communities

The university's dean of faculties and chief academic officer appointed the Service Learning Advisory Committee for University College in 1997 to advise faculty and instructional teams on integrating service-learning into the curriculum of first-year courses and to promote co-curricular service opportunities for entering students. The Service Learning Advisory Committee comprised faculty, staff, community agency representatives, and students. The committee reviewed literature, gathered program information from other campuses, conducted a focus-group of IUPUI students who had participated in service and service-learning, interviewed six IUPUI service-learning instructors, and spoke with three community agency partners. This work led to the conclusion that designing community-based service experiences for first-year students is different than designing such activities for upperclass students who are typically more skilled, more experienced in managing academic responsibilities, and more confident in their career direction. The Service Learning Advisory Committee concluded that service-learning is an effective strategy to promote active learning and active citizenship; however, it must be well structured to meet the developmental needs of first-year students so that they can contribute effectively to a community agency. The committee provided a list of recommendations (e.g., group projects rather than individual projects, involvement of instructional team, clear rationale on syllabus) that is regularly distributed to LC instructors (Figure 1).

Although the one-credit hour course limits the amount of community service that can be expected of the students, a number of instructors have integrated a service component into their LC class (Table 1). The Kelly School of Business is the only school to date that requires service-learning for all entering students (approximately 600 each year). A partnership with Junior Achievement of Central Indiana, Inc., involves teams of first-year business students in presenting lessons on basic business and economic concepts to elementary students. Junior Achievement provides the curricular materials, and classroom teachers monitor the student presentations. A professional staff member in the Kelly School of Business coordinates program logistics. The goals of this service-learning component are for students to (a) learn to give back to the community, (b) develop group skills, and (c) acquire project management skills. The primary reflection activity is a required written report that includes lesson plans and asks students to think about the service component. Students who work during the day are expected to make special arrangements to complete the service component. The partnership with Junior Achievement has laid the foundation for the Kelly School of Business to develop other campus-community projects (e.g., Boys and Girls Clubs of Central Indiana).

Another way to involve LCs in service-learning is to ask college students to host campus visits for middle school students. Campus tours provide an opportunity for college students to share their knowledge of the campus and to discuss educational aspirations with the visiting middle school students. The Center for Service and Learning distributes a Middle School Campus Visit Packet to instructional teams that includes information on arranging tours, names of middle school counselors and coordinators of after-school programs, tips on working with middle school students, and reflection activities. University College provides funds for transportation and refreshments. Students in LCs design campus tours based on the learning objectives of the course. For example, a communications class designed a letter exchange program between college students and middle school student pen pals and then hosted their pen pals for a campus visit.

Service-Learning in Gateway Courses

Due to large enrollment, integrating service-learning into a gateway course is, in many ways, a logistical challenge. The Center for Service and Learning (CSL) offers workshops on designing service-learning classes in gateway courses, consults with faculty on course design and implementation, and assists faculty with curricular development proposals. The CSL also offers Service-learning Assistant Scholarships ($750 to $1,500). These scholarships are awarded to students who assist with the implementation of service-learning in large enrollment classes.

Figure 1.

Recommendations on Integrating Service into First-Year Courses
(IUPUI Service Learning Advisory Committee in University College)

◆ Design group service projects, rather than individual service activities, for entering students so that the service component is a way to build peer relationships and strengthen communication between the students and the instructional team. Group projects can lessen the anxiety that may be associated with venturing out into the community. Offering opportunities for first-year students to interact with faculty and staff in diverse roles is very beneficial.

◆ One-time service projects (e.g., painting a room at a community center, environmental cleanup activity, hosting a campus visit for middle school students) are recommended for entering students. While this is not always possible, it allows students to complete a project with a sense of accomplishment. A group of Learning Communities (LC) could commit to a larger, ongoing service project (e.g., preparing a vacant house for renovation) and "pass the torch" from one LC to the next over the semester in order to complete a larger service project.

◆ The LC instructional team can assume a variety of roles in the design, implementation, monitoring, and structured reflection of a service-learning component. Student mentors can be instrumental in assuming some responsibilities for details associated with integrating a service experience. The instructional team should plan, if possible, to supervise the service activity, so that the burden of supervision does not lie solely on the community agency.

◆ Include a clear description of the service component on the syllabus so that entering students are well aware of this course expectation and can plan accordingly. Entering students benefit from having a clear rationale for course expectations. Make the learning objectives of the service experience explicit in the syllabus, in class discussions, and in the reflection activities.

◆ Identify, early on, a community agency or school partner. Meet with agency staff to discuss, plan, and assess the service component. Work toward developing a partnership with the community agency or school, rather than simply a placement site. Invite the community partner to visit class prior to the service experience.

◆ Consider blocking out class time for the service experience, in the same way that one would block out time to visit the Career Center or complete a lab project. Or, plan for all of the LC classes from one school to convene on a Saturday to complete a school-wide service project. Provide dates on the syllabus.

◆ Recognize and celebrate the involvement of first-year students in the service project by providing pictures to the campus newspaper or school newsletter. Hold a celebratory event with community partners and invite students to participate in the campus-wide recognition hosted by the Center for Service and Learning.

Table 1.
Examples of Service-Learning in First-Year Courses at IUPUI

School and Course Title	Community Partner and Service Activity	Number of Course Credits	Required or Optional Service	Group Project or Individual Service	Number of Service Hours
Business Learning Communities	Teach Junior Achievement curriculum in elementary schools	1	Required	Group project for entire class	10
Criminal Justice Learning Communities	Visit Indiana Boys School and sponsor a social event for young men	1	Optional	Group project	5
Liberal Arts Learning Communities	Write pen pals in middle school and host a campus tour	1	Required	Individual; Group project	8
Liberal Arts Communication Voice & Diction	Read stories to children at the campus Center for Children	3	Optional	Individual	10
Engineering Introduction to Construction Technology	Work on construction site with Habitat for Humanity	3	Required	Group project for entire class	6
Education Examining Self as Teacher	Tutor children in after-school programs at community centers	3	Required	Individual	10
Science Environmental Geography	Plant trees and environmental cleanup at the White River	3	Optional	Group project	6
Science Psychology as a Social Science	Read with elementary students at Riverside School	3	Required	Individual	30

Another strategy for integrating service into gateway courses is the Service-learning Option. The Center for Service and Learning has developed a Service-learning Option Packet for students to contract individually with a faculty member to complete a service-learning component in a course. Gateway instructors receive information about the service-learning option, and although to date it has not been widely used, instructors who have had positive experiences with a small number of service-learning students will hopefully be more likely to design a service-learning course in the future.

A gateway course that has been developed as a campus prototype for service-learning (Bringle & Hatcher, 1996) is Environmental Geology. Coordinated by the faculty and staff in the interdisciplinary Center for Earth and Environmental Science, the service-learning component is part of a comprehensive and ongoing project to restore the banks of the White River, just west of the campus. Tree plantings, water testing, and environmental cleanups provide opportunities for many students to be involved at the same time and for students to conduct field-based research over time. Service-learning assistants provide support for implementing these service-learning projects. Because of the success of this service-learning class, other gateway courses have become involved in the project (e.g., Introduction to Oceanography, Physical Systems of the Environment, Introduction to Environmental Sciences). Environmental Geology makes extensive use of the web (www.cees.iupui.edu) for students to learn about the service-learning projects, sign on for project activities, complete volunteer forms, and keep up to date on project development.

Co-Curricular Service for First-Year Students

An increasing number of entering students arrive on campus with prior experience in voluntary service (Sax & Astin, 1997), and this is the case for many IUPUI students. A survey conducted by the Center for Service and Learning (CSL) of 550 entering students at IUPUI found that 63% of the students had participated in community service during the previous year, with a median of 20 hours of service being reported, while 75% reported participating in community service during the previous five-year period. The survey also asked entering students about their interest in various types of community service; 86.6% of the respondents indicated that they would be "somewhat interested" or "very interested" in one-time service projects, followed by interest in contracting with an instructor for a service-learning option (80.8%), paid community service (76.2%), short-term service projects (65.3%), international projects (54.9%), service-learning classes (52.5%), and immersion projects (31.1%) (Bringle, Hatcher, & McIntosh, 1999).

These results indicate the importance of designing both curricular and co-curricular service opportunities for entering students that allow students to build on their past experiences, continue their involvement, respond to their interests, and become part of a culture of service during their first year on campus. The CSL has made significant progress in establishing onetime service events as a part of the educational culture of IUPUI. Since 1994, the campus has collaborated with United Way of Central Indiana to engage teams of faculty, students, and staff in a "Day of Caring" at United Way agencies during September. Since 1998, the CSL has also organized community service projects for teams to celebrate Dr. Martin Luther King, Jr. Day as a "Day-On of Service" in January. In addition, CSL sponsors the "Jam the Bus" food drive in November, "Holiday Assistance Program" in December, and "Into the Parks" in April. These group service projects are promoted to LC instructional teams as a way to involve first-year students in campus activities and to promote camaraderie among students.

To increase student participation in all forms of community service, a professional staff position, the Coordinator for Community Service, was created in 2000. This position is jointly funded by the Center for Service and Learning and the Student Life and Diversity Programs in Student Affairs as an intentional way to bridge the gap that often exists between academic affairs and student affairs. The Coordinator for Community Service consults with instructional teams on middle school campus visits and onetime group service projects, provides program information for University College publications distributed to all entering students, works with student organizations on designing service projects, and collaborates with other student affairs staff to develop community service as a component of student life. Impressive results have occurred in a short amount of time as more and more students now participate in co-curricular service activities.

Freshman Service Scholarships

IUPUI has made a significant decision to recognize community service as an area of merit in awarding campus scholarship dollars. The Center for Service and Learning coordinates an extensive Community Service Scholarship Program drawing upon $100,000 of campus scholarship funds dedicated annually to recognizing students who have demonstrated a commitment to community service. The Community Service Scholarship Program is composed of five types of scholarships: Freshman Service Scholarships ($2,000), Community Service Scholarships ($3,000), Community Service Leader Scholarships ($3,000), America Reads Team Leader Scholarships ($2,000), and Service-learning Assistant Scholarships ($1,500). The Freshman Service Scholarship provides an important means of attracting entering students who have had prior experience in service and service-learning. A cohort of 15 Freshman Service Scholars enrolls in a service-learning class (specifically, Psychology as a Social Science) during the fall semester, participates in three hours of community service each week during both semesters, participates in two group service projects, and attends monthly meetings with all Service Scholars in the spring. The Freshman Service Scholarship blends curricular and co-curricular community service experiences and develops connections among students and contacts on campus and in the community. In this way, the scholarship program can play a significant role both in the recruitment and the retention of first-year students.

Assessment

The Office of Service Learning made an early commitment to develop a culture of evidence to assess the outcomes of service-learning. A research project conducted in 1994 suggests that first-year students in a service-learning class benefit in multiple ways. Journals of 133 first-year students who participated in Project X/L, a study skills class that linked underprepared first-year students with eighth grade students in a tutoring relationship for 10 weeks, were evaluated to assess self-reported learning outcomes. College students reported positive gains in self-confidence, improved perceptions of themselves as learners, stronger academic skills and competence, a better understanding of career and educational goals, and the ability to develop interpersonal relationships with peers (Hatcher & Oblander, 1998). An end-of-course survey was developed by the Office of Service Learning in 1997 and distributed to all service-learning instructors to administer at the end of the semester. This survey included items to assess students' progress towards the

Principles of Undergraduate Learning. The Principles of Undergraduate Learning (i.e., core communication skills, quantitative skills, critical thinking, integration and application of knowledge, intellectual depth and breadth, adaptiveness, understanding society and culture, values and ethics) provide a framework for the development of a common undergraduate experience at IUPUI. When respondents in service-learning classes were compared to a random sample of continuing IUPUI students, students in service-learning classes scored significantly higher on in-depth understanding of course material, ability to relate knowledge with practice, understanding different people and traditions, and appreciation of ethical standards (see Table 2). In addition, the researchers compared students in three-credit hour service-learning classes to students in three-credit-hour classes that did not include a service component and to students in one-credit-hour Learning Communities that included a service component. Higher scores were reported for students in three-credit-hour service-learning classes on all items associated with IUPUI's Principles of Undergraduate Learning, except quantitative skills and computer skills (Bringle,

Table 2.

Comparison of Service-Learning Students to Returning Continuing Students on IUPUI's Principles of Undergraduate Learning

Item	Service-Learning Students	Continuing Students
In-depth understanding of course material	3.77	3.32*
Ability to critically examine ideas and issues	3.86	3.20*
Ability to relate knowledge with practice	4.09	3.29*
Ability to express facts or ideas in writing	3.60	3.34*
Speaking in a small group setting	3.67	3.22*
Speaking to a large group	3.16	2.69*
Ability to integrate knowledge from several fields	3.55	3.15*
Ability to view events from different perspectives	3.87	2.97*
Developing a sense of values and ethical standards	3.64	2.76*
Ability to make sense of personal and social experiences	3.84	2.87*
Understanding different people and traditions	3.79	2.87*

* $p < .05$

Hatcher, & McIntosh, 1999). These results testify to the considerable academic role that service-learning can play in support of student learning. As IUPUI more carefully examines and discusses general education for undergraduate students, it will be important to inform the campus community of the potential of various educational strategies, including service-learning.

Conclusion

Although many of the factors that lead to student success and persistence are pre-entry attributes that are not easily influenced by academic culture such as goals, commitments, family level of education, institutional experiences (e.g., formal interactions with faculty and staff, out-of-class interactions with peers, informal interactions with others) can be designed to support more fully the academic and social integration of first-year students (Bean, 1986). Research indicates that active involvement in coursework is critical for first-year success. Perhaps the single most important factor contributing to campus climate is what occurs in the classroom. Because service-learning shows promise for improving first-year learning outcomes and contributing to first-year persistence, its potential is valued by University College. Furthermore, service-learning is valued at IUPUI as an important institutional strategy to create a campus climate that supports student engagement in the community (Boyte & Hollander, 1999).

References

Astin, A. W., Vogelgesang, L. J., Ikeda, E. K., & Yee, J. A. (2000). *How service-learning affects students: Executive summary.* Los Angeles Higher Education Research Institute, University of California.

Bean, J. P. (1986). Assessing and reducing attrition. *New Directions for Higher Education, No. 53 Managing College Enrollments, 14*(1), 47-61.

Boyte, H., & Hollander, E. (1999). *Wingspread declaration on the civic responsibility of research universities.* Providence, RI: Campus Compact.

Bringle, R. G., Games, R., & Malloy, E. A. (Eds.). (1999). *Colleges and universities as citizens.* Needham Heights, MA: Allyn and Bacon.

Bringle, R. G., & Hatcher, J. A. (1996). Implementing service-learning in higher education. *Journal of Higher Education, 67,* 221-239.

Bringle, R. G., & Hatcher, J. A. (2000). Institutionalization of service-learning in higher education. *Journal of Higher Education, 71,* 273-290.

Bringle, R. G., Hatcher, J. A., & McIntosh, R. (1999). *Student involvement in service and service-learning.* Paper presented at the Association for Research on Nonprofit Organizations and Voluntary Action, Washington, DC.

Bringle, R. G., & Velo, P. M. (1998). Attributions about misery. In R. G. Bringle & D. K. Duffy (Eds.), *With service in mind: Concepts and models for service-learning in psychology* (pp. 51-67). Washington, DC: American Association for Higher Education.

Eyler, J., & Giles, D. E., Jr. (1999). *Where's the learning in service-learning?* San Francisco: Jossey-Bass.

Gabelnick, F., MacGregor, J., Matthews, R. S., & Smith, B. L. (1990). Resources on learning communities. *New Directions for Teaching and Learning, 41,* 95-102.

Gray, M. J., Ondaatje, E. H., & Zakaras, L. (1999). *Combining service and learning in higher education: A summary report.* Santa Monica: RAND.

Hatcher, J. A., & Oblander, F. (1998). *The promise and pitfalls of service-learning for entering students.* Presentation at the 17th Annual Conference on the First-Year Experience, Columbia, S.C.

Jewler, A. J. (1989). Elements of an effective seminar: The university 101 program. In M. L. Upcraft & J. N. Gardner (Eds.), *The freshman year experience: Helping students survive and succeed in college* (pp. 198-215). San Francisco: Jossey-Bass.

Kuh, G. (Ed.). (1991). *Involving colleges: Successful approaches to fostering student learning and development outside the classroom.* San Francisco: Jossey-Bass.

Levitz, R. S., & Noel, L. (1989). Connecting students to institutions: Keys to retention and success. In M. L. Upcraft & J. N. Gardner (Eds.), *The freshman year experience: Helping students survive and succeed in college* (pp. 65-81). San Francisco: Jossey-Bass.

Osborne, R. E., Hammerich, S., & Hensley, C. (1998). Student effects of service-learning: Tracking change across a semester. *Michigan Journal of Community Service-learning, 5,* 5-13.

Pascarella, E. T., & Terenzini, P. T. (1991). *How college affects students: Findings and insights from twenty years of research.* San Francisco: Jossey-Bass.

Sax, L. J., & Astin, A. W. (1997). The benefits of service: Evidence from undergraduates. *Educational Record, 78*(3-4), 25-32.

Tinto, V. (1987). *Leaving college: Rethinking the causes and cures of student attrition.* Chicago: University of Chicago Press.

Tinto, V. (1999). Taking retention seriously: Rethinking the first year of college. *NACADA Journal, 19*(2), 5-9.

Upcraft, M. L., & Gardner, J. N. (Eds.). (1989). *The freshman year experience: Helping students survive and succeed in college.* San Francisco: Jossey-Bass.

Zlotkowski, E. (Ed.). (1998). *Successful service-learning programs: New models of excellence in higher education.* Bolton, MA: Anker.

Inquiry as a Mode of Student Learning at Portland State University: Service-Learning Experiences in First-Year Curriculum

Dilafruz Williams
Judy Patton
Richard Beyler
Martha Balshem
Monica Halka

Much of the literature on service-learning argues that students who learn experientially and actively by serving the community in meaningful ways benefit from their experiences. The student learning outcomes associated with service-learning include (a) attainment of valuable skills such as communication and problem-solving (Eyler & Giles, 1999); (b) ability to deal with diversity and that which is unfamiliar (Williams & Driscoll, 1996); (c) the development of a sense of personal efficacy in terms of recognizing one's strengths, weaknesses, and personal biases (Astin, 1992; Reeb et al, 1998; Waterman, 1997); (d) social activism (Cushman, 1999); and (e) a better understanding of academic content, better insofar as the service activity is tied to a specific course curriculum (Astin & Sax, 1998; Cumbo & Vadenboncoueur, 1999; Eyler & Giles, 1999).

Recognizing these potential benefits and the power of service-learning as a form of inquiry and application, we have deliberately made service-learning an integral part of the undergraduate curriculum at Portland State University (PSU). Almost a decade ago, PSU aligned its curricula, academic programs, scholarship and research, and community outreach to reflect its commitment to a newly defined "urban" mission that placed student learning and student experience at the heart of the educational enterprise. Taking seriously its motto *Let Knowledge Serve the City*, PSU characterizes itself as an institution whose identity and future are intimately connected with the metropolitan region. This urban self-identification works not as a limiting factor but as a core value that helps to strengthen the university's vision and direction. Among the institutional changes that have served to transform PSU, one of the most important was the adoption of a new University Studies program, which joined the Honors program as a general education option in 1994.

University Studies is a four-year interdisciplinary program with a curriculum that has four explicit goals: (a) inquiry and critical thinking, (b) communication, (c) the diversity of human experience, and (d) ethical issues and social responsibility. These goals are based on research that investigates how general education can improve student learning and retention (Astin, 1992; Boyer, 1987; Chickering & Gamson, 1987). Service-learning functions as one of the key strategies by which we operationalize our goals and simultaneously practice our "urban" mission of partnering with the metropolitan community. It is typical for PSU students to be engaged in the communities beyond the four walls of the classroom and to address communal and societal issues through direct involvement. Faculty development support for service-learning is provided by Community-University Partnerships at the Center for Academic Excellence located in the Office of Academic Affairs. Faculty receive assistance not only in finding relevant community organizations as sites for service but also with curriculum design, pedagogical issues, and assessment tools associated with service-learning.[1]

Although the senior-level capstone course is the culminating service experience in the University Studies curriculum, many faculty integrate an introductory community experience into their Freshman Inquiry (FRINQ) course, using inquiry as a mode of student learning. Through inquiry, students are exposed to a process of learning that establishes a framework for identifying critical questions for a topic, finding or collecting evidence or data to support possible answers to those questions, and analyzing the understanding gained to make informed decisions or recommendations. Early exposure to community-based work is important because it not only meets the learning goals of the program but also serves as a gateway to other service-learning courses in the four-year curriculum. Furthermore, we believe that cumulative service experiences enhance the ability of students to do well in their senior-level capstone.

The entry-level FRINQ course is a three-term sequence (5 credits per term) designed to support students in their year-long transition to higher education, in its broadest sense. Teams of faculty from different disciplines design thematically based courses that address the four goals of University Studies through a rich and challenging content. Each faculty member is paired with an undergraduate peer mentor. They work closely together, with peer mentors serving as communication bridges between the students and faculty. FRINQ courses meet as a whole (a maximum of 36 students, a faculty member, and a peer mentor) twice a week for 75 minutes. In addition, each student attends two weekly sessions led by a peer mentor. The curriculum for the mentor sessions is developed by the entire team and individualized by specific professor/mentor partners.[2] Themes for FRINQ courses change as faculty from disciplinary departments move in and out of the program, having made a commitment to teach for two to three consecutive years. Some of the course themes are: "The Columbia Basin;" "Human/Nature;" "Faith and Reason;" "Knowledge, Art, and Power;" "Metamorphosis;" and "The Cyborg Millennium."

In this chapter we will describe a range of service-learning activities included in our FRINQ courses and focus on two distinct kinds of experiences in and structures for service-learning. We will illustrate ways in which service-learning activities are explored, set up with partners, and undertaken by students. We also discuss student responses.

Varieties of Service-Learning: Early Exposure in Freshman Inquiry

It is our belief that providing students with exposure to a variety of service-learning experiences in their first year not only strengthens the integrity of the general education program but also develops a familiarity with and expertise in service-learning that will stand students in good stead throughout their careers at

PSU. While some of these service-learning experiences may include intensive one-day experiences in the community, others might require weekly contact for an entire term, and still others may involve year-long commitment at the same site in the community. By letting FRINQ faculty experiment with community-based work without imposing a particular model, we have found greater willingness on their part to incorporate service-learning into their courses. Incentive mini-grants have also been employed toward this end. As a result, we have noticed over the last six years an increasing number of FRINQ faculty have adopted service-learning and have encouraged students to reflect on their experiences and include these in their portfolios.

A typical scenario for setting up a service-learning project is as follows. During FRINQ faculty orientation at the beginning of a new academic year, staff from the Office of Community-University Partnerships introduce faculty to support programs available for linking academic content with appropriate and relevant service opportunities. Incentive mini-grant applications are distributed if grant monies are available. Faculty contact the Partnership office to initiate an exploration of possible sites. Once partnership opportunities have been presented and service-learning sites/experiences have been agreed to, the office helps faculty develop service-learning projects that are appropriate for specific FRINQ themes and place students with a variety of community organizations. Examples of service-learning syllabi, reflection exercises, assessment forms, and scholarship and publication opportunities are shared and discussed. Depending on faculty interest, the Partnership office also discusses liability issues, partner expectations, and transportation options with a faculty member's students, doing so well before students are expected to visit their service sites.

Among the wide variety of service-learning opportunities in FRINQ courses, the following are representative:

- Students electing the "Knowledge, Art, and Power" theme have worked with the Portland Art Museum to guide middle school students through current exhibits and to research and write exhibition catalogues.
- Students electing the "Portland" theme have worked on several projects in conjunction with the City of Portland. For example, one of these dealt with a study of how citizens access the city; another was a tree count recording the location, size, type, and condition of trees within the city limits.
- Students electing the "Pluralistic Society" theme have participated in tutoring among newly arrived immigrant populations, with a large percentage of FRINQ students choosing to continue to tutor even after the assignment has ended.

In their reflection exercises, students have reported an increased sense of self-confidence, a feeling of connection to those with whom they have worked, and a greater awareness and understanding of different populations in Portland.

Service-learning projects such as these reflect the interdisciplinary nature of the FRINQ courses and focus on the goals of the University Studies program. Typical in this regard is the "Einstein" FRINQ class that taught physics to first and third graders. The FRINQ students maintained a relationship with the younger students and researched different learning styles during the course of an entire academic year. Through the use of visual presentations, technology to enhance those presentations, and a variety of research methods, FRINQ students studied how well the younger students were internalizing information and content from their class. Using the data gathered, they then identified those aspects of Einstein's work and Newtonian physics most likely to interest elementary school children. When the FRINQ students were assessed as part of an on-going evaluation of service-learning at PSU, they identified their service-learning project as one of the most meaningful aspects of their course.[3]

Also typical is the "Columbia Basin" FRINQ class taught by Monica Halka. Halka's students, in collaboration with the coordinator of the Forest Park Ivy Removal Project, planned and carried out an experimental study to test the best method for removing English Ivy in order to inhibit its regrowth. The project linked well with the academic content and themes of *Human Management of the Columbia Basin* and *The Future of the Basin,* for winter and spring quarters respectively. Relatively little is known about English Ivy (*Hedera helix*), a species non-native to Oregon that is taking over forests in the region. Portland's Forest Park, America's largest urban forest, is especially at risk because this invasive plant has been introduced into gardens by surrounding homeowners. It has spread to the forest because the ivy grows rapidly and has no natural enemies in the local ecosystem. In Forest Park, where it has become widely established, it suffocates ground cover and native plant seedlings, climbs and destroys native shrubs and trees, and provides no food for native wildlife. Many homeowners, like many of the students in the class, have had the misconception that ivy is a good ground cover for erosion control. However, its shallow roots and waxy leaves make it, in fact, unsuitable for this purpose while native plants that do serve as natural filters and control erosion on stream banks can be crowded out by the ivy, thereby degrading local water quality.

After a presentation by the Coordinator of the Ivy Removal Project that explained the issues of invasive plants to the class, it became clear that any service project aimed at removing invasive ivy from Forest Park would have to be grounded in scientific knowledge. Hence, FRINQ students helped design an experiment to test which of two ivy removal methods would best prevent or impede its regrowth: a pull-and-drop or a pull-and-remove method. Class discussions of the scientific method led to a plan for pulling and monitoring two neighboring plots in the park. During the winter quarter, students in groups of four or five pulled ivy for three two-hour periods on their assigned plot, using the method designated for that plot. During the spring quarter, students were separated into different groups to avoid bias. The groups then monitored re-growth of ivy on the plots. Both groups determined that the pull-and-drop method was the better choice, and their results were statistically significant. They hypothesized that the probable reason for the superiority of this method is that the dropped vines effectively blocked sunlight from new shoots.

For this service-learning project, students had to develop scientific skills including careful observation, inquiry, hypothesis formation and testing, data collection, identification of invasive and native plant species, collection of statistical information, and use of computer programs for database development and analysis. They also had to practice group work skills by establishing and following a protocol and by discussing and coming to a consensus on their findings. Initially, many students were skeptical about the educational value of pulling ivy, but once they recognized the pervasiveness of the non-native-species problem and understood that they would be performing a scientific study to help find solutions, they were open to it. After the study was finished, journal entries by the students indicated that they all thought the project to varying degrees had been beneficial to themselves, the university, and the community. One group wrote a letter to the landscapers at PSU to urge them to remove ivy from campus or at least to stop planting it but they were disappointed by the reply, which indicated that no action would be taken. Overall, however, students said they had enjoyed feeling like a part of the solution rather than part of the problem. Many said they now looked at forests with new eyes, and there were even some who expressed their intention to continue helping to pull ivy in Forest Park on available Saturday mornings.

Examples of Course-Based Service

Freshman Inquiry Topic: Human/Nature

In 1999, 90 students participated in four sections of a new FRINQ course, Human/Nature. The course was taught by an interdisciplinary team of faculty, including Richard Beyler. A main focus of this FRINQ was to understand human interaction with nature. This included an examination of how human life affects the natural environment and vice versa, confrontation of environmental problems, and comprehension of related environmental policy debates. However, instead of simply covering the concepts through texts, the course required students to participate in carefully structured service-learning projects. Clearly, the purpose of these projects was to expose students to a kind of learning atypical in most higher education institutions by directly connecting their "academic" work with service-based experiences.

The choice of service options depends on the closeness of the experience offered to the course theme as well as the flexibility of the project's schedule (e.g., including weekends and evenings for those students who work). The activities included ivy and foreign species removal at local parks, animal exercise and care, Earth Day celebrations, and river cleanup day. The community organizations that sponsored these activities included the Friends of Tryon Creek, the Oregon Humane Society, Portland Parks and Recreation, Metro Regional Parks and Greenspaces, Friends of Columbia Gorge, and SOLV (Stop Oregon Litter and Vandalism).

Many of the students' portfolios attested to the impact the service component had on participants. The course instructors identified projects that were logical extensions or examples of the class themes that served to point the way toward other content areas (e.g., the scientific, historical, and social background of particular policy issues). From the office of Community-University Partnerships, the faculty team obtained information on the kinds of community organizations working in the environmental area and on the possibility of connecting with these organizations. With this knowledge, they were then able to design an appropriate syllabus and begin planning the course's service projects. The team's ability to integrate traditional course content with service projects was, in part, a result of its members' prior experience in integrating service-learning into FRINQ courses.

Syllabus/content clarity. The following explanation was provided to participating first-year students in the course syllabus:

Our course's theme (Human/Nature) is an exploration of two seemingly simple but, in fact, quite complex concepts: "human" and "nature." What do these ideas mean, and how does our understanding of them affect how we live our lives individually and collectively? What does it mean to be human? What are the significant dividing lines—if any—between humans and other living beings? Are there qualities that are essential or intrinsic to all humans, and if so, where do they come from? How does our view of the essentials of human nature affect the way we organize our society and vice versa?

In the spring quarter, the course focused primarily on "human interactions with nature," specifically on questions of public policy, ethics, social responsibility, and political decision-making. Practical confrontation with these issues occurred on a regular basis through the organizations listed above, and service projects were thus viewed as a potentially critical nexus between theories and abstractions and practical, concrete initiatives.

Service-learning assignment. Students were asked to choose two different service sites/opportunities from a "menu" of several different possibilities that had been arranged with the appropriate agencies before the beginning of the term. Each project was monitored by at least one member of the faculty team or by a peer mentor from one of the four sections of the class. Students were instructed to write a three-part reflective journal after completing each of their chosen projects, including the following: (a) anticipation of the project; (b) narrative of service experiences; and (c) connections between the service experience and concepts, theories, and/or analyses presented in assigned readings or class discussions. Figure 1 presents guidelines for these journal assignments.

Student responses: *Why service-learning matters.* Based on student responses to the assignments, the four course faculty members unanimously felt that the service-learning project formed a valuable, indeed crucial, part of the course. While some missteps occurred in planning and executing the service component, both the formal assignments and the informal reactions of students indicated that the component effectively advanced the identified learning goals—and also had some unanticipated benefits. A large majority of the students included their journal reflections in their course portfolios to demonstrate their "progress" toward meeting key objectives of the general education program. In one section of 22 students, 13 chose to use the service-learning journal to illustrate their work towards the goal of ethical and social responsibility, three chose it in connection with diversity awareness, and two chose it as an example of written communication. Moreover, a detailed examination of these reflections showed a number of ways in which students found that the service-learning experiences contributed to their understanding of the course content of Human/Nature. Representative comments can be organized under several themes.

♦ *Connections to course content.* Making connections to the content of the course, one student wrote, "[A] greater respect and appreciation of nature can be gained by getting our hands a little dirty . . . Human interaction with nature is unavoidable, but by working in nature and defining what we believe nature is, our impact on the health of the environment can be a positive one." Similarly, another student noted, ". . . it makes me sad that I live my life so cut off from nature.... If people would not view the natural work as a commodity or destination, but instead look at it as an intrinsic part of our world, no matter where one lives, perhaps it would be in a much better state."

Figure 1.

Guidelines for Service-Learning Journal

One of the major assignments this term involves work different from that which we have been doing so far and from typical college fare. Namely, you will spend some time in two or so brief service-learning projects, working directly in or about the natural world. The service projects are all, in some way or another, a positive contribution to the community in which we live; in this sense they have a value in themselves apart from our class. However, these experiences also provide an opportunity to reflect on and understand the themes of our class in a "hands-on" way, distinct from the conventional academic mode of theoretical discussion. To that end, we are asking you to describe and reflect on the experience itself and then to link those reflections to the theme of the class.

The following instructions are written under the assumption (which applies to most members of the class) that you have been assigned to two different service assignments in public places (e.g., parks) If this doesn't apply to you, please consult me about an appropriate modification of the assignment.

For both of the two service projects that you undertake, write the following three journal entries (thus six entries in all):

1. Beforehand, write a relatively brief entry (approximately a half page) in which you describe what you anticipate the project will be like. Perhaps you have done something similar before and can imagine some probable likenesses. Perhaps you haven't; in that case, try to imagine what you think might happen. To what are you looking forward? What are you expecting in a negative sense? For the *second* project, this entry should include some comments based on your experience with the first.

2. As soon as possible after the project, write an entry (1-2 pages) in which you describe your experience doing the work itself. Describe what you actually did. Describe the environment in which you were working. What did you see, hear, touch...? How did it feel physically? How did it feel emotionally (e.g., exciting, boring, stressful, relaxing) and why? For the *second* service project, be sure to include some comments on any striking differences from or similarities to the first.

3. You should then write an entry (2-3 pages) of reflection, in which you attempt to link this experience to one or more of the themes or theoretical perspectives on human/nature interactions which we have considered. As a starting point, you might consider one of the following sets of questions (not all questions will be appropriate to all service projects):

♦ In what sense is the place you were working a "commons" in Hardin's sense[1]? What are the literal and figurative uses of this place? Is there any evidence of a "tragedy of the commons" occurring there? Is it appropriate that you (or any other individual) should be doing work there? To put it another way, why does the Parks Department, for example, need volunteers to do work anyway? What benefits do you (or any other individual) get from this "common ground"? What responsibilities do you have toward it?

♦ White's essay comments vividly on the fact that many people today, including many professed environmentalists, do not experience the natural world through work/labor but only through recreation/leisure.[2] Does this description apply to you? How does it relate to this particular service project? What are the consequences of primarily working and living in a largely human-made environment? What are the consequences of having life and work experiences primarily based on physical contact with the natural (non-human-made) world?

♦ A set of readings in Unit 4 discusses several key ecological concepts that may be relevant to your service assignment: habitat, biodiversity, and alien (or exotic) species. Discuss the broader importance of the service project in terms of one or more of these concepts, identifying if possible the particular species, interactions, processes, etc., that are involved in the case you worked with. What are the problems, causes, and solutions?

These journal entries are not intended to be formal academic essays; nevertheless, you should use language carefully. Try to express your observations and your ideas vividly and clearly. Final entries should be typed. If you feel so inclined, illustrations or graphics are quite welcome. Journal entries must be based on your assigned service project(s).

1. Hardin, G. (1968, December). The tragedy of the commons. *Science, 13,* 243-48.
2. White, R. (1996). Are you an environmentalist or do you work for a living?: Work and nature. In W. Cronon, (Ed.), *Uncommon ground: Rethinking the human place in nature* (pp. 171-85). New York: W. W. Norton.

♦ *Appreciation of input from community partners.* "I learned a lot about the organization and the types of things a person could get involved in," one student wrote, acknowledging the contribution made by her community partner. "It was cool to see a person so close to my age so passionate about preserving the area so that everyone can enjoy it. She was also knowledgeable about the local plant life."

♦ *Enjoyment and value of the experience.* For a number of students, the service learning experience clearly represented something of intrinsic value. As one student wrote, "I loved hearing the creek running nearby, the chirping of the birds, and even the sound of some of the other volunteers singing . . . Even though the actual work itself was exhausting, I relaxed as the day progressed." And another remarked, "It is so much different from anything else I do as a student. It is refreshing and in some ways it feels more real. I could see my progress first hand, I wasn't working towards some abstract goal."

♦ *Inspiration for community participation.* Reflecting a positive developmental experience, a student noted in his journal, "We all have the capability to do something important and morally worthwhile, and it starts with ourselves." Similar in thrust was the suggestion that "Hopefully, the coming generation will be educated to the simple fact that everyone makes a difference and finally we will take responsibility."

♦ *Community-building in class.* "You had to work as a team," was one prevalent theme. Another common observation, "While doing work, students were able to talk to each other and enjoy the time they spent together," echoed this theme.

A sample of 23 journal entries was analyzed for other themes and patterns. Sometimes contradictory responses were noted. Among the generally positive emphases, 78% found a clear connection to class themes whereas 4% found no connection. Furthermore, although 13% found class themes challenged or contradicted by their service projects, such a finding only points to the fact that an understanding of service as it relates to course content is something that has to be teased out and explicated without discounting—still less dictating—how students gauge the connections. Indeed, since the approach through the year had been to present assigned readings more as starting points for discussion and debate, students who perceived a contradiction between the theoretical perspectives presented in readings and lectures and their concrete experience were in many cases taking a significant step towards independent critical thinking.

Typically, instructors find it very challenging to bring first-year college students to a more complex understanding of the relationship between the abstract/theoretical and concrete experience. Conversely, it is often difficult for first-year students to take the critical step of shifting from merely going through experiences to using them as platforms for analysis and reflection. For many first-year students, the service-learning project in the Human/Nature course provided a venue for precisely the complex kind of learning mentioned here. From their journal comments, it was clear that students were grappling with complex issues on multiple levels:

♦ Human attempts to "manage" nature have been of ambiguous value, especially given the frequent occurrence of their unintended consequences. An especially forceful example of this was provided in those projects that involved the removal of non-native species such as English Ivy and Himalayan blackberries, whose "escape" from lawns and gardens is having a dramatic, potentially disastrous impact on some local forests. Students whose community service took them to the Humane Society also had to confront the difficulties caused by humans' ignorance or willful neglect of problems related to domestic animals.

♦ Throughout the year, the course examined various ways in which our understanding of "nature" is laden with cultural values. Several projects provided students with an opportunity to reflect on the multifarious public meanings of parks and green spaces, used for human recreation and as natural preservation. Other projects, such as participation in Earth Day celebration activities, led students to unpack and comment on the social values represented in the environmental movement.

♦ Several assigned readings discussed the consequences of the fact that, apart from recreation, modern life is increasingly removed from physical contact with nature, a separation that has dramatically changed our image of and relationship with nature. This general truth was brought home to many students in the hard—and often boring—work of pulling ivy vines or cutting blackberry shoots for several hours at a time.

♦ Another important idea discussed during the spring term was the problem of the "tragedy of the commons"—the process by which competing individual uses of and responsibility for common resources can lead to a degradation of those resources as a whole. Several students saw practical reflections of this in projects that involved cleaning up parks and other public spaces: as long as access is open to anyone, we run the risk of diminishing the experience for everyone.

♦ As a corollary to the previous point, the course examined public policy questions concerning the creation and management of parks and recreational areas. What purposes do they serve? What are the rights and responsibilities of public access? How should such areas be developed and maintained? Almost all of the service projects posed these questions in one form or another. A number of students confronted the fact that they were providing free labor for ostensibly publicly funded resources (parks).

In addition to providing substantiation of the thematic content of the class, the service assignments had the not insignificant, albeit unplanned, benefit of building community within individual sections of the class and even among sections (since, as was noted above, students from each of the sections participated in each project). Many students commented in their journals on the enriching experience they had had because of the opportunity to interact with other students and with instructors and peer mentors outside of class in an informal setting. It seemed that some of the inhibitions imposed by classroom roles dissolved when working together with young children during a community-park activity day or pulling vines in the woods—everyone's hands get dirty and everyone's backs get sore the same way. Friendships formed between individuals who had shared a classroom but had somehow avoided personal interaction. In some cases, animosities were diminished or quelled between students who had become antagonists over the course of several months of discussion and debate. The experience also provided many students with an opportunity to become familiar with places in the Portland area that were new to them (even for those who came from the Portland area) and with community organizations of which they had not been aware.

Problems encountered and lessons learned. Problems with the community service projects did arise. Some were at the level of logistical detail; others were of a more pedagogical/philosophical nature. The most tractable projects were those in which the community partners had an ongoing volunteer program into which we could "plug" the PSU students at a given time and place. More difficult were those placements involving special arrangements that entailed assigning students to activities/times/places on an individual basis. Despite all efforts at advanced planning, a few cases of miscommunication about specific projects did arise (e.g., community organization liaisons not meeting up with student groups at an expected time or place). Avoiding such cases in the future is partly a matter of all participants learning from experience. Another lesson learned is that projects with several different sub-components or that lack a single supervisory figure tend to be more problematic. Service projects that required an exact number of students or that had an inflexible maximum or minimum were also difficult to handle logistically; even with advanced sign-up, it proved impossible to determine precisely how many students would actually participate in a given project. Transportation to and from service sites also proved to be a problem in some cases. Not all students had cars, and public transportation was not always an option. Moreover, providing car or van pools in university vehicles was itself a sizeable logistical hurdle relative to the numbers of students involved.

Besides these practical problems, instructors also had to confront and discuss some broader questions. For a significant number of students, albeit a minority, the community service project was an unsatisfactory or, at best, a mixed learning experience as the journal entries cited below indicate.

- *Relationship to class unclear or problematic.* "How did the project relate to this class?" one participant asked, noting that "lack of information made the students restless; concepts should be spelled out more clearly."
- *Problems with community partners.* One student noted that he "thought the organization was not very serious about the tasks," while another pointed to a "lack of communication and organization."
- *Work found to be objectionable, trivial, futile.* For a few students the service experience was simply not worthwhile: "I felt the day was a waste of time"; "I love the outdoors very much, but not when it requires me to use a lot of energy; maybe I am just lazy"; "I felt that the work I was doing was futile, as the ivy would eventually grow back."
- *Imposition on time.* Lamented one student: "One of the most stressing factors about this project was finding time to schedule in the project during our daily routine . . . .Taking into consideration most people in class are full-time students holding down a part-time or full-time job . . . it was hard to find time."
- *Been there, done that.* "When I was in high school, it was required for graduation to volunteer 20 hours of community service" and "I grew up with a mother who used to make me work in the garden for hours on end during summer vacation" were comments suggesting that several students did not feel they needed more of the "same" service experience they had already had elsewhere.

Faculty discussed these concerns, focusing particularly on ensuring that the service projects were integrated as closely as possible with the cognitive content of the class. While this integration was successful for a majority of the students, there remained troubling cases of students who saw the activity as, at best, superfluous "make-work." In retrospect, the instructors felt that perhaps some of the service projects were less appropriate than others—not through any fault of the organizers but simply due to a less obvious connection with course content. One of the lessons learned was that while it is difficult to arrange for speakers to come to class, when community partners came and shared the purposes of their work, students got a clearer sense of the broader context of their service. A problem that remains unsolved is that many students felt acutely burdened by having to add service activities to full class loads, heavy work schedules, and family obligations, especially since scheduling service-learning is not like finding time for other forms of homework.

Freshman Inquiry Topic: Community and Conflicts

Sometimes a community service project can be designed to fit the needs of a particular group of students, if planning and implementation can be done within the time frame of the term. This was the case with PSU/Nike P.L.A.Y. (Participate in the Lives of America's Youth) Day. This project was undertaken by the students in a section of the FRINQ course entitled "Community and Conflict" taught by Martha Balshem. In this class, issues such as community boundaries, social discrimination within and between communities, and the interplay between individual freedom and social connection were explored. Ironically, these same issues complicated social relations within the class. Sixteen of the 42 students were student athletes, eight of them on the football team. A subgroup of the football players constituted a "pre-existing community" (Ramette, n.d.), whose members demonstrated what Baiocco and DeWaters (1998) refer to as "required course apathy," exerting negative social pressure on any player who engaged in class discussion. According to the course evaluations at the end of the first term, other students in the class hesitated to participate in discussion for fear that they, too, would be ridiculed. Explicit reference to this problem had no effect on student behavior. Clearly, the only solution lay in academically engaging the student athletes and their allies in the class.

To accomplish this, it was necessary to redefine the class's unusual characteristics as strengths, not weaknesses. Two observations were helpful in doing this. First, the results of a Keirsey-Bates personality test (Keirsey, 1998) showed the class to be overwhelmingly dominated by extroverts. Defining the social intelligence of the students and the pre-existing friendships among them as class strengths led the instructor to posit social learning modalities as likely to be unusually successful with this group. Second, as the instructor, via the students, became more conversant with common practices in high school and college athletics programs, she became aware that student athletes are generally required through their programs to do a great deal of community service, much of it involving work in athletic programs for children. In a school-based service project, therefore, her student athletes would be in a familiar environment in which they had previously enjoyed success. It remained to find the right project for this particular group of students.

"PSU/Nike P.L.A.Y. Day" was originally conceived by staff in the Portland State University Department of Athletics. The Nike P.L.A.Y. Corps is a program designed to encourage college students to coach in children's athletics programs in underserved areas. The Department of Athletics sought to work through the Nike P.L.A.Y. Corps to bring a group of elementary school children to campus for a day of sports and educational activities. The university's purpose was to introduce PSU, an institution of opportunity for lower-income and first-generation college students, positively to children who might not imagine college as part of in their future.

Seeing this project as an excellent fit for her students, Balshem offered to use her class to organize the P.L.A.Y. Day and to serve as coaches and campus guides during the event. Mindful of school schedules for both the college students and the children, the P.L.A.Y. Day was scheduled on a Saturday. Considerable FRINQ class time was spent organizing the event. The students divided themselves into four groups, each responsible for one group of children. They designed four activity modules through which each group would rotate during the day. Via the Department of

Athletics, all the children and students were also invited to attend a PSU men's basketball game for free. This meant arranging dinner for the participants and designing a system for ensuring the safe pick-up of all children following the game. The FRINQ students participated in all of this planning.

Two of the four activity modules for PSU/Nike P.L.A.Y. Day involved sports activities. In one room, a group of students led a football clinic, demonstrating tackling and blocking skills and teaching how to throw and catch a football. In a small gymnasium, another group of students led basketball shooting and passing games. A third module, led by Nike staff, involved glue, regrind material from recycled sneakers, and eggs dropped onto the resulting surface from various heights. In leading a fourth activity, a campus tour, the students were instructed to include those places on campus where they spent the most time. Thus, the tour included the new campus practice field (donated by Nike and made from sneaker regrind), the student center, the park that runs through campus, the dormitories, the book store, the cafeteria, and the library.

Sixty-five children attended PSU/Nike P.L.A.Y. Day, and 24 FRINQ students served as organizers and guides. Children were recruited through the Boys and Girls Clubs of Portland, the Police Athletic League, and a local mentoring program for underserved youth. The four groups moved successfully through the activity modules, and all participants gathered for a nine-foot-long subway sandwich dinner and then attended the basketball game together. During dinner, the college student athletes autographed P.L.A.Y. Corps tee-shirts provided by Nike.

Although no formal evaluation data are available, the reaction of the children to the PSU/Nike P.L.A.Y. Day, judging from their level of excitement and their attachment to their college student leaders, was overwhelmingly positive. Evaluation of the effect of this service experience on the FRINQ students was based on an in-class debriefing, which involved freewriting and a guided class discussion, and on reflective essays written approximately three weeks later for end-of-term portfolios. The predominant theme in both the debriefing and the reflective essays was the FRINQ students' poignant realization of how quickly the children had attached themselves to them and how much the children admired them. In the debriefing discussion, one student, a football player, stated that he had been emotionally affected by the extent to which the children had looked up to him, considering that "I feel like I'm just a kid myself."

Debriefing PSU/Nike P.L.A.Y. Day was an opportunity for many students to display an unusual level of emotional engagement during class discussion. The energies brought into the class through the service-learning project carried through the rest of that term and animated discussions about individual and community responsibility and social inequality. One major lesson drawn from this experience echoes lessons drawn from most service projects: Class time and student energy spent planning and debriefing a project create powerful links between the service project and the learning goals of the course. The PSU/Nike P.L.A.Y. Day experience, however, suggests an additional best practices issue: Different projects play differently for different groups of students, and best practice demands adapting service-learning projects to specific circumstances. Because of the lengthy planning time such projects often entail, it is not always feasible to do this. However, it is important for instructors to consider whether adaptations can be made to improve the fit between particular service-learning opportunities and particular groups of students.

Conclusion

After reviewing studies on learning within and outside instructional settings, Mandl, Gruber, and Renkl (1996) conclude that in traditional forms of university instruction, "students often acquire inert knowledge" that cannot be transferred into complex problems typical of everyday or professional life (p. 394). They argue that in order to become lifelong learners students must gain "flexible expertise" by becoming participants in a "community of practice." This point is affirmed by Colby and Ehrlich (2000) who argue that through active pedagogies of engagement, students can grapple with tough moral and civic issues in their communities. Interdisciplinary FRINQ courses in the general education University Studies Program at PSU attempt to introduce students to a way of teaching and learning that engages them in serving their communities while simultaneously addressing a wide variety of cognitive content areas. Furthermore, the permeable boundaries between the university and the community help FRINQ students learn to appreciate the complexities of our pluralistic, democratic lives.

The sheer scope of service-learning at PSU brings vitality of engagement to the forefront as hundreds of students each year participate in a broad range of service-learning activities in the metropolitan region. This requires flexibility if instructors are to undertake a shift in pedagogy that feels comfortable to them. It also requires support and faculty development provided through organizations that are centrally located and visible—such as the Center for Academic Excellence. We have found that service-learning enhances understanding of academic content, builds a sense of community among students, and provides practical hands-on experience. It also affects our students' affective domain since many of them continue to serve in organizations long after they have met their academic requirements.

Notes

1. Simultaneous with the adoption of the University Studies general education program, the Center for Academic Excellence was created with three components: Teaching and Learning, Assessment, and Community-University Partnerships. Because of its central location in the Office of Academic Affairs, the Center has visibility, and faculty and community partners can easily access it.

2. Peer mentor sessions enroll no more than 14 students, meet twice a week for 50 minutes each time, and take place in specially designed computer labs with a computer for each student and a central area for discussion and group projects. Peer mentors are drawn from a variety of majors, thus increasing the multidisciplinary perspectives of any given course. They actively participate in the service activities along with the first-year students.

3. In addition to formal evaluation results, student reflections included in course portfolios also indicate students viewed their service experience in this way.

References

Astin, A. W., & Sax, L. (1998). How undergraduates are affected by service participation. *Journal of College Student Development, 39*(3), 251-263.

Astin, A. W. (1992). *What matters in college: Four critical years revisited.* San Francisco: Jossey-Bass.

Baiocco, S. A., & DeWaters, J. N. (1998). *Successful college teaching: Problem-solving strategies of distinguished professors.* Boston: Allyn and Bacon.

Boyer, E. L. (1987). *The undergraduate experience in America.* New York: HarperCollins.

Chickering, A., & Gamson, Z. E. (1987, March-April). Seven principles for good practice in Undergraduate Education. *AAHE Bulletin.*

Colby, A., & Ehrlich, T. (2000). Higher education and the development of civic responsibility. In T. Ehrlich, (Ed.), *Civic responsibility in higher education.* Phoenix, AZ: Oryx Press.

Cumbo, K., & Vadenboncoueur, J. (1999). What are students learning?: Assessing cognitive outcomes in K-12 service-learning. *Michigan Journal of Community Service-learning, 6,* 84-96.

Cushman, E. (1999). The public intellectual, service-learning, and activist research. *College English, 61,* 328-336.

Eyler, J., & Giles, D.E. (1999). *Where is the learning in service-learning?* San Francisco: Jossey-Bass.

Keirsey, D. (1998). *Please understand me II: Temperament, character, intelligence.* Del Mar, CA: Prometheus Nemesis.

Mandl, H., Gruber, H., & Renkl, A. (1996). Communities of practice toward expertise: Social foundation of university instruction. In *Interactive minds: Life-span perspectives on the social foundation of cognition.* Cambridge: Cambridge University Press.

Ramette, C. (n.d.). Unpublished notes from classroom observations. Portland, Oregon: Center for Academic Excellence, Portland State University.

Reeb, R., Katsuyama, R., Sammon, J., & Yoder, D. (1998). The community service self-efficacy scale: Evidence of reliability, construct validity, and pragmatic utility. *Michigan Journal of Community Service Learning, 5,* 48-57.

Waterman, A. (1997). The role of student characteristics in service-learning. In A. Waterman (Ed.), *Service-learning: Applications from the research.* Hillsdale, N.J.: Erlbaum.

Williams, D., & Driscoll, A. (1996). Connecting curriculum with community service: Guidelines for facilitating student reflection. *Journal of Public Outreach, 2*(1), 33-42.

A Positive Impact on Their Lives: Service-Learning and First-Year Students at LeMoyne-Owen College

Barbara S. Frankle
Femi I. Ajanaku

"LeMoyne-Owen College, a historically Black liberal arts teaching institution, prepares students in a nurturing and student centered community for lives of success and service." Mission Statement of LeMoyne-Owen College

A Defining Tradition of Service

Throughout their histories, historically Black colleges and universities (HBCUs) have assumed a dual mission of educating youth for leadership roles and preparing them to be active players in the African-American community and the broader American society. Combating the segregation imposed from without, HBCUs consciously created oases of hope, cultural opportunity, and political action. They provided lyceums, enrichment programs for children, political discussion groups, and even places of refuge for southern travelers who could not find lodging in Jim Crow territory. Frequently the only place in town where members of the White and Black communities could meet, the campuses became important centers for social action. The members of these communities in their turn supported the effort to educate their youth, whose concept of service included an obligation to lead in the civic, economic, social, and political advancement of their race. Located in, and drawing students from, economically deprived backgrounds, the HBCUs built bridges instead of fences and reached out to their communities. Thus the concept of service lies at the heart of the experience of LeMoyne-Owen and its fellow HBCUs.

LeMoyne-Owen College traces its founding to the service commitment of the American Missionary Association of the Congregational Church, whose schools taught basic literacy to freed men and women in the final days of the Civil War. After violent race riots in 1866 left the association's Memphis facilities a charred ruin, abolitionist and philanthropist Julius Francis LeMoyne gave funds to build a new school, which its benefactor proclaimed should be nonsectarian and "open to any class and color." The institution named for him merged in 1968 with Owen Junior College, established in 1954 by the Baptist Missionary Educational Convention.

Both of these original institutions, and the resulting LeMoyne-Owen College, embraced from the start a commitment to community. In the tradition of the HBCUs, the college has equated service with leadership, giving a practical spin to W.E.B. DuBois' charge to educate the "talented tenth" by instilling in graduates the necessity of uplifting the community. LeMoyne-Owen College has indeed educated African-American leaders, numbering among its graduates the vast majority of African-American professionals in the mid-south region—its Black teachers, doctors, and civic leaders. During the 1960s, LeMoyne-Owen students and faculty were on the front line in civil rights marches and demonstrations. The campus was a center for planning and strategizing. Once the movement had helped to bring about a shift in political and administrative power, LeMoyne-Owen alumni assumed key offices, providing Memphis's first African-American mayor, several members of the city council and county commission, members of the judiciary, and the superintendent of the school system. Key national figures like Benjamin Hooks, retired head of the NAACP, and mayors of other major cities have been products of LeMoyne-Owen.

Living its commitment to all members of the community, the college also provides programs to enrich the life of its neighborhood—a community of economically and educationally deprived citizens, many dwelling in the public housing development directly across the street from the campus. Cultural events, mentoring to school children, symposia on community issues, tax preparation, business consultation for small entrepreneurial enterprises, health fairs and screenings, and enrichment programs for youth—just a few of the college's community initiatives. The library is open to all its neighbors, and its students find themselves surrounded by curious adolescents in the afternoons, often becoming de facto mentors to middle schoolers struggling with their first written reports.

Building concretely from a mission statement that avows the importance of service, the college's current strategic planning goals address the enhancement of civic participation. The College pledges to "promote leadership qualities among students" by providing them with "leadership opportunities on and off campus" and "more opportunities for community involvement." Further, it pledges to "develop an integrated Community Service Plan," weaving together its active Community Development Corporation, academic service programs, and its role in the evolution of a neighboring music museum and academy capable of providing music education and cultural enrichment for neighborhood youth (LeMoyne-Owen College, Strategic Plan, 2000-2001).

Concretely, the College program seeks to develop in students the capacity to be active contributors to the social good. By providing field experience combined with reflection, the College attempts to instill in its students a sense of responsibility to the wider community, to build confidence, to help students evaluate the relationship between personal experience and social circumstances, and to make students aware of the contributions they can make. We seek to make them reflective citizens with the analytical, communication, and organizational skills of civic leaders—qualities best learned and expressed through active involvement in their communities.

Continuing its tradition of community involvement, the College seeks to be a good neighbor by offering its human, physical, and intellectual resources to improve the conditions of the contiguous federally designated enterprise zone. As an educational institution, especially one which has traditionally provided opportunities for a minority underserved population, LeMoyne-Owen is committed to playing a role in the entire educational life of the city and is involved in a number of programs to assist in the development of the K-12 system.

Service-Learning at LeMoyne-Owen College

Service-learning at LeMoyne-Owen is thus embedded in a rich tradition of community responsibility. Building on its long history of involving students in civic action, the college, in 1996, redefined its approach to student participation with the implementation of a structured service-learning program. The Ford Foundation/United Negro College Fund (UNCF) Community Service Partnership Program, Learn and Serve America of the Corporation for National Service, and the Council of Independent Colleges all provided funding and networking opportunities to help establish a sound program. Following best practices, the college carefully integrated solid academic study and reflection with active field experience to give students intellectual insight into social issues while directly engaging them in social action. Given the centrality of service to the institution's mission, the College decided to require one first-year service experience (described in the following sections of this chapter) and two elective experiences for upper-level students. The first option, an interdisciplinary service-learning course, involves a flexible number of credit hours and, in different semesters, different experiences. The other option involves adding an extra academic credit to any course students may be taking if, in negotiation with the instructor and the service-learning coordinator, they undertake a social action project directly related to the content of that course. Both options may be taken more than once.

However, as central as service is to its mission, the college did not want to leave service-learning to the students' chance selection of courses, preferring instead to ensure that all students have at least one such experience. In this regard, the college is fortunate in having a highly structured core curriculum as its general education program. This core provides a set of course sequences required of every student and includes a first-year seminar as well as interdisciplinary courses in communications, mathematics, the natural sciences, the social and behavioral sciences, the humanities, and health and wellness. Such a structure enables the faculty to embed material and competencies they consider essential to student growth in courses students will be certain to take. It also allows them to locate activities at those points in the academic program when student development suggests they will most benefit from such activities.

Thanks to this structured core, first-year students benefit from an educational experience not confined to a single course or seminar, but spread across their entire curriculum. Service-learning was deemed so important to personal and academic growth that the faculty decided students should encounter it at the very beginning of their college careers. Faculty also believed this experience would be so rewarding it would encourage service in subsequent years. Consequently, service-learning was integrated into the first-year level social science class Power and Society.

First-Year Students and the Junior Achievement Service-Learning Project

A fortunate chance blossomed into a happy opportunity when Junior Achievement (JA) invited the college to join its team of instructors in the Memphis City Schools. JA has developed a curriculum of economic and social structures for children in grades one through six and trains community members to present this curriculum in the schools. Alleviating pressure on faculty time, JA makes all the administrative arrangements. Most important, its class materials relate directly to the subject matter of Power and Society.

Recognizing that the best way for students to learn course concepts would be to have them teach them to others, the social science faculty was attracted to this serendipitous opportunity. Indeed, the JA invitation coincided with a concern that students enrolled at LeMoyne-Owen were not getting enough experience in oral presentations—a key component of the JA project. Experience had already shown that LeMoyne-Owen students respond best to service programs involving children and that many seek ways to inspire youngsters to achieve academically and to aspire toward college education. Thus, the JA partnership represented an excellent match, and the resulting experience has met expectations on all counts.

Student voices offer the most eloquent testament to the impact JA has had on LeMoyne-Owen students. Contrary to the constant complaint that students do not write well, we find that they express themselves poignantly when describing their experience in the schools. When students are involved in their subject matter, they can communicate tellingly. Following good service-learning practice, the students reflect on their experience in journals and evaluation papers. Their essays reveal they believe they have matured most in the areas of self-confidence and self-presentation, career development, and awareness of the rewards of service.

These student-selected themes relate directly to seven of the eight course objectives, which themselves derive from the following 10 competencies all students are expected to attain before graduation. The competencies include the ability to

1. Think creatively, critically, logically, and analytically using both quantitative and qualitative methods for solving problems
2. Communicate effectively (listen, read, speak, and write) on formal and informal levels
3. Distinguish, clarify, and refine personal values for the attainment of richer self-perception and relate those values to the value systems of others
4. Express an appreciation, understanding, and knowledge of the foundations of the Afrocentric perspective
5. Express an appreciation, understanding, and knowledge of the foundations of diverse cultures in the context of a global community
6. Express an appreciation, understanding, and knowledge of the principles, methods, and subject matter which underlie the major discipline
7. Accept social responsibility and provide service to humankind
8. Achieve technological literacy in order to understand the impact of science and technology on individuals, society, and the environment
9. Exhibit motivational, personal management, and interpersonal skills and resourcefulness, which will form the basis for a career and/or further educational experiences
10. Hone critical skills of reference and understanding to appreciate and discriminate artistic achievement

Although the themes found in student writing refer more frequently to affective behaviors than to the social science content of Power and Society, the JA program does reinforce course content, providing concrete examples of power imbalances; the educational patterns of urban children; class and gender circumstances; community and organizational structures; differential community resources; and civic activism. However, students often do not explicitly recognize these subject matter connections; therefore, the faculty are currently examining new ways to help them do so.

As has already been mentioned, faculty were enthusiastic about the JA program because of the opportunity it presented for oral presentations, related to the second competency area. As the following two statements attest, students often have to overcome a fear of speaking formally in front of strangers:

"I know that I will have to overcome my fear in order to succeed in my career." (Student Y)

"This experience has helped me face one of my phobias. Talking to the third graders, I was able to forget my anxiety and apprehension of public speaking." (Student T)

These statements also suggest the ninth objective has been met. Certainly the need to interact with the Junior Achievement trainers, the teachers, and the children has helped students improve their interpersonal skills. Furthermore, the logistics of organizing trips to schools, planning and replanning presentations, and finding ways to schedule these visits in the midst of busy lives has helped them to exercise the resourcefulness and managerial skills expressed in competency area nine.

During a program orientation, the JA coordinator, while assuring students they have enough resource support to complete the assignment successfully, stresses the importance of student responsibility in making contact with the school and the classroom teacher, of arriving on time, and of dressing appropriately. For instance, students are warned to expect a variety of situations, but they are also reminded that the coordinator is available if there appears to be any impediment that cannot be resolved with a classroom teacher.

Some students have resisted the program, complaining of not having transportation or clothing other than blue jeans (which are not permitted). Expecting such complaints, the coordinator holds in reserve some assignments in schools close to the college. Still other students are enthusiastic but not confident of their ability to communicate before an audience. One student, who chose the elementary school she herself had attended because she "wanted to go back to contribute . . . to see my old teachers," experienced shyness and hesitation in talking to a large audience. The first day, despite her classroom teacher's attempts to ease her fright, her discomfort was so noticeable one of children asked her directly, "Are you nervous?" She later reported that the more times she went, the better she felt (Student Y).

Indeed, students have learned that imagination and resourcefulness can transform negative experiences into positive ones. One regrouped and creatively met the objections of her class: "The kids told me not to come back because the assignments were boring. So I went home and made up a game for them to play" (Student Q). In the end, these once reluctant children expressed real enthusiasm: "The children wrote me little notes about how much they liked me and they drew me pictures" (Student Q). Another student wrote about making adjustments due to miscommunications between the school and JA regarding host teachers.

The program also contributes career development experiences. It gives most students an opportunity to assume the new role of teacher, with the accompanying responsibility of managing a classroom. For those students who already have some interest in teaching as a career, this experience can strengthen their inclination. A young woman planning to major in education said her participation "added height" to her educational experience (Student U). Although another student originally had only a "slight interest" in teaching, she appreciated the "hands-on experience" (Student E). A third reflected on what day-to-day professional practice might entail: "I always thought that teaching was easy, but as I found out, making out lesson plans and teaching them was not an easy task, but in the end it was very rewarding" (Student B). Still another student was so inspired by learning to handle a class that he became sure he wanted to work with children and rationalized futuristically: "Even if I can't make a lot of money in the field, I will just have to deal with it" (Student J).

Such a statement attests to a growth in self-confidence that can, in turn, lead to additional achievements. A student who started out "disgusted" with the JA requirement concluded that being an instructor had, in the end, raised her self-esteem and self-confidence (Student T). This young woman's characterization of her development is echoed by another student:

> In the beginning, I was too nervous. I stumbled over my words so much; my sentences wouldn't connect for some reason. I thought it was going to be a flop but I finally began to flow. My words became a part of one another. (Student E)

Because LeMoyne-Owen is surrounded by an African-American community, participating elementary school populations are overwhelmingly Black. Yet there still exists ample opportunity for experiencing diversity. Since the elementary students come from a variety of socioeconomic backgrounds, LeMoyne-Owen students can develop considerable sensitivity to class as well as racial stereotypes. One student wrote about working with a "biracial child," another about her experiences at an integrated magnate school. Addressing issues of class and socioeconomic awareness, she noted that "the program helped me to better understand some of the things and people in society that we as a group of people as a whole, not just Blacks take for granted" (Student R). Furthermore, unlike many more traditional assignments that exclusively stress objectivity in conducting analytical, social scientific observations, the JA assignment allows students to examine their own participation in accepting or challenging concepts and practices they perceive as positive or negative. While they learn to analyze the problems of society in general as well as the particular problems associated with African and African-American cultures and other racial/ethnic groups, they also learn to solve problems—thinking creatively, critically, logically—using both quantitative and qualitative methods.

One final aspect of the students' reflections deserves mention: their awareness of the value of community service. Whatever negative experiences may have occurred, the students most often conclude on the positive note that they were able to do something for the children with whom they worked. The following three responses are exemplary of the many comments on this accomplishment.

> "I felt I had contributed to changing the lives of some of these youngsters forever."

> "Knowing that I have helped a kid, or two, makes me feel like I have made a difference."

"I got to do what I love best in a way that would let me represent myself and my college."

Some students, especially males, have used the term "role-model" to express how they saw themselves at various stages of the program: "I found out that for some of these kids, I was the only real male role model they have ever had" (Student K). Two young men who partnered for one assignment considered the positive effect of having the "children get a chance to see two young black males that are positive role models" (Student F). Indeed, comments sometimes suggest a new awareness of just how important such role modeling can be:

> I thought that the Junior Achievement program was good for the children, especially the thought of black college students showing the younger students that they can do whatever they want to do if they plan to work hard to get it. (Student A)

Students also recognize that community service is reciprocal. While they are giving their time, "their" students are giving them an opportunity to enlarge their self-development. Some students have observed that the elementary school students helped them in their first presentations by "smiling when they entered." One student addressed reciprocity in these words: "I got a chance to know the kids and they got a chance to know me" (Student O). Another noted hopefully, "I am happy that JA gave me an opportunity to meet some of our future leaders" (Student K).

Examples like these demonstrate how readily students respond to new ideas, information, and responsibilities. They also point convincingly to the ways in which service-learning supports several course objectives and desired competencies, including critical thinking, an understanding of diverse cultures, an understanding of the Afrocentric perspective, communicating effectively, clarifying personal values, accepting social responsibility, and achieving self-management.

Conclusion: Expansion of Student Horizons

The Junior Achievement program has indeed expanded the horizons of Lemoyne-Owen students, leading them to new visions of service and teaching them to act beyond the confines of the project. Assessment has demonstrated the achievement of the service goals that drive the institution. The evaluation includes a review of student reflections on their experience, the cooperating teachers' analysis of the students' performance, and a follow-up of subsequent student activities in the service arena. The students' own commentaries reveal that they have realized their ability to be active contributors to the community and are committed to service. Their words and actions suggest that the goals of preparing students to be civic leaders and of instilling an ethic of service are furthered through this project. Most significantly, the program develops self-confidence and motivation to "accept social responsibility and provide service to humankind."

The institutional goal of providing support to the community, particularly in the K-12 educational sector, is also enhanced. Assessment of this aspect of the program occurs through an analysis of the comments of the participating teachers and of the Junior Achievement program. The simple fact that we are able to provide at least 150 volunteers per year to Junior Achievement testifies to the solidity of the service.

Some students have continued to visit their JA classes after the conclusion of their assigned times; some have sought a broadening of the project, and others have continued their commitment to serve in other ways. The impact of the program on the development of first-year students is clear, and the powerful combination of service and reflection has helped them to articulate and appreciate that impact in ways that suggest a lasting impression. Thanks to the program, the college has been able to develop several attitudes and competencies it recognizes as important in its mission statement, its strategic planning, and its curricular design.

As anticipated, the placement of the requirement in the first year has spurred students to seek out further service opportunities as they continue their college careers. One student reported that as a result of her first-year JA experience, she developed a passion for helping others. Even during her first college year, she sought other ways of serving. She helped the college by volunteering in the admissions office and in the community by working with the nearby Boys and Girls Club during Christmas break. Directly following her involvement in the Junior Achievement project, she, as a sophomore, became involved in a Memphis City Schools mentoring program at an elementary school one block from the campus. Through this mentoring program, she met weekly with a child, reading to him and discussing with him the challenges he confronted at home and at school. Later, she volunteered daily to assist a disabled youngster in a home environment. Now a junior, she is an AmeriCorps volunteer and works for the Regional Intervention Program, helping youngsters with behavioral problems and their parents. Clearly, she has come to see service as a lifetime commitment, using as her motto, do unto others as you would like others to do unto you. We conclude with a particularly compelling statement, a statement demonstrating a rich understanding of children, leadership, and service.

> My students were second graders, the kind who are just old enough to talk back to you if you let them . . . So, I would pick the baddest or noisiest child to be my class helper. So, I got to know Freddie, Eddie, Demetricus, April, Jasmine, and Charrice very well. These kids were my 'Wild Bunch'; they were at times, uncontrollable, loud and downright disrespectful to their teacher, but not to me. I would put on that deep resonance in my voice like James Earl Jones and it would reach into the bottom of the shoes to say to them "straighten your butt out or I'll do it for you." I knew I would have to keep on them, but it did work . . . I really saw a great improvement in their listening skills, and we generally had a good time. I had one young lady, April, who was a foster child whom I kind of took to. She was not the most well-behaved child and her reading was below the class level. But, she was a nice kid, and I brought her lunch and bought her some supplies because she had run out of paper. If I can, I will check back on her because she made me appreciate how much I love my children and want them to be happy. (Student K)

This student's response is an inspiration to all of us to continue to refine the role of service learning in our general education program.

Service-Learning in a Learning Community: The Fullerton First Year Program

Kathy O'Byrne
Sylvia Alatorre Alva

The First-Year Experience

In recent years, growing numbers of colleges and universities across the nation have begun efforts to focus attention on their new students. Although the particular details of first-year programs vary from institution to institution, these initiatives share several commonalties. First, all of them are deliberately designed to help first-year students adjust more successfully to campus life—as Gardner (1986) puts it, "to provide a rite of passage in which students are supported, welcomed, celebrated, and ultimately (hopefully) assimilated" (p. 266). Second, many first-year experiences incorporate the element of linking entering students with a role model or mentor on campus. Third, first-year experiences typically provide entering students with resources, information, and opportunities not only to develop academic skills but also to increase personal involvement.

In spite of the growing history of such programs and the enthusiasm they often generate, only recently have researchers begun to assess their effectiveness. A growing body of literature now suggests that first-year experiences have a wide range of positive outcomes for participating students: increased recruitment, retention, and graduation rates; improved grades and academic skills; increased extracurricular involvement; expanded use of student services; increased health and wellness behaviors; greater clarification of academic and career goals; increased satisfaction; an enhanced sense of internal locus of control; stronger feelings of connection to the university; and even the possibility of increased alumni giving (Barefoot, 1993; Gardner, 1986; Geraghty, 1990).

Structured Learning Communities

Even more recently, educators have begun to discuss the positive outcomes associated with first-year programs within an even larger context—the formation and structure of learning communities. Gabelnick, MacGregor, Matthews, and Smith (1990) define learning communities as "curricular structures that link different disciplines around a common theme or question. They give greater co-herence to the curriculum and provide students and faculty with a vital sense of shared inquiry" (p. 6). Indeed, research shows that the more students engage in discussion with peers and faculty members about what they are learning, the higher their levels of critical thinking and intellectual development (McMillan, 1987) and the higher their satisfaction with the overall college experience (Pascarella, Duby, Terenzini, & Iverson, 1983; Pascarella & Terenzini, 1991; Tinto, 2000; Terenzini & Pas-carella, 1977).

In addition to bringing greater coherence to the curriculum and the learning experiences of students, learning communities also can function to link the cur-ricular and co-curricular experiences of students (Astin, 1996; MacGregor, 1991; and Schroeder & Hurst, 1996). Indeed, there is ample research that shows that when service-learning activities are also integrated into learning communities, stu-dents connect the texts of the classroom to the rich array of learning opportunities provided in and through service to the larger community (Cross, 1998; Gray, 2000).

A Learning Community for First-Year Students: The Fullerton First Year Program

In 1998, a structured learning community of first-year students, faculty mem-bers, librarians, and student affairs professionals was created at California State University, Fullerton. This learning community was called the Fullerton First Year Program, and its goal was to enhance learning by creating more integrated aca-demic experiences for first-year students. Too often undergraduates experience the college curriculum as fragmented. Separate courses and different academic disciplines typically stress specific content areas and particular approaches, rather than searching for commonalities or making connections between areas. More-over, among too many first-year students, the general education program is made up of courses one has to get out of the way before one can start taking the courses that "really matter" (i.e., the courses in one's major).

The Fullerton First Year Program is structured as a yearlong undertaking that includes enrollment in a first-year seminar, a computer and electronic library skills course, a set of linked general education courses, and a 30-hour service-learning project that integrates students' classroom learning with productive contributions to communities outside the classroom. All students involved in the Fullerton First Year Program are required, through classroom assignments, to participate in some form of service-learning, typically through an activity that engages them in un-paid, community-based public service related to the content of a course in which they are enrolled during the spring semester. For example, students in a political science course might act as interns for a local city council, coordinate a voter regis-tration drive, or help teach citizenship classes. Students in the required speech communication course might become proficient on a particular topic (health is-sues, civic involvement) and then give presentations on that topic in community contexts (e.g., schools, youth groups, the campus community).

The Office of Freshman Programs supports the students and instructors in the service-learning course by maintaining a database of community sites, sponsoring a community fair to help the first-year students connect with representatives from those sites and tracking the degree of student involvement and the outcomes asso-ciated with the projects.

Service-Learning Outcomes

In 2000, the third class of new students in the Fullerton First Year Program was asked to complete a questionnaire before and after their community service experience to assess the learning outcomes tied to their service-learning projects. The faculty member who taught the service-learning course (Political Science 100, American Government) that spring semester administered the questionnaire, which was adapted from the survey and interview questions used by Eyler and Giles (1999) in their seminal book *Where's the Learning in Service-Learning?* The questionnaire took about 40 minutes to complete and asked the students to rate several statements related to service and civic responsibility, using a five-point Likert scale in which 1 = Strong Disagree, 2 = Disagree, 3 = Uncertain, 4 = Agree, and 5 = Strongly Agree.

A Sense of Duty and Social Responsibility to Serve Others

As summarized in Table 1, the students in the program expressed attitudes reflecting a greater sense of duty to serve others as well as a greater sense of civic responsibility; they also identified personal benefits with their service-learning experience.

Table 1.
Student Attitudes Toward Duty and Social Responsibility

Survey Item	Pre-service	Post-service
Adults should give some time to the good of their community.	2.13	3.56
It is important to me personally to volunteer my time to help people in need.	3.73	3.33
It is important to me personally to become a community leader.	2.62	3.21
It is important to me personally to have a career that involves helping people.	3.24	3.20
I feel that social problems are not my concern.	3.59	2.25

There is quite a bit of evidence linking community service to an increased sense of duty and social responsibility (Johnson & Bozeman, 1998; Nnakwe, 1999; Parker-Gwin & Mabry, 1998; Smith, 1994). Consistent with these findings, the students in the Fullerton program became more aware of their responsibilities to others and the role they could play in shaping their communities. Upon completion of their service projects, they were more likely to endorse the belief that adults should take an active role in providing service to the community. The biggest attitudinal change between pre- and post-service was in their belief that "adults should give some time to the good of the community." On the other hand, the post-service survey indicated a decrease in attitudes regarding the importance of "volunteering my time to help people in need." This decreased interest in "volunteering" may reflect the first-year students' preference for an organized, structured program such as service-learning in FFY. As individuals, they are anxious about new situations, but as a group they are more confident risk-takers, willing to encounter those who may be "in need."

Civic Responsibility

As Ehrlich (2000) argues, "a democratic society is one in which informed citizens interact with each other, learn from each other, grow with each other and together make their communities more than the sum of their parts" (p. ix). Similarly, in her article "Embracing Civic Responsibility" (2000), Ramaley notes that good citizens are open-minded, informed and emphatic. "They also have some understanding of the idea of the public good and a sustained desire to work toward achieving the common good and a common ground" (p. 1). To determine the extent to which students in the Fullerton First Year Program embraced and accepted this belief in civic responsibility, responses to seven questionnaire items were compared before and after the students' community service. The students in the program demonstrated only minor changes in their attitudes toward civic responsibility, with the largest change occurring in their belief that "people who receive social services largely have only themselves to blame for needing services" (Table 2). At first sight, this finding was somewhat surprising. While we strongly believe the particular course supporting the service-learning component (American Government) is a natural fit for infusing the theme of civic responsibility into the curriculum, in hindsight, we also have come to recognize that we should have been much more intentional in aligning civic responsibility with the learning goals and structure of the course.

Table 2.
Student Attitudes Toward Civic Responsibility

Survey Item	Pre-service	Post-service
I think our social problems can be solved by the community.	3.14	3.07
Government should get out of the business of solving social problems.	2.73	2.43
People who receive social services largely have only themselves to blame for needing services.	3.59	2.55
We should reach out to specific people in need rather than create programs to address social problems.	3.39	2.86
I feel positive about my community's ability to solve its social problems.	3.76	3.00
Communities should provide social services to their members in need.	3.52	3.58
People who work in social service agencies can do little to really help people in need.	2.52	2.57

Findings in this portion of the survey may also reflect students' newfound perspective that the problems they encountered through their service-learning experiences are complex and require longterm solutions involving multiple systems. The students often reported feeling overwhelmed by the depth and breadth of the problems that confronted those they meet. They had come to understand that non-profit organizations often work in a particular area of need for many years and frequently report slow progress in correcting problems or remediating skills. The decline in responses to items 1 and 5 may reflect this awareness.

Systemic Views of Poverty and Social Disadvantage

We also found that issues of diversity and social opportunity were a common theme in classroom discussions and reflection papers. Indeed, we found that the students talked a lot about the diversity of the individuals and families they met at their service-learning sites and how that diversity altered their perceptions of the community in which they were working. From the findings below, it is evident that students held stereotypical assumptions about those who live in low-income neighborhoods prior to their community service, but together with their coursework and personal reflection, their service experiences helped many of them to begin to challenge those assumptions (Table 3).

Table 3.
Student Attitudes Toward Poverty and Disadvantage

Survey Item	Pre-service	Post-service
If I could change one thing about society, it would be to achieve greater social justice.	2.92	3.48
Social problems are more difficult to solve than I used to think.	3.09	3.02
The problems that cause people to need social services are frequently the result of circumstances beyond their control.	3.35	3.11
For the most part, each individual controls whether he or she is poor or wealthy.	3.55	2.96
I feel uncomfortable working with people who are different from me in such things as race, wealth, and life experiences.	2.73	2.60

Individual Skills Development

Recent findings on the relationship between service participation and leadership development are some of the most fascinating in the service-learning field. For example, Astin (2000) notes that service participants report that community service helps them develop leadership skills. While service may indeed be helpful in fostering the development of leadership skills, our findings also suggest that we must be more intentional in creating a link between service activities and both leadership development and career preparation. In our study, service participants did not see an enhanced connection between their service work and their career goals and aspirations (Table 4). This is not entirely surprising. With early adulthood marked by an extensive exploration of career and identity issues, many first-year students do not yet have a clear sense of their own career identities and, thus, do not readily see connections between service and career preparation (Arnett, 2000). However, given the need entering students have to explore occupational paths and prepare for adult work roles, service-learning may well provide a useful vehicle for achieving this—but only if we are intentional in structuring experiences that make that connection explicit.

Table 4.
Student Attitudes Toward Skill Development

Survey Item	Pre-service	Post-service
Community service will help me develop leadership skills.	2.05	3.34
Skills and experiences that I gain from community service will be valuable in my career.	3.73	3.21

Personal Benefits of Community Service

Previous studies (Giles & Eyler, 1994; McElhaney, 1998; Rauner, 1995; Rosenbaum, 1997; Rhodes, 1997) have reported a number of student-identified benefits of service-learning. After completing their community work, students in the Fullerton program were asked to rate how important each of these benefits were to them, using a three-point Likert scale in which 1 = Not Important, 2 = Somewhat Important, and 3 = Very Important. In descending order, the five most important benefits associated with service-learning projects reported by participants include feeling a sense of reward from helping others, learning how to work with others effectively, understanding oneself better/personal growth, appreciating different cultures, and identifying community programs that address social problems. Table 5 includes student ratings of all program benefits.

Many of the students described their service-learning experiences as the first time they ever felt they could make a difference in the world.

"My service learning experience taught me a lot about responsibility and commitment to others."

"The service-learning helped me build my confidence, be responsible to others, and it helped my resume."

"One person can make a difference."

"When I had to leave from service-learning sites for the semester, some of the kids were crying. It was the first time that it really hit me—Wow, I had really made a difference in these kids' lives."

Table 5.
Student Descriptions of Personal Benefit

Student Response	Post-Service
How rewarding it is to help others.	3.00
How to work with others effectively.	3.00
Understand myself better/personal growth.	2.98
To appreciate different cultures.	2.84
To identify many community programs that address social problems.	2.83
How complex the problems faced by people I worked with are.	2.64
To see social problems in a new way.	2.59
Spiritual growth.	2.52
Deeper understanding of things I already had learned about in my classes.	2.30
That the people I served are like me.	2.15

Conclusions and Recommendations

The Fullerton First Year Program has shaped its identity around the theme "Education, Social Responsibility, and Community." As a learning community for first-year students, it contributes significantly to creating an educational environment where all students have the opportunity to succeed and where a welcoming, supportive climate engenders satisfaction in students as well as in faculty, staff, and others who interact with them. As a learning community, the program also strives to extend the concepts of service, leadership, and civic responsibility beyond the university to surrounding communities.

In accord with the developmental level of first-year students, we focus on selected service-learning issues. We don't push discussions of the contributions of specific disciplines and careers so much as the importance of using knowledge and skills in a responsible, ethical way. We talk about the necessity of students' becoming community leaders after graduation: Where will each student make her mark in society? We talk about the need to have a life and a career that are not only financially rewarding but personally satisfying. We pose rhetorical questions such as "Why do you think the world needs more (fill in the blank) majors?" or "Why do we live in a world, or a society, where there is a need for a nonprofit organization such as this?" These questions invite students to articulate why they came to college in the first place, and to take an active role in their education.

However, as important as the Fullerton First Year Program can be in enabling Cal State Fullerton to realize its academic mission, structured learning communities may not meet the needs of all students in a highly diverse student population. For example, they require that students enroll more or less full-time, that they commit a significant block of time for the entire year to curricular and co-curricular activities, including a 30-hour service project.

Our last four years of experience in implementing a learning community that includes service-learning have taught us that such a program should remain an elective activity and that colleges and universities should carefully consider policies that require all first-year students to provide service. We have, therefore, revised our program recruitment materials and publications to make sure potential applicants know there is a community service project required of all students who elect to be part of this learning community.

Our experience also has taught us a great deal about how to refine the service-learning component of the program. For example, we have become much more sensitive to the needs of students by expanding the number and type of service-learning sites available. We have expanded our placement list to include sites in a greater number of communities to meet the needs of commuter students and those who work full- or part-time. We have also included on-campus service sites to accommodate the needs of residential students who lack transportation. Finally, we have been able to create a more sophisticated set of service options that are closely tied to the goals and content of the sponsoring course.

With regard to faculty and staff training, the service experience has become more structured over the years, and more time is spent preparing students as well as faculty and staff for the service experience. The creation of a structured learning community requires arrangements that value collaboration and shared ownership of the learning process. Creating such arrangements among the various constituencies that make up a learning community, including community partners, is a time-consuming process. The work of creating a common vision for the learning community and a common view of desired learning outcomes takes genuine effort.

All of the faculty and student affairs professionals in the learning community participate in a week-long instructional planning retreat during the preceding summer and attend monthly planning sessions throughout the academic year to identify the curricular linkages between and among the various courses in the learning community. As a result, more class time is now devoted to service-related topics such as diversity and multiculturalism in the first-year seminar, University Studies 100, to support the reflection and learning that is taking place in the disciplinary course that carries the service-learning component.

We also have restructured our relationships with community partners and have tried to strengthen their roles as "co-educators" through the types of sessions we regularly schedule, the feedback and communication systems we employ, and the syllabi we make available to them. We have scheduled more time for planning retreats, which we use to discuss issues of syllabus development and ways to link classroom activities and readings across courses more effectively, thereby more fully using the service-learning experience as a "text" for interdisciplinary work.

Finally, we now co-sponsor, along with several other units on campus, an all-day community service fair. This event makes it easier for faculty and staff to work more closely with agency representatives in designing service-learning requirements. The fair also allows students to meet with and interview potential supervisors from various community sites, helping students identify a good fit between their needs and those of participating agencies. Responses to the community service fair by faculty, students, and community representatives have been very positive.

Perhaps most important, we continue to listen to student feedback on their service experiences and to find new and better ways to assess the concomitant learning. Our plans are to move beyond the data available through scaled surveys and integrate student assessments with graded assignments. This will give us a better understanding of student perspectives that can continue to inform our work. Although we are encouraged by what we have seen in terms of student attitudes and the benefits of their service involvement, we believe we can do much more to address the needs of all our constituencies.

References

Arnett, J. L. (2000). Emerging adulthood: A theory of development from late teens through the twenties. *American Psychologist, 55*(5), 469-480.

Astin, A. W. (1996). The role of service in higher education. *About Campus*, 14-19.

Astin, A. W. (2000). Comparing the effects of community service and service-learning. *Michigan Journal of Community Service Learning*, 25-34.

Barefoot, B. O. (Ed.). (1993). *Exploring the evidence: Reporting outcomes of freshman seminars and the freshman year experience*, (Monograph No. 11). Columbia, SC: University of South Carolina, National Resource Center for The Freshman Year Experience and Students in Transition.

Cross, K. P. (1998). Why Learning Communities. Why Now. *About Campus*, 4-11.

Ehrlich, T. (Ed.). (2000). *Civic responsibility and higher education*. Phoenix, AZ: Oryx Press.

Eyler, J., & Giles, D. E. (1999). *Where's the learning in service-learning?* San Francisco: Jossey-Bass.

Gabelnick, F., MacGregor, J., Matthews, R., & Smith, B. (1990). *Learning communities: Creating connections among students, faculty, and disciplines*. San Francisco: Jossey-Bass.

Gardner, J. N. (1986). The freshman year experience. *The Journal of the American Association of Collegiate Registrars and Admissions Officers, 61*(4), 261-274.

Geraghty, M. (1990). More students quitting college before sophomore year, data show. *The Chronicle of Higher Education*, A35-A36.

Giles, D. E., & Eyler, J. S. (1994). The impact of college community service laboratory on students' personal, social, and cognitive outcomes. *Journal of Adolescence, 17*, 327-339.

Gray, M. J. (2000, May/June). Making the commitment to community service: What it takes. *About Campus*, 19-24.

Johnson, S. D., & Bozeman, M. (1998). Service learning and the development of social responsibility. Paper presented at the Annual Convention of the Central States Communication Association, Chicago IL.

MacGregor, J. (1991). What difference do learning communities make? *Washington Center News, 6*(1), 4-9.

McElhaney, K. A. (1998). *Student outcomes of community service learning: A comparative analysis of curriculum-based and non curriculum-based alternative spring break programs*. Unpublished Dissertation, University of Michigan.

McMillan, J. (1987). Enhancing college students' critical thinking: A review of studies. *Research in Higher Education, 26*, 3-29.

Nnakwe, N. E. (1999). Implementation and impact of college community service and its effect on the social responsibility of undergraduate students. *Journal of Family and Consumer Sciences, 91*(2), 57-61.

Parker-Gwin, R. P., & Mabry, J. B. (1998). Service-Learning as pedagogy and civic education: Comparing outcome for three models. *Teaching Sociology, 26*, 276-291.

Rauner, J. S. (1995). *The impact of community service-learning on student development, as perceived by student leaders*. Unpublished Dissertation, University of San Diego.

Rhoads, R. A. (1997). *Explorations of the caring self: Rethinking student development and liberal learning.* Paper Presented at American Education Research Association, Chicago, IL.

Rosenbaum, V. M. (1997). *Understanding college age volunteers' behavior.* Unpublished Dissertation, LeHigh University.

Smith, M. (1994). Community service-learning: Striking the chord of citizenship. *Michigan Journal of Community Service Learning, 1,* 37-43.

Pascarella, E., Duby, P., Terenzini, P., & Iverson, B. (1983). Student-faculty relationships and freshmen year intellectual and personal growth in a nonresidential setting. *Journal of College Student Personnel, 24,* 395-402.

Pascarella, E., & Terenzini, P. (1991). *How college affects students.* San Francisco: Jossey-Bass.

Ramaley, J. (2000). *Embracing civic responsibility.* Campus Compact Reader: Service-learning and civic education. Providence, RI: Campus Compact.

Schroeder, C., & Hurst, J. (1996). Designing learning environments that integrate curricular and cocurricular experiences. *Journal of College Student Development, 37*(2).

Terenzini, P., & Pascarella, E. (1977). Voluntary freshman attrition and patterns of social and academic integration in the university: A test of a conceptual model. *Research in Higher Education, 6,* 25-43.

Tinto, V. (2000). What have we learned about the impact of learning communities on students? *Assessment Update: Progress, Trends, and Practices in Higher Education, 12*(2), 1-2, 12.

Writing as Students, Writing as Citizens: Service-Learning in First-Year Composition Courses

Thomas Deans
Nora Bacon

Composition, as a discipline, has been an "early adopter" of service-learning. Two programs developed in the late 1980s—the Community Educator Project at UCLA and the Community Service Writing project at Stanford—were widely discussed, replicated, and adapted throughout the 1990s so that, by the end of the decade, service-learning was well established in the discipline. Community-based writing assignments have been integrated into courses in community colleges, four-year colleges, and universities, at every level from basic writing workshops to graduate courses in rhetoric. When the American Association for Higher Education (AAHE) launched its influential series on service-learning in the disciplines in 1997, the first book to see print was *Writing the Community;* its appendix includes profiles of 25 service-learning programs in composition, just a sampling of the dozens of programs then in existence. Today, the Campus Compact web site for service-learning educators (www.compact.org) posts more syllabi from English than from any other discipline, and the National Council of Teachers of English hosts its own service-learning web site (www.ncte.org/service) with resources for teaching and research as well as descriptions of over 60 curriculum-based community writing initiatives.

Scholarship on service-learning in composition courses has kept pace with course development. At the annual Conference on College Composition and Communication, the principal national conference for composition studies, the number of papers on service-learning mushroomed from six in 1992 to more than 70 in 2002; a thorough bibliography of service-learning in composition now includes textbooks, monographs, special issues of *The Writing Instructor* (Winter, 1997) and *Language and Learning in the Disciplines* (October, 2000), as well as a long list of articles. *Reflections on Community-Based Writing and Learning*, a quarterly publication, is devoted entirely to service-learning and writing studies.

This rapid growth is not difficult to explain: Composition, as a site for service-learning projects, is a natural. Because composition courses are seen as initiatory, service-learning projects that acquaint new students with a campus and its surrounding community can find a natural curricular home there—especially since the reflection component of service-learning so readily takes shape as a series of writing assignments. The most widely required undergraduate course, first-year writing, is a good place to begin the "continuum of service" that service-learning educators like to envision. Furthermore, since writing is a *practice* rather than a *body of knowledge*, the composition curriculum is unusually plastic. What's essential is that students get writing practice and feedback; beyond that, composition instructors have more freedom to experiment than teachers in other disciplines who feel compelled to cover a defined slice of disciplinary knowledge.

Even more important is the congruence of service-learning with the issues currently motivating research and theory in the field. In the early 1980s, composition studies took a "social turn": We began to conceive of writing not only as a set of skills, not only as a process whereby words appear on paper, but as a situated social activity. In a shift that might be viewed both as a step forward into postmodernism and a step back toward our historical roots in rhetoric, composition theorists and researchers focused on exploring writing as a practice embedded in its social context. A consequence of this shift was a heightened awareness of the limitations of the classroom as a setting for learning to write. In composition, theory and teaching practice are never far apart. With renewed interest in the social dimension of literacy, composition teachers quickly embraced community-based writing assignments as an opportunity for students to deploy critical thinking and writing skills in analyses of social issues, to develop the rhetorical awareness and flexibility necessary for writing in unfamiliar settings, and to find their places and their voices both within and beyond the academy.

This chapter provides a brief overview of service-learning in composition. The meat of the chapter appears in three sections describing models for integrating community-based service-learning into composition courses: Students can be asked to write *about* the community, *for* the community, or *with* the community (these terms will become clear as we proceed). But while all three models have proven successful in first-year writing courses—and we include sketches of exemplary programs of each type—the models differ in significant ways. The point to which we will return most emphatically is this: The sort of service activity students undertake must be carefully designed to advance the particular goals and theoretical commitments of a particular course in its particular institutional home. To begin, then, we identify the range of goals that composition courses address. Next we describe the models, and finally we consider the challenges composition programs face in developing service-learning initiatives as well as the administrative support they require.

The Purposes of First-Year Writing

Because of the pervasive fear of writing in our culture and the low status accorded "service" courses in the university, students often enter writing classes reluctantly. Yet what most find in composition is a small, interactive class that stands in sharp contrast to large lecture courses. Composition courses offer students not only space for creative and critical thinking but also an invitation to the modes of research and writing valued in the academy.

Shared Characteristics of Composition Courses

As students enter their first-year writing experience, they are likely to encounter courses grounded in widely accepted understandings of writing and writing instruction:

- *Writing as a vehicle of reflection and action.* Whether emphasizing personal inquiry or cultural critique, composition instructors generally see writing not only as a way to communicate thinking but also as a means to explore experience, reflect on ideas, and act in the world.

- *Writing as audience-directed.* Moving away from exclusively rule-based writing instruction, most composition teachers emphasize how writing is shaped by audience expectations, whether that audience is a specific constituency, the community of writers in the class, the academic community, the local community, or the general public.

- *Active and collaborative learning strategies.* Problem-solving activities, small group work, peer workshops on drafts, in-class writing, and other forms of active and collaborative learning have become the norm.

- *A process approach.* Most instructors emphasize writing as a complex, recursive process that involves planning, drafting, revising, and editing. With respect to instruction, this means that rather than simply assigning a topic and then grading the final product, instructors encourage students to write drafts, share them with peers, and engage in substantial revision, thereby replicating the practices of most professional writers.

- *Social and developmental goals.* Many instructors articulate course goals that extend beyond simply equipping students with skills to succeed in the academy and workplace. These often include encouraging students to explore their own histories and values, to develop critical consciousness of social injustice, and to use writing as a means of democratic action.

Many of these understandings predispose composition to service-learning. Still, while compositionists largely agree on some core issues, their conceptions of the curricular aims of first-year writing can vary enormously. Both content and approach differ from college to college, often from course to course, and understanding the variety of approaches to first-year writing instruction is critical to program development in community-based writing.

Differing Conceptions of Composition

Constituencies of teachers and scholars in composition conceptualize the role of first-year writing differently, with each approach based on its own distinct curricular and ideological assumptions.

- *Composition as initiation to academic discourse.* In this view, composition is a "service" course in the sense that it serves other disciplines by preparing students to adopt the writing strategies and conventions valued by academic disciplines (particularly analysis, synthesis, and research, as well as the stylistic features of academic prose).

♦ *Composition as response to a variety of literary genres.* This mode of instruction overlaps with the one above but focuses on one particular kind of academic discourse: literary criticism. Most writing instructors are trained in literature and their inclination is to choose short works, such as short stories or classic essays (like those of George Orwell or E. B. White), as prompts for student papers.

♦ *Composition as a place for personal inquiry and creative nonfiction.* This approach, often called expressivism, values writing as a means for students to render their own experiences and ideas, usually in narrative. The emphasis is on the personal essay, on writing as self-inquiry, and on ways to relate one's own thinking and values to those of the larger culture.

♦ *Composition as cultural studies or critical pedagogy.* This approach emphasizes the analysis of culture and ideology, often from a neo-Marxist perspective, and aims for "critical consciousness." Students are taught methods of abstract thinking and cultural critique, which are then expressed in the critical essay genre.

♦ *Composition as introduction to argument.* This mode of instruction recalls the roots of writing instruction in rhetoric, sometimes emphasizing classical rhetorical theories like those of Aristotle and other times contemporary theories of argument like those of Stephen Toulmin.

This list is not exhaustive. For example, some consider composition a place simply to learn generalizable skills like standard grammar and usage or conventional academic genres like the essay and research paper. And to complicate things further, many, perhaps most, instructors blend elements of more than one approach in the same course—for example, by including both personal and analytical essays.

In sum, those committed to service-learning in composition should devote attention not only to the disciplinary culture of English studies but also to the curricular and ideological dispositions of particular departments and writing programs. Selecting a kind of community-based writing that is aligned with departmental or program values makes for a strategic first step in successful program development.

Varieties of Service-Learning in Composition

As service-learning has taken hold in composition, three main paradigms have emerged (Deans, 2000):

♦ *Writing **about** the community.* These courses use writing as a way to describe, analyze, or contextualize experiences emerging from, or social issues related to, student outreach activities.

♦ *Writing **for** the community.* In these courses, students become writers for local nonprofit agencies, where they compose purpose-driven documents like newsletter articles, brochures, and internal research to meet the needs of the organization.

♦ *Writing **with** the community.* These courses emphasize the direct collaboration of students and local citizens, who together use writing to raise awareness of pressing social issues or to solve local problems.

Sorting by categories often betrays the complexities of reality, and some courses combine different paradigms (Cooper & Julier, 1997). Still, describing categories provides an overview of current practices and raises important questions about the range of, and purposes for, community-based learning in first-year writing.

Writing About Community

Since the emergence of composition courses in the 19th-century American university, students have been asked to write essays about personal, aesthetic, and social matters. Service-learning composition courses that adopt a writing-about-the-community approach continue in this established tradition but recalibrate the curriculum to focus explicitly on social concerns, to encourage critical reflection, and to value community outreach experiences as a motivation and source of material for emerging writers. Students in writing-about-the-community courses are concurrently involved in community service work (often tutoring youth), and students turn to that experience for writing and research topics.

Depending on the instructor's goals, students sometimes write about ways to address the pragmatic problems they encounter in their outreach work, in which case they might, for example, research second language acquisition patterns to help them better assist ESL students (Brack & Hall, 1997), or they might reflect more generally on the ethical complexities of service, unpacking the concept of *noblesse oblige* or exploring the dynamics of reciprocity. In some cases, students engage in community-based research, perhaps conducting interviews and drawing on their own experiences to write a profile of a local nonprofit organization. Alternatively, students might be asked to focus on the broader systemic and institutional forces that constitute the context for their service, in which case they might investigate how tracking systems in American schools shape student achievement or how race and class function to help or hinder success (Herzberg, 1994). Some courses ask students to write personal narratives that give expression to human encounters or learning moments that emerge from service experiences. Still other writing-about-the-community courses are centered on a particular theme such as homelessness, domestic violence, or HIV/AIDS, introducing literary, historical, and analytical readings that resonate with the students' community work (Comstock, 1994; McGuinness, 1995; Novak & Goodman, 1997; Vermillion, 2000). In all these cases, students write about, and reflect on, social issues, and their community work serves as a touchstone for writing. Essentially, outreach experiences are accorded the status traditionally reserved for course readings.

This approach is distinguished by the fact that student writing itself does not constitute a service to the community; rather, the community service is a resource for student writing. The student provides a valuable service such as tutoring youth, answering the phone at a crisis center, or working at a homeless shelter, and such experiences are translated into texts when students reflect on and write about them. The writing reveals the quality of student reflection. Such writing usually remains within the classroom, read by teachers and peers, and the discourses look largely like those performed for most composition courses, even if the topics, the degree of student investment, and the experiential richness of the material are markedly different.

This makes the writing-about-the-community approach appealing to those instructors and programs that value the traditional modes of academic thinking and writing (such as the critical essay) but still wish to make their curricula more so-cially engaged. It also means that instructors need not learn a whole collection of new teaching strategies; they can rely on the methods they have been using for years, adjusting the content to match the course theme or the students' outreach experiences. And in doing so, many have noted a substantial boost in their own and their students' motivation (Adler-Kassner, Crooks, & Watters, 1997; Deans, 2000). Furthermore, reflection is integral to service-learning, and writing has al-ways been an indispensable mode of reflection. Writing-about courses leverage the power of service-learning to animate and enrich reflective writing.

Writing for the Community

Writing-for-the-community programs have arisen in response to one of the most stubborn problems in composition pedagogy. While good writing is defined above all by its effectiveness in communicating with an audience, composition courses have traditionally asked students to write paper after paper for the same reader, the English teacher. Even in courses in which students respond to drafts of each other's papers, peer-review groups often function as stand-ins, helping the stu-dent writer prepare to address the teacher, the reader who finally counts (Heilker, 1997). When student writers do not get practice shaping their texts to meet the needs of varying audiences, they are unlikely to develop the rhetorical flexibility expected of mature writers.

Writing-for-the-community courses circumvent the problem of "dummy run" assignments by giving students real occasions to communicate with real and vary-ing readers. A class of 15 students, working in groups, might serve as volunteer writers at half a dozen community agencies. Imagine that one group creates a news-letter for a women's shelter, the second works on a press release for an after-school tutoring program, the third designs a brochure for the campus radio station, the fourth researches and writes a fact sheet detailing the obstacles faced by immi-grants negotiating the social-service maze, the fifth writes an exposé of discrimi-nation against gays for the campus newspaper, and the sixth writes fundraising letters for the local free clinic. As they make connections with these organizations, analyze the tasks, and work through drafts with their classmates, these students get first-hand exposure to different discourse communities, different writing goals, different readers, different genres. The idea that one writes to accomplish specific purposes with a specific audience is no longer an abstraction but a fact of life that both motivates students and demands their thought and action.

Service-learning courses of this type are organized around a predictable set of steps. A crucial first step is the match: students need to write for organizations whose missions they can endorse (in many cases, student writers temporarily speak for the organization) and whose writing needs are a good fit with their abilities and their course's goals. Experienced instructors learn to avoid tasks that are too simple (e.g., editing existing documents), too extensive for one semester (e.g., con-ducting a community survey and composing a needs assessment), or too depen-dent on insider knowledge (e.g., most grantwriting). While some instructors en-courage students to make their own connections with community organizations—and this can be an important part of the learning experience in pre-professional writing courses (Henson & Sutliff, 1998; Huckin, 1997)—most instructors in first-year writing courses like to develop relationships with community partners be-fore the semester begins, working collaboratively to select assignments that meet the needs of both the agency and the student writers. It's the rare community agency that doesn't have a list of writing needs from which to choose.

Students typically work in pairs or small teams. They visit the community agency's office for an orientation and conversation about the writing task; write a contract or a memorandum of understanding spelling out mutual expectations (about the text's purpose, the readership, recommended sources of information, length, format); familiarize themselves with any model documents available; gather information about the topic; submit drafts to the teacher, classmates, and the community-based editor or supervisor; then edit, proofread, and submit a final draft, sometimes for the agency's internal use, sometimes for publication.

Most students find writing for the community a stretch, intellectually and emotionally. They proceed through the stages first observed by Anson and Forsberg (1990): high hopes, disorientation and a crisis of confidence, and finally resolution as the document begins to take shape. Instructors have developed strategies for supporting students' work and maximizing their learning. Students might, for example, be encouraged to perform direct service (similar to volunteer activities) at the organization before they accept a writing task so that they have some time to develop a comfortable niche in the social network of the agency. Many instructors devote class time to problem-solving discussions and design supplementary writing tasks such as a profile of the organization, an analysis of a sample text in the assigned genre, or regular reflections in a community service journal.

Like other service-learning projects, writing-for-the-community courses require extra effort from teachers. To their other responsibilities, such courses add a layer of planning, relationship-building, and monitoring of multiple projects (Sayer, 2000). In addition, teachers often find it challenging to assess students' work; there is no one-size-fits-all grading rubric for community-based documents. Nevertheless, many teachers integrate community-based writing assignments into their courses year after year. These assignments provide an invaluable lesson in rhetorical awareness. Because they perform genuine communicative work and because they introduce a wide range of genres into the course, community-based tasks give meaning to key rhetorical concepts—audience, purpose, discourse community—that might otherwise remain mere abstractions. Equally important, they give students a chance to experience the power of writing not just to earn a grade but to move other people to new understandings, beliefs, or actions.

Writing With the Community

As with the writing-for approach, writing-with-the-community initiatives structure opportunities for students to craft texts that readily enter the public sphere. However, such projects emphasize the direct collaboration of student writers and local community members, unmediated by nonprofit agencies. Writing-with programs and courses take many forms, but they generally hinge on processes—compositional, artistic, or problem-solving—that are shared by students and local community members. Moreover, they usually adopt a grassroots sensibility and often entail cross-cultural partnerships. Because such initiatives are more often housed in upper-division than in first-year courses, this approach may be of less immediate usefulness to first-year instructors. What follows are sketches of three ways in which college writing courses have scaffolded opportunities for students to write with local citizens: community problem-solving, oral history recovery, and creative expression projects.

Writing-with-the-community initiatives that center on problem solving foreground the role that writing can play in addressing local concerns. A problem-solving approach invites community members and college students to identify a pressing local issue and then set a strategic agenda for using writing and rhetoric to address the matter. One compelling example of this kind of problem solving can be found in the Community Literacy Center (CLC), a partnership of the English Department at Carnegie Mellon University and a literacy center on the north side of Pittsburgh. In an eight-week cycle, local citizens (often urban teens) and college students work together to explore and address a community problem through discussion and collaborative writing. For example, they might address the high number of suspensions at district schools or the difficulty of finding good jobs. Students and teens "rival" alternatives, exploring different possibilities, and then the CLC brings all the stakeholders together—teens, parents, teachers, local officials, university researchers—for a "community conversation," a kind of town meeting at which teens and mentors share their written and oral performances to help spark productive dialogue and problem solving among all stakeholders (Deans, 2000; Peck, Flower, & Higgins, 1995).

Another problem-solving approach involves proposal writing, where college students and citizens identify a problem and craft a letter or proposal addressed to those who have some power over the matter. Proposals for solutions to community problems can target local or state constituencies (Stotsky, 1996), or they can address campus concerns (Schulz & Gere, 1998). Rather than place students in a client relationship to nonprofit agency personnel, projects such as these situate students in direct collaboration with local stakeholders and showcase the pragmatic role that writing can play in addressing problems and injustices.

A different writing-with approach can be found in service-learning projects where the goal is to record oral histories, particularly of those community members who have been overlooked by our culture. For example, Susie Lan Cassel of California State University, San Marcos, has developed a course called "American Immigrant Testimonials." In this course students not only study the tradition of immigrant narratives in American culture (which in turn reveals much about our ethnic and racial history) but also collaborate with first- or second-generation immigrants to recover, record, and render life narratives (which are then, if participants wish, published). Similar projects have focused on inter-generational exchanges through which students record the oral histories of elderly Americans (Haussamen, 1997; Talarico, 1995).

Writing as creative expression also holds enormous potential for service-learning. Some college students already engage in creative writing as part of their college coursework, and many community members employ modes of creative expression outside of school structures. A community-based creative writing project can bring the classroom into contact with the community by emphasizing how art, self-expression, and art-play can instigate social change. For example, in Michael John Martin's (2000) courses at San Francisco State University, students have visited with children at an after-school center to write, perform, and publish poetry. Students serve as mentors and "ambassadors from the conceptually distant university" (p. 14). They share their literate experiences with disadvantaged children while simultaneously arriving at critical insights about literacy, education, and socio-linguistics. Children and youth are a natural fit for these kinds of initiatives, but similar service-learning projects have been successful with other constituencies, such as adults (Adams, 1998), senior citizens (Talarico, 1995), and prisoners (Hastings, 2001; Mastrangelo, 2001; O'Connor, 2000; Pifer, 2001; Trounstine, 2001).

While writing-about-the-community projects depend largely on academic expectations and school literacies (which are relatively uniform across institutions), and writing-for projects depend largely on agency structures and workplace literacies (which are relatively uniform across communities and regions), writing-with initiatives are less beholden to existing institutional structures and therefore more attentive to community needs as articulated by local citizens. Such organic and democratic partnerships are not easy to establish, but when done well they engender creative opportunities for students and community members to pursue social change together as writers.

In choosing among service-learning approaches, instructors must consider not only community needs and their own theoretical preferences but also the backgrounds and abilities of their students. As Zlotkowski observes in this volume, "service-learning in any introductory course must be designed in ways that stretch but do not break the first-year student's sense of competence" (p. 34). While all three approaches to community writing have been used effectively in first-year composition courses, all three are challenging. First-year students cannot be thrown into the community and expected to swim; service-learning courses for these students require close attention to partnership building, course design, task selection, and orientation to community-based work.

Institutional Challenges

Students frequently observe that writing about, for, or with the community is more meaningful than classroom-based writing because the stakes are higher: students recognize that when their writing represents or influences the lives of real people, they incur a responsibility to choose words with care. When we design courses that involve the off-campus community, we incur a similar responsibility. Faculty and administrators planning service-learning projects in composition need to take a clear-eyed view of the challenges that can be anticipated. We need to take advantage of—if necessary, to create—enabling mechanisms to support teachers' efforts.

The principal challenge is that service-learning involves a considerable investment of faculty time. The same features of service-learning that account for its power to transform teaching and learning—the inclusion of multiple perspectives in the construction of knowledge, the opportunity to form relationships supporting teaching and research, the interdisciplinarity of real-world issues—make service-learning labor intensive. Faculty members need time to meet with community partners; to plan, monitor, and support students' service experiences; to systematically assess the effect of the work.

As we have indicated above, the nature of the faculty-community partnership varies with the model of service-learning being employed. Generally speaking, though, the faculty member and the community partner will collaborate more closely in writing-for projects than in writing-about projects, and more closely still if students are writing with the community. Other variables affecting the partnership include the presence or absence of a community-service center on campus, the number of sites where students serve, the size and maturity of the program (the better established the program, the smoother the road for individual instructors). But it is always true that the faculty member and community partner need to spend enough time together to achieve a shared understanding of what students will do, what purposes drive the work from the community's point of view, and how the work advances academic goals.

Faculty must also set aside time for transforming their courses to maximize the learning value of the service experience. Many writing instructors have found that the first time they incorporate service into a course they conceive of it as an add-on, perhaps even presenting the service to students as an option for extra credit. But as they see the effects of the service, as they come to appreciate its potential to challenge and extend their students' (and their own) conceptions of literacy, they relocate the service experience to a central position in the course, rewriting other assignments to support the service work. The students' sense that service-learning involves "extra work" is alleviated by the movement toward integration.

But the work for service-learning educators continues as they find themselves addressing new questions. Some of these are practical or logistical questions: How can students be prepared for their service experiences? How should their work be graded? How can the community preference for longterm relationships be reconciled with the constraints of a 15-week semester? How can interdisciplinary projects be organized to meet the real, complex needs of the community? These are most likely to be solved if faculty have access to the experience of their colleagues through service-learning workshops, "teaching circles," and the professional literature. Other questions are theoretical: Does conventional writing instruction prepare students for literacy practices outside the university? Should it? How can those literacy practices be characterized? How do they develop, and how do they change over time? Whose interests do they serve? Does the community-based experience politicize the classroom? Should it? Questions like these may prompt more extended investigations through empirical research and ethical inquiry.

The point is that service-learning, when done well, cannot be done hastily. The service-learning literature has, in recent years, begun to explore the question of what faculty members need to know, possess, and do if they are to make a continuing commitment to service-learning (Deans, 1997; Morton, 1996; Zlotkowski, 1996). Service-learning educators in every discipline need institutional support through such mechanisms as release time or summer funding for curriculum development, funding for conference travel and other professional development activities, and recognition of service-learning course development and scholarship in tenure and promotion procedures.

In composition, the issue of institutional support is complicated by a history of exploitative hiring practices. Many composition courses are taught by adjunct faculty and graduate students who teach the most demanding courses on campus for the lowest pay (MLA Committee on Professional Employment, 1997). When they integrate service into their courses, they do so out of a personal commitment to their students and their communities. In this case, the institution has an especially compelling obligation to provide adequate support. At some institutions, adjunct faculty are actually barred from participation in faculty development opportunities. The movement toward integrating service-learning into composition and other first-year courses provides an opportune moment to correct this inequity.

A final and related consideration is the authority structure of composition programs. In many cases, composition programs are headed by one tenured or tenure-track faculty member who is responsible for curriculum design, either individually or as part of a program committee. The Writing Program Administrator may articulate course goals, select textbooks, and determine the assignment sequence, or instructors may make these decisions autonomously. Certainly if a service-learning component is to be integrated program-wide, it will be important to implement a collective decision-making process that ensures the full understanding and commitment of every instructor who teaches the course.

Service-Learning in Composition: A Utopian View

Structuring opportunities for students to write in community contexts not only resonates with the experiential learning and ethical leadership imagined by progressive American educators like John Dewey but also recalls the roots of writing instruction in rhetoric, the art of public discourse. The ancient Greek rhetorical tradition was directed not at teaching students to succeed in school but rather at equipping citizens for active participation in the public sphere. Relatedly, the works of Roman rhetoricians such as Cicero and Quintilian underscored the imperative that rhetorical skills ought to serve the civic good— that the speaker/writer should employ language not only eloquently but also ethically. From the middle ages through the 19th century, rhetoric stood at the center of European and American university curricula, as one of the core liberal arts. By acting on the affinities between college writing and service-learning, we can reanimate the rhetorical tradition and more fully embrace an action-oriented and civic-minded perspective on writing instruction in particular and higher education more generally.

As educators we should, ideally, create opportunities for student writers to act as "rhetors," in the richest sense of that term. Rather than position the college student as a pupil who requires remediation, service-learning encourages the student to adopt the role of authentic rhetor, emerging professional, and active citizen (Bacon, 1992). Community-based writing invites students to be agents in their learning rather than spectators to instruction, educated citizens rather than consumers of education. Students in these courses practice writing both as a means of intellectual inquiry and as a mode of democratic action.

While first-year writing has often been considered a "service" course, in the sense that we do academic housekeeping for other disciplines, the "service" in service-learning speaks to broader aspirations of engaged citizenship. This reframing of composition holds enormous potential for both the discipline and the entire first-year experience. As students enter college, they open themselves to new worlds of knowledge, and, we hope, to transformative learning experiences. Composition is positioned in the curriculum as a gateway course, taken by nearly all incoming students, and as such it can set the tone for academic experiences that follow. If students just entering higher education encounter an academically rigorous, rhetorically oriented, and ethically provocative first-year writing course, they will likely be predisposed to other service-learning and outreach opportunities. If colleges and universities hope to pursue their civic and academic missions in concert—participating in Ernest Boyer's

(1994) vision of "concerned institutions" that are "committed to improving, in a very intentional way, the human condition" (p. 48)—then gateway courses like composition are an apt place to begin.

References

Adams, H. (1998). A grassroots think tank: Linking writing and community building. In W. Ayers, J. A. Hunt, & T. Quinn (Eds.), *Teaching for social justice.* New York: Teachers College Press.

Adler-Kassner, L., Crooks, R., & Watters, A. (Eds.). (1997). *Writing the community: Concepts and models for service-learning in composition.* Washington, DC: American Association for Higher Education/NCTE.

Anson, C. M., & Forsberg, L. L. (1990). Moving beyond the academic community: Transitional stages in professional writing. *Written Communication, 7,* 200-231.

Bacon, N. (1997). Community service writing: Problems, challenges, questions. In R. Crooks, L. Adler-Kassner, & A. Watters (Eds.), *Writing the community: Concepts and models of service-learning in composition* (pp. 39-56). Washington, DC: American Association for Higher Education/NCTE.

Boyer, E. (1994, March 9). Creating the new American college. *Chronicle of Higher Education,* p. 48.

Brack, G., & Hall, L. (1997). Combining the classroom and the community: Service-learning in composition at Arizona State University. In R. Crooks, L. Adler-Kassner, & A. Watters (Eds.), *Writing the community: Concepts and models of service-learning in composition* (pp. 143-152). Washington, DC: American Association for Higher Education/NCTE.

Cassell, S. L. (2000). Hunger for memory: Oral history recovery and community service learning. *Reflections on Community-Based Writing Instruction, 1*(2), 12-17.

Comstock, C. (1994). Literature and service learning: Not strange bedfellows. In R. Kraft & M. Swadner (Eds.), *Building community: Service learning in the academic disciplines.* Denver: Colorado Campus Compact.

Cooper, D. D., & Julier, L. (1997). Democratic conversations: Civic literacy and service-learning in the American grains. In R. Crooks, L. Adler-Kassner, & A. Watters (Eds.), *Writing the community: Concepts and models of service-learning in composition* (pp. 79-94). Washington, DC: American Association for Higher Education/NCTE.

Deans, T. (1997). Writing across the curriculum and community service learning: Correspondences, cautions, and futures. In R. Crooks, L. Adler-Kassner, & A. Watters (Eds.), *Writing the community: Concepts and models of service-learning in composition* (pp. 29-38). Washington, DC: American Association for Higher Education/NCTE.

Deans, T. (2000). *Writing partnerships: Service-learning in composition.* Urbana, IL: NCTE.

Flower, L. (1997). Partners in inquiry: A logic for community outreach. In R. Crooks, L. Adler-Kassner, & A. Watters (Eds.), *Writing the community: Concepts and models of service-learning in composition* (pp. 95-118). Washington, DC: American Association for Higher Education/NCTE.

Hastings, P. (2001, March). Beneath the ivy, behind the bars: Linking writers in college and prison composition classes. Conference on College Composition and Communication. Denver, CO.

Haussamen, B. (1997, October). Service-learning and first-year composition. *Teaching English in the Two Year College,* 192-98.

Heilker, P. (1997). Rhetoric made real: Civic discourse and writing beyond the curriculum. In R. Crooks, L. Adler-Kassner, & A. Watters (Eds.) *Writing the community: Concepts and models of service-learning in composition* (pp. 71-78). Washington, DC: American Association for Higher Education/NCTE.

Henson, L., & Sutliff, K. (1998). A service-learning approach to business and technical writing instruction. *Journal of Technical Writing and Communication,* 28(2), 189-205.

Herzberg, B. (1994, October). Community service and critical teaching. *College Composition and Communication,* 307-19.

Huckin, T. N. (1997). Technical writing and community service. *Journal of Business and Technical Communication,* 11(1), 49-59.

MLA Committee on Professional Employment. (1997, December). Final report: MLA committee on professional employment. Submitted by Sandra M. Gilbert to the Delegate Assembly Meeting of the Modern Language Association.

Martin, M. J. (2000). Merging voices: University students writing with children in a public housing project. *Reflections on Community-Based Writing Instruction,* 1(1), 14-16.

Mastrangelo, L. (2001, March). Freshman composition and women in prison: Service-based writing and community action. Conference on College Composition and Communication. Denver, CO.

McGuiness, I. (1995). Educating for participation and democracy: Service-learning in the writing classroom. *The Scholarship of Teaching,* 1(2), 3-12.

Morton, K. (1996). Issues related to integrating service-learning into the curriculum. In B. Jacoby & Associates (Eds.), *Service-learning in higher education: concepts and practices* (pp. 276-296). San Francisco: Jossey-Bass.

Novak, C. C., & Goodman, L. J. (1997, Winter). Safe/r contact zones: The call of service-learning. *The Writing Instructor,* 16(2), 65-77.

O'Connor, P. (2000). *Speaking of crime: Narratives of prisoners.* Lincoln, NE: Bison Books.

Peck, W. C., Flower, L., & Higgins, L. (1995). Community literacy. *College Composition and Communication,* 46(2), 199-222.

Pifer, M. (2000). Out with it: Audience as a space of resistance in service-learning. Conference on College Composition and Communication. Denver, CO.

Sayer, C. (2000). Juggling teacher responsibilities in service-learning courses. *Reflections on Community-Based Writing Instruction,* 1(1), 20-23.

Schultz, A., & Ruggles Gere, A. (1998). Service-learning in English studies. *College English,* 60(2), 129-149.

Stotsky, S. (1996). Participatory writing: Literacy for civic purposes. In A. H. Duin & C. J. Hansen (Eds.), *Nonacademic writing: Social theory and technology* (pp. 227-256). Mahwah, NJ: Erlbaum.

Talarico, R. (1995). *Spreading the word: Poetry and the survival of community in America.* Durham, NC: Duke.

Trounstine, J. (2001). *Shakespeare behind bars: The power of drama in a women's prison.* New York: St. Martin's Press.

Vermillion, M. (2000). Community-based writing instruction and the first year experience. *Reflections on Community-Based Writing Instruction,* 1(1), 5-9.

Zlotkowski, E. (1996). Linking service-learning and the academy: A new voice at the table? *Change,* 28(1), 20-27.

Section 4

Summing Things Up

What, So What, Now What:
Reflections, Findings, Conclusions, and Recommendations on Service-Learning and the First-Year Experience

John N. Gardner

In this monograph we have been treated to an examination of service-learning as an educational reform concept and pedagogy in its relationship to myriad topics and contexts. Some of these include:

♦ Developing and mobilizing an entire campus culture for service to the surrounding community

♦ Incorporating service-learning into other established reform practices and structures such as learning communities, first-year seminars, and an integrated first-year experience program

♦ Using service-learning to resuscitate the moribund and unengaging introductory course in multiple disciplines

♦ Basing college level service-learning on the rapidly growing service-learning experience in secondary schools

♦ Adapting service-learning to an institutional mission statement

♦ Adapting service-learning to adult and "nontraditional" students as well as to those of traditional college-aged status

♦ Linking service-learning to the most ubiquitous course in the first-year curriculum, the first-year writing course

Thus, it would seem easy and obvious to conclude that service-learning is now a "mature" educational reform concept and practice with advocates spanning a wide variety of pre-secondary, secondary, and post-secondary educational institutions and the ranks of the teaching faculty, student affairs and guidance personnel, and administrators in those institutions. In this chapter, I identify what I see as some of the principal insights emerging from this monograph and draw some key recommendations from those insights.

Community Service Versus Service-Learning

Perhaps the first, and central, observation that follows from this monograph is the distinction between community service and service-learning—a distinction best captured by Jayne Richmond in her description of the University of Rhode Island's move from community service to service-learning in the context of the first-year seminar. Approximately 74% of post-secondary institutions have such a course; nearly three fourths of those institutions grant baccalaureate degrees, and one quarter are two-year colleges (National Resource Center for The First-Year Experience and Students in Transition, 2000). Moreover, it is highly likely that the service incorporated into the first-year seminar is community service rather than true service-learning. This certainly is a confession I would have to make about the service component I introduced into the University 101 first-year seminar at the University of South Carolina.

True service-learning in the context of the first-year seminar, or any course for that matter, is more than the simple performance of service. It represents a much more involved process of assessing student learning; developing requisite, multiple, and varied community partnerships and contexts for service; and providing faculty development. It also involves establishing very specific goals and priorities for the service component of the course. Depending on the size of the institution, it may well involve the establishment of a special unit or center to support service-learning faculty development. It is absolutely critical, as Zlotkowski argues in his chapter, that the "community-based work . . . be carefully linked to course objectives . . . [which] may include—or even stress—such non-content-specific skills as team building, interpersonal communication, sensitivity to diversity, practical problem solving, and personal empowerment" (p. 34).

Thus, an explicit and clear rationale for service-learning work should be provided in all first-year course syllabi and should be further discussed in class. The chapter by Hatcher, Bringle, and Muthiah presents a model for doing this. Moreover, any campus that includes in its institutional mission statement an objective of preparing students for lives of service to community and nation or for having the campus itself engaged in providing service to its local community, region, or nation should examine whether service-learning is not an under-used, under-appreciated, less-than-fully-developed resource to achieve such ends. As a natural part of the re-accreditation process, all of our campuses must periodically re-examine their mission statements and the activities that relate to them. Thus, all of us have a natural opportunity to examine the potential vitality of this connection. There are few institutions that are sufficiently intentional about their educational and operational effectiveness. The first-year seminar represents an ideal forum for introducing students to this institutional mission of service.

Service-Learning in High School

Extent of Prior Experience

As I indicated in my preface, the extent of service-learning in the precollege sector surprised me. A study of first-year programs at 600 post-secondary institutions revealed that 41.6% of baccalaureate institutions have service-learning components in the curriculum; 28.7% of two-year colleges feature them (Barefoot, 2000). These findings echo what Duckenfield and Furco report in their chapters on the extent of high school service-learning experiences: From one third to nearly a half of all public high schools incorporate service-learning in the curriculum. Furthermore, one cannot fail to be impressed by Duckenfield's account of the number and type of federal, state, and private agencies and foundations involved in promoting high school service-learning.

Turning to the data on precollege students themselves, Vogelgesang, Ikeda, Gilmartin, and Keup cite data from the Cooperative Institutional Research Program's Freshman Survey, indicating that the percentage of entering first-year students reporting participation in volunteer work has increased each year since 1990, reaching 81% in 2000. However, as these researchers from UCLA also report, this level of prior participation in service does not necessarily translate into continuing service work in college. To the contrary, they found "a formidable gap between service participation in high school and service expectations for the college years" (p. 16). Thus, one of our challenges as college educators would seem to be to build more effectively on students' prior service experiences. What kind of commentary on higher education is it if college students are *less* likely to serve their communities than are high school students?!

One way to ensure continued service participation for college students may be to create more and better articulation between the K-12 and higher education service-learning fields. This needs to be done at the campus level, particularly by those institutions that recruit primarily from the local area. An excellent national resource for implementing more effective school/college collaboration and partnerships is the Education Trust, located in Washington, D.C. Furthermore, a powerful and logical way to connect these two service-learning sectors would be to design settings where both college and high school students can work together and share in the reflective process. I would even conjecture that there exists here an excellent opportunity for college students to serve as mentors for high school students, thereby enhancing the college students' motivation and skills.

Because of the extensive service experience many first-year students have recently had in high school, it is imperative that college-level service-learning faculty and program designers give consideration to the extent of this prior experience. As Furco argues in his chapter, care must be taken to design service-learning experiences that appropriately challenge these students. To do this, we at the college level need to learn from these students more about their high school service-learning experiences—what did and did not work for them. Prior to reading this monograph, I had incorrectly assumed that service-learning would be one of the newer elements of the college experience. Not so. We must challenge our assumptions that somehow college will be automatically and inherently more engaging for students than high school. Indeed, for many of our students, high school experiences may have served to raise their expectations as to the level of service-learning they will find in college. We must not frustrate or lower these expectations.

Moreover, we need to recognize that expectations play an important role in how and why students make decisions about where to attend college. Students may use positive service-learning experiences as criteria for selecting a college; thus, appropriate linkages should exist between campus officials responsible for service-learning and those who design enrollment management and student recruitment strategies and literature. I would, in fact, argue there is greater potential for the influence of such criteria on choosing a college in the post-September 11th environment.

Outcomes

One cannot fail to be struck by the impressive outcomes reported for high school students who have participated in service-learning and by their striking similarity to outcomes for college students at a later point. Such congruence testifies to the power of the service-learning process per se regardless of the specific education level at which it is found. Discussing high school students, Furco cites research reporting benefits such as increased motivation, more regular class attendance, higher levels of social and personal adjustment, higher self-esteem, reduced alienation, and less involvement in high-risk behaviors. Complementing this, Duckenfield reports on high school service-learning participants who are more likely to have chosen career goals, have more prior experience in reflection, have more insight into how real and powerful learning takes place for them, and have a greater awareness of how a variety of educational approaches affects them as learners. Clearly, there also needs to be much more research on the effect of high school service-learning on students' adjustment to college. This, it seems to me, is particularly true with regard to academic performance.

Strengthening the Delivery of Service-Learning Through Alliances with Other Curricular Innovations

A recent national study of first-year programs found that 36.8% of four-year institutions and 23.5% of two-year institutions had learning communities. Nearly 80% of the four-year and 62.1% of the two-year campuses offered a first-year seminar of some type (Barefoot, 2000). These data have important implications for achieving more partnerships and greater synergy between these curricular reform efforts and service-learning initiatives. In fact, the portraits of best practice at the colleges and universities both profiled and referenced in this volume provide strong evidence for integrating service-learning into such initiatives as first-year seminars, learning communities, first-year writing programs, and academic affairs/student affairs partnerships. What is most striking by its absence is the representation of service-learning as a stand alone intervention. The moral of this story should be clear. The impact of curricular innovations is heightened by partnerships, alliances, and broad structural and institutional arrangements that reach beyond any one particular course or intervention. Since such innovations, when taken individually, have frequently enhanced student success and persistence, it only follows that those innovations' potential effect should be heightened when combined and integrated. This was certainly my own experience with regard to retention when we integrated the first-year seminar and living-learning programs at the University of South Carolina.

O'Byrne and Alva suggest still another rationale for such an integrated approach to first-year enhancement by pointing out how compatible the goals of first-year service-learning courses can be with programs to enhance the first-year experience. Both involve (a) a deliberate design to help first-year students in their academic adjustment to higher education; (b) an effort to link them with role models and mentors; and (c) a strategy to provide them with the resources, information, and opportunities they need to develop leadership skills and to increase personal involvement.

Given the demonstrably positive results of student participation in such discrete interventions as first-year seminars, on-campus residential living/learning environments, learning communities, out-of-class interaction with fellow students and faculty as well as service-learning, it would make sense to attempt to connect these initiatives. Indeed, a campus-wide structural design to coordinate and integrate such programs would seem to be in order. Based both on what I have read in this volume and on what I have observed and practiced in my own career, I would strongly recommend the joint integration of first-year seminars, learning communities (see Levine, 1999), Supplemental Instruction (see Martin & Arendale, 1993), first-year writing courses, and service-learning, with the last as the curricular and pedagogical glue that binds, reinforces, and spans all the other discrete components.

The Critical Role of Service-Learning Support Units

From the program examples included in this volume it seems clear that, for service-learning to fulfill its potential, faculty development support must be provided. While faculty may have sufficient interest and motivation to introduce service-learning components into their courses, the likelihood is they had neither service-learning experiences as undergraduates nor service-learning preparation in graduate school. In all probability, faculty will also need assistance from professional staff familiar with both the campus and the community in identifying appropriate service opportunities, dealing with transportation and liability issues, and handling a host of other practical matters related to off-campus work. This, in turn, can result in an organizational paradox. While student affairs personnel can provide much excellent and needed support, the fact that service-learning is rooted in the formal academic curriculum suggests that support centers and personnel also need reporting lines to the academic side of the house. Somehow the divide between student and academic affairs must be bridged, no matter where faculty support is technically housed.

Because quality service-learning demands faculty development and support, and because faculty support is a need shared with other first-year reform initiatives such as first-year seminars and learning communities, there exists a compelling rationale for taking a coordinated, integrated, shared-resources approach to providing such support. The bottom line here is this: If we encourage faculty to engage in practices for which they have not been prepared, they are much more likely to be successful if we recognize and institutionalize their need for further development and support. The key integrating theme here is, of course, support for improving first-year courses. All disciplines have a stake in this. Hence the beauty of service-learning as a cross-disciplinary phenomenon.

Service-Learning Activities Designed for Specific Populations of Students

The key to success for service-learning programs is careful consideration of the particular needs and experiences of the students for whom those programs are designed. One size does not fit all. As Hatcher, Bringle, and Muthiah point out, more advanced students are typically more skilled in managing their academic responsibilities and more focused on and confident about their career directions. Hence, service-learning for first-year students must not assume skill and maturity levels that typically develop later in college. For example, first-year students are more likely to benefit from a group focus or project than an individual one. Such a group focus is more likely to ensure that students have sufficient contact with faculty, professional staff, and other students. Reinforced by colleagues from IUPUI and Portland State, O'Connell makes clear that service-learning also has an important role to play in the education of so-called "nontraditional" students. But instructors and program directors must be open to the range of experiences (and the variety of outside commitments) that adult learners and part-time students bring to the classroom. For this reason, O'Connell argues that one must take care that the service work be perceived as an integral and not an "add-on" component.

Service-Learning as a Manageable Variable

As a variable affecting first-year student success, service-learning is far more under our control than are many other variables such as family income and educational status, specific courses taken in high school, and community location of secondary school. Thus, by intentional leveraging of this intervention, we may be able to offset the disadvantages some of our students bring with them to college. This follows from the fact that service-learning provides an educational context where many of the interventions shown by research to have a positive influence on student success and retention can take place.

The Traditional First-Year Survey Course

Considerable evidence exists, much of it reviewed by Zlotkowski, that the standard first-year survey course—regardless of the discipline—is "broken" and needs "fixing." A thorough and thoughtful examination of the customary pedagogy used in such courses, when juxtaposed with the characteristics of today's first-year students, suggests that many of these courses are not well designed for what they seek to achieve, especially since "many of the students filling the seats in introductory courses have already developed habits and attitudes that represent a barrier to sustained attention and meaningful intellectual engagement" (Zlotkowski, p. 28). While service-learning is not a panacea for such problems, a careful examination of what service-learning can do in the context of first-year courses highlights why so many of our students find their courses dreadfully boring and unengaging. Zlotkowski's chapter also suggests a further rationale for service-learning in the introductory course: namely, the hope that students may learn to integrate into their other non-service-learning courses some of the skills and habits they develop in these courses (e.g., use of reflective writing and thinking, group project work, research and learning in community-based settings, application of course principles in social action contexts, and more out-of-class faculty-student interaction).

Indeed, the analysis of the traditional first-year survey course offered here is so disturbing that it calls for a more extended investigation of this topic as well as an extended blueprint for reform. I would especially welcome an examination of specific differences that are a function of disciplinary cultures and increased buy-in from faculty across the disciplines. I have increasingly concluded from my own work on enhancing student retention in the first college year that many of the efforts to achieve this have occurred, for very understandable reasons, in contexts outside the curriculum, in particular, without reference to the most commonly taken first-year courses. But it is within the curricular context that the heart of the unfinished first-year retention agenda remains. Service-learning, learning communities, and Supplemental Instruction are the three reform interventions that bear most directly on improving student success in the most common first-year courses.

The Potentially Powerful Connection and Synergy Between First-Year Service-Learning and First-Year Writing Courses

In their chapter, Deans and Bacon make a compelling case for the first-year composition course as a natural curricular home for service-learning. On many campuses, the course most likely to be taken by all first-year students is first-year composition. One of the themes I have been promoting as critical to enhancing the first-year experience is "community," developing and requiring a set of "common" experiences for students with the hope that these experiences will help bond them to each other and the institution. First-year composition courses are one site where such community can develop, and a focus on group service-learning experiences can certainly enhance that community. At the risk of pointing out the obvious, let me note that the list of characteristics shared by both service-learning and first-year composition courses is a long one. This congruence can be extended by noting the connections between the role of writing in both the reflection component of service-learning and the significant role writing plays in many first-year seminar/learning community programs.

I conclude from all of this that there are strong reasons for first-year programs to consider more active partnerships not only with advocates of service-learning on their campuses but also with first-year composition faculty and programs. In this regard, I would especially welcome the collaboration of those professional faculty groups concerned with writing instruction.

Service Scholarships

Hatcher, Bringle, and Muthiah's description of first-year service scholarships at IUPUI is another gem of an idea that had not occurred to me prior to reading this monograph. The basic concept here is to recognize community service as an example of meritorious conduct and skills demonstrated at the precollegiate level and as a basis for awarding scholarships. If we pay for what we value—such as prior achievement and excellence in academic endeavors, athletics, and the arts—why not also "pay" for service? Such scholarships can also serve as a recruitment incentive, allowing us to attract precisely those students who share such an important value with us.

First-Year Service-Learning and Career Decision Making

As the research discussed by Vogelgesang et al. demonstrates, first-year service-learning experiences can have an effect on students' subsequent selection of a service career and their decision to continue performing service after graduation. Given the country's need for skilled workers in both the public and the nonprofit sectors, these findings constitute a powerful argument in favor of service-learning as a mandatory experience for all first-year students. Thus, the working relationship among service-learning programs, practitioners, and units responsible for providing career planning needs to be strengthened and made more intentional. Given the findings from UCLA's Higher Education Research Institute's 2000 study of the effects of service on the cognitive and affective development of students, especially the finding that such participation in service has a significant positive effect on students' choice of a service career and plans to participate in service after college, we cannot afford to leave use of this connection to serendipity. Furthermore, the first-year seminar represents a logical delivery vehicle for integrating career planning services and service-learning activities.

Service-Learning and the Overall First-Year Experience

Contributors to this monograph largely agree that service-learning positively affects first-year students in numerous ways. For example, our colleagues from CSU Fullerton, O'Byrne and Alva, report that their students expressed a greater sense of duty to serve others, a greater sense of civic responsibility, a newfound understanding that social problems are complex and in need of longterm solutions, and a belief that diversity altered their perceptions of the communities they served. At the same time, Frankle and Ajanaku, writing from the perspective of a historically Black campus, describe how their students have reported increased self-esteem and self-confidence. They also join many of the other chapter authors in reporting that their students, once introduced to service-learning in the first year, are spurred on to seek out additional service-learning courses and opportunities voluntarily as they continue their college careers. In the case of Portland State, Williams, Patton, Beyler, Balshem, and Halka describe students as gaining valuable skills in

- ◆ solving problems and communicating effectively
- ◆ dealing with diversity and, more fundamentally, that which is unfamiliar
- ◆ developing a sense of personal efficacy and greater self-understanding
- ◆ achieving and sustaining social activism
- ◆ understanding academic content insofar as the service activity is tied to specific course objectives

But perhaps the single most compelling statement on the potential power of service to affect student success is Vogelgesang et al.'s summary of what UCLA's Higher Education Research Institute has discovered about the relationship between service and the overall undergraduate experience:

> ... undergraduate service participation shows significant positive effects on all 11 outcome measures: academic performance (GPA, writing skills, critical thinking skills), values (commitment to activism and to promoting racial understanding), self efficacy, leadership (leadership activities, self-rated leadership ability, interpersonal skills), choice of a service career, and plans to participate in service after college ... (p. 16)

This theme is so dominant and so consistent that it requires both careful consideration and appropriate subsequent action.

The Need for More Research on and Assessment of the Impact of Service-Learning on the First-Year Experience

Vogelgesang et al. articulate this need succinctly when they note that there is in general a scarcity of studies that consider the relationship between service-learning and students' first year in college" (p. 19). I have already mentioned the need for more research on the relationship between high school service-learning experiences and first-year success. This recommendation can be expanded. In spite of the positive evidence, findings, conclusions, and testimonials provided by the chapters in this volume, the recommendations of these practitioners and researchers indicate that much more assessment is needed. Those who are just launching a service-learning program should build an assessment dimension into their work from the very beginning, starting with program design. An expanded research/ assessment agenda should include quantitative as well as qualitative studies, the voices of students and community members as well as of faculty.

Two new instruments are now available to assist in these efforts. First, the National Survey of Student Engagement, developed by George Kuh of Indiana University and in use at hundreds of institutions, can be used to look at populations of students who have or have not experienced service-learning in their first college year. The First-Year Initiative, just completing its first pilot year of administration in Fall 2001 to over 50,000 students at 62 institutions, all enrolled in first-year seminar courses, is an effort to benchmark first-year seminars among peer institutions. This instrument measures how student perceptions of the first college year experience relate to what students have learned and experienced as participants in first-year seminars. Because service-learning has been widely incorporated into first-year seminars, this instrument, as it is refined and gains expanded use, may provide additional evidence concerning the value of service-learning in such courses. Finally, it should be pointed out that UCLA's Higher Education Research Institute is expanding the number of students and institutions participating in the 2002 Your First College Year Survey to approximately 125 institutions.[1] This expansion should result in even more valuable data on the role of service-learning and will enable HERI researchers to build on the findings they report in their chapter in this monograph.

One additional assessment-related resource deserves mention. An immediate and practical way to increase the amount of assessment of service-learning would be for those developing programs in service-learning, first-year seminars, learning communities, and Supplemental Instruction, and those researchers working with them, to share precious institutional research resources by combining forces. Since these initiatives have so much in common—including not only many of the same students, faculty, and student affairs personnel but also the experience of being held to a higher standard of accountability—the logic of such a move seems self-evident and might even help eliminate unnecessary competition for scarce resources.

Conclusion

I conclude with one final recommendation: Readers should consider establishing a special group to reflect on the questions of "what," "so what," and "what next" prompted by this monograph. How can the lessons and the recommendations I have identified be used to strengthen both service-learning and the entire first-year experience on each campus? This monograph can serve as a catalyst to bring together some of the best, most creative, and most enthusiastic minds on your campus working in service-learning, first-year seminars, learning communities, Supplemental Instruction, first-year composition, living/learning communities, and academic/student affairs partnerships. Hopefully, the insights I have gleaned will point the way to insights of your own, insights you can put directly to work in enhancing your students' first-year experience.

Notes

1. Both the First-Year Initiative and Your First College Year surveys have been developed under subcontracts awarded by the Policy Center on the First Year of College, directed by this author and funded by The Atlantic Philanthropies and The Pew Charitable Trusts.

References

Barefoot, B. O. (2000). National survey of first-year curricular practices. [Survey results]. Available: http://www.brevard.edu/fyc/survey/Curricular/survey.htm

Levine, J. H. (Ed). (1999). *Learning communities: New structures, new partnerships for learning* (Monograph No. 26). Columbia, SC: University of South Carolina, National Resource Center for The First-Year Experience and Students in Transition.

Martin, D. C., & Arendale, D. R. (1993). *Supplemental instruction: Improving first-year success in high-risk courses* (Monograph No. 7). Columbia, SC: University of South Carolina, National Resource Center for The Freshman Year Experience.

National Resource Center for The First-Year Experience and Students in Transition. (2000). 2000 national survey of first-year seminar programs. [Survey results]. Available: http://www.sc.edu/fye/research/surveys/survey00.htm

Appendix: Additional Program Profiles

The Communication and Culture Freshmen Interest Group at Humboldt State University

Armeda Reitzel

Each August the instructors of the Communication and Culture Freshmen Interest Group (FIG) at Humboldt State University in northern California meet to finalize their syllabi for the next cohort of incoming first-year students. These meetings help reunite and revitalize three veteran instructors who have a strong commitment to teaching first-year students and serving the local community.

The Communication and Culture FIG involves an anthropology professor who teaches cultural anthropology, an English instructor who teaches English composition, and me, a communication professor who teaches fundamentals of speech communication. Students take these general education courses together as a package and earn from 9 to 11 units of credit. Three aspects of this FIG make it a unique offering: (a) It is a residential FIG (all students live in the residence hall and all FIG classes meet in the residence hall); (b) classes are block-scheduled in two- to-three hour time periods so that there is internal flexibility in planning class time (e.g., to allow for field trips and workshop days); and (c) the three classes are integrally woven together by a common service-learning project involving an exploration of the community through an oral history project.

The Communication and Culture FIG follows a set of simple, sequential steps that facilitate the development of knowledge and skills in our first-year students.

1. Students are given an orientation to the community and its co-cultures. We take the students on field trips to introduce them to the area. Our trips have included a walking tour of Old Town Eureka with a local history buff as a guide (during which the students learn about the logging and fishing industries), a visit to the local PBS station (which, for some reason, delights the students when they learn that our PBS station is the smallest one in the contiguous 48 states), and a half-day exploration of Patrick's Creek State Park (where our students discover the traditions and contributions of our local Native American tribes). We debrief after each trip to see what interested and impressed each student. Their questions give us insights into how to proceed with our discussions about culture and co-cultures.

2. As a long-time instructor of intercultural communication, I share my personal definition of culture with the students: "Culture refers to the products and processes that define the ways of thinking, believing, and behaving of a group of people." Co-cultures are those "mini-cultures" that are sometimes known as "sub-cultures" in other disciplines, but because of the possible negative connotations of "sub" (which might suggest "less than" or "inferior" to some people), I ask my students to use the term "co-culture" instead. We generate a list of possible co-cultures that they could explore for the oral history project. Co-cultures have included loggers, environmentalists, the Portuguese, the Hmong, the Hupa, skateboarders, surfers, the homeless, and returned Peace Corps Volunteers. During this

discussion we inevitably start talking about stereotyping and its influence on how we perceive people we do not personally know. Critical thinking, listening, and speaking skills are employed during these discussions.

3. Students then select their group members and form research teams of three or four people. Each team chooses a co-culture to explore. No more than one team can select a particular co-culture.

4. Students are given extensive preparation in researching and interviewing before they go out into the community. Basic anthropological concepts and research skills are covered early in the semester. The students visit the Humboldt Room in the university library where maps, photographs, articles, and books archive the rich history of the area. In their English class, they keep oral history journals in which they record their research progress. In the communication course, I have them practice their interviewing skills. I include a paired interview speech as a precursor to the actual co-culture interviews. The students find a newspaper article that they summarize. They then generate three to five interview questions about the topic. After the questions have been analyzed and given the "okay" by classmates, each pair conducts a minimum of 10 short interviews with people outside of class. The results of the interviews are summarized and reported back to the class in the form of a short three-minute speech. This first step in interviewing has really helped students in critically constructing, conducting, and condensing their oral history interviews into significant and meaningful presentations.

5. The majority of the semester is spent on the teams' research and reports on the oral history projects. Students spend time reflecting on what they are learning about the community and about themselves.

6. For the communication class, the pinnacle of the semester-long project is reached at the oral history conference. The oral history conference is a formal occasion during which each team presents its oral history report and reflections in a symposium format. Each team is allotted 30 to 40 minutes for its presentation. We make this a festive occasion. Community members, administrators, and the local press receive formal invitations. We provide a large brunch buffet for the half-day event. (This is especially impressive to the residence hall students who have been eating cafeteria food for four months or so.) We ask the students to come dressed up for the occasion (which actually impresses us instructors since the fact that we teach all of our classes in a residence hall classroom means we sometimes see the students in their bedroom slippers and bathrobes!). The students express a keen sense of accomplishment when they see their efforts recognized by their instructors and others in such a grand way.

7. Students turn their written reports and journals in to the anthropology and English instructors at the end of the semester. Their writings reflect their questions, insights, frustrations, and solutions as they worked on their oral history projects. The instructors look for the analysis, synthesis, and application of course content in the students' writing.

What Do the Students Gain From the Communication and Culture FIG?

They develop a knowledge and an appreciation of the local community. Many of the students begin volunteering their time and talents to community endeavors because they now feel a connection to the community. They cultivate speaking, listening, reading, writing, and research skills that will be beneficial to them throughout their academic and professional careers. They fulfill 9 to 11 units of general education during their first semester of college. They reap the benefits of working on a major project from a variety of disciplinary perspectives and discover that what they learn in one class can be applied in another class. As first-year students living in the residence halls and learning together as a cohort, they develop collegial relationships that often blossom into friendships. Some of the students have stayed on at Humboldt State as peer mentors and living group advisors in the residence halls, working with FIG students in subsequent semesters.

What Do the Instructors Gain From the Communication and Culture FIG?

I have developed a close, working relationship with two campus colleagues. Although we are in different departments and disciplines, we share our expertise and experiences with one another. This has contributed to our own professional development. From a pragmatic standpoint, we can schedule our classes in such a way that if one of us is gone to a conference, someone else can fill in so that no class time is lost. We meet several times before, during, and after the semester to report, reflect, revamp, and rejuvenate. We work together as a team, in much the same way that our students collaborate and cooperate in their oral history teams. The co-culture that we instructors "investigate" is the co-culture of our FIG cohort.

What Do the Co-Cultures in the Community Gain From the Communication and Culture FIG?

Our students give back to the community through their oral presentations, which are now being videotaped and edited to become part of a video archive about the local community. We plan to publish some of the students' writing on the web and in hard copy form. Local community members are invited to be part of this archiving process. The community also learns more about Humboldt State University students, and this helps build bridges between the "town" and "gown" co-cultures.

The FIG concept, especially when it unites different disciplines through a fully integrated, carefully sequenced community service-learning project, is a powerful instructional approach to teaching first-time first-year students. One of the greatest thrills for me as an instructor in the Communication and Culture FIG occurred a few years ago when one of my students went from an "Us" versus "Them" mentality when talking about the community at the beginning of the semester to saying "We here in Humboldt County" during his speech at the oral history conference. In just four short months, this student made the connections for which I had hoped. Such linkages are what make FIGS successful, not only for the students, but also for their instructors and their communities.

An Overview of IMPACT: A Residential Learning Community at the UMass, Amherst, Focused on Community Service-Learning

John Reiff

"The opportunity to be in close proximity with people who have the same love and desire for service is why I joined the program . . . I like having the opportunity to talk with other people about their experiences without having to leave my floor or even my room, for that matter!"

The statement above, made by a student in the 2000-2001 program year for IMPACT, captures some of the goals of the program. IMPACT is a residential learning community for first-year students at the University of Massachusetts, Amherst. Where other learning communities in the university focus on disciplines such as engineering or biology, IMPACT's focus is on community service-learning (CSL). Students admitted to the program must demonstrate a history of community service and a commitment to continue community service as university students. They find themselves living and working with other students who have similar values and a passion for service; they become part of a network of social support that can catalyze their own growth and development.

History and Structure of the Program

The 1999-2000 academic year marked the change of the Honors Program at UMass, Amherst, into the commonwealth Honors College. In late spring, 1999, IMPACT was created and scheduled with about 10 other Commonwealth College (ComCol) learning communities in residence halls in Orchard Hill. Nine honors students were recruited; they were placed together in a CSL course in the fall (which required them to spend about three hours per week in community service placements of their choice) and were asked to take another CSL course together in the spring.

Now in its third year, the program has become a CSL learning community for the whole campus; it is still run by the honors college, but it is open to both ComCol and non-ComCol students. Before classes begin, IMPACT students go on a weekend retreat together to begin building community and exploring the nature of CSL. They take two classes together in the fall, Introduction to Anthropology and Peer Leadership, and they choose one of three CSL placements for three to four hours each week—working in the after-school program at Ware Middle School; in the free lunch, food pantry, and free store of the Amherst Survival Center; or with senior citizens living at The Arbors. In the spring, they choose one of several CSL courses and meet together in a one-credit weekly integrative seminar.

Living in the residence hall with the IMPACT students is a former IMPACT student who has returned as the Academic Program Assistant, serving as a peer mentor and helping the students develop programming. Co-teaching the Peer Leadership course is an AmeriCorps VISTA volunteer assigned to the campus; she works with the Learning Communities Coordinator and the Director of Community Service Learning to provide further support to the IMPACT students.

Goals of the Program

Like every other learning community on campus, IMPACT has the goal of making the big university smaller—creating a community of learners who take courses together, live close to one another, share common interests, and become a network of social support for each other—thereby enhancing learning and also increasing retention of first-year students. The program has four additional goals:

1. To provide support for students who have a passion for service, so they will be encouraged and enabled to act on that passion
2. To help these students link service and learning through CSL
3. To serve as a reliable source of student workers for community-based organizations that are core partners with the UMass Office of Community Service Learning
4. To serve as a feeder to the Citizen Scholars Program (a more intensive two-year CSL program involving five CSL courses, 60 hours of community service each semester, and a focus on social justice and public policy) and as a support for student leadership regarding CSL

Outcomes

Below are the outcomes for the four specific CSL goals. A study conducted by Tania Mitchell, the program evaluation specialist in the CSL Office, provided data from the 2000-2001 cohort in response to the first two goals:

1. Support for service: The living/learning environment provided significant support for students. Students reported on their relationships with one another, on the ways in which their service experience had become significant, and how they found themselves connected to the larger community.
2. Linking service and learning: This goal requires linking the right courses to the program (see Challenges below), but even without the best match, at least some of the students have met it.
3. Providing student workers to "core partners": The Office of Community Service Learning has entered into relationships with six community-based organizations (CBOs) that it calls its "core partners" in the community. These relationships involve quarterly retreats and substantial additional time planning how CSL can be structured and implemented in ways that meet the needs of both the university and the CBOs. One need articulated by the CBOs is for longterm, dependable student workers. To address this need, two of the three placements for this year's IMPACT students are with the core partners.
4. Feeding the Citizen Scholars Program and providing student leadership for CSL: Two of this year's 19 new Citizen Scholars were in IMPACT last year; one is also the student who returned to work with IMPACT this year as an Academic Program Assistant. We've started on this goal and hope to see it grow.

Challenges

The first cohort of students in IMPACT was recruited without sufficient clarity regarding the expectation of service in the program; several of them complained continuously about this expectation and undermined the integration of service into the IMPACT fall CSL course. The instructor teaching that course did not want to link up with IMPACT the following year, so another first-semester CSL course was designated for the program. Recruiting for that year focused much more clearly on the service component; the 10 students in the program, who were indeed committed to service, strongly critiqued their fall CSL course for not integrating service fully enough into the curriculum.

This year, we have found the right balance between recruiting and curriculum: students are showing a strong commitment to service and appear to see the links between their service experience and the content of their two new IMPACT courses. The Introduction to Anthropology course is taught with a strong emphasis on diversity and social justice, which provides a meaningful context for the students' community service; the Peer Leadership course involves them in collectively planning and organizing a service project, allowing them to try out their leadership skills in service.

Challenges remain. One is recruiting. Planned with a capacity of 24 students, IMPACT has grown over three years from 9 to 16 students. We're still exploring how to make the program more visible in the university's recruiting process and how to reach out directly to catch the attention of high school students who might want this kind of experience.

The new focus on student leadership poses challenges for the Office of Community Service Learning: What structures and roles should it develop to support emerging student leaders and how should it draw on those students in building CSL at UMass?

IMPACT moved this year to a smaller residence hall, occupying much of one floor that also has several single rooms reserved for upper-level students. The space creates the potential for developing a multi-year residential learning community focused on CSL.

Our third challenge, then, is how to seize this potential—what students to recruit, what roles to create, how to build a multi-year CSL learning community.

The Future

Looking past next year, several possibilities beckon. Once the program reaches its maximum of 24 students, might a second CSL learning community be started? Residential learning communities at UMass are limited to first-year students, but could a shared service experience be a basis for building a residential learning community across class years—perhaps especially including former IMPACT students who continue to work at the same service sites? Might the residence hall that IMPACT shares with three other learning communities eventually become a CSL residence hall, with several course/placement combinations that create subcommunities within the population of over 100 students? Might part of this learning community comprise a section of the curricular Alternative Spring Break program, which is currently one of our most successful CSL offerings? Might another part focus on mentoring and tutoring youth—an area in which several CSL initiatives have started over the past year? How might IMPACT link with the other progressive learning communities on campus, such as the student businesses?

In our third year, we've gotten the basic elements of the program established enough that we can begin to dream of the steps after the next steps.

Building Awareness: Environmental Action Projects at Philadelphia University

Anne Todd Bockarie

"What seemed to be a painful activity to be doing on a Friday afternoon turned out to be an experience of a lifetime. It made me feel good about myself in that I was giving back to the community."
—Carrie Sobkow, Fashion Design Major in the Stream Watch Project

Program Development

Philadelphia University has wholeheartedly embraced the concept of service-learning by institutionalizing Environmental Action Projects into the university's general studies program. A pilot research study with 90 first-year non-science majors enrolled in the required environmental science class indicated that students learned more course content, were able to apply the knowledge to their daily lives, participated more actively in class, and received higher course grades if they completed a semester-long, hands-on project with an environmental organization. By linking our students' creative skills in architecture, business, design, fashion, and textiles with community groups to address real world environmental issues in the city, both students and the environment benefited. The projects involve students working between 15 and 25 hours on a current environmental issue that a citizen group is tackling, writing a three-to-five page reflection paper about their experience that includes 10 references from background research, and presenting a poster in class to faculty judges describing what they learned.

From 1999 to 2001, with support from the Philadelphia Higher Education Network for Neighborhood Development and an internal university grant, the Environmental Action Program developed a student handbook, an annual faculty workshop, an environmental projects web site (http://www.philau.edu/ssh/es/Service_Learning.html), a library tutorial on how to research environmental issues (http://www.philau.edu/library), and a partner agency evaluation form to assess student participation. Five part-time faculty members coordinate the projects. The coordinators meet with partner agencies to develop new projects, work with students on finding a project that meets their interests and time commitments, hold in-class discussions on what students are learning, organize poster-session judging, and grade reflection papers.

The program has expanded so that annually more than 600 first-year students and 10 faculty members partner with 40 different government, nonprofit, and grassroots community organizations to improve the environment in the nation's fifth-largest city. The teams work together to catalyze and support community action in recycling and solid waste management, environmental education, wildlife conservation, tree planting and tree health assessment, trail repair, cost analysis of green architecture alternatives, use of endangered species in fashion, graffiti removal, mural arts for urban renewal, restoration of historic structures, and monitoring of drinking water quality, to name just a few project types. Some of the students' more unusual and significant accomplishments include a map of environmental hazards (invasive plants, graffiti, dumping, erosion) in West Park; a cost analysis for aluminum recycling in a HUD housing project; restoration of the roof and windows of Rockland Mansion (built in 1747); designing, planting, and monitoring a butterfly garden on campus; and creation of a web page for K-12 teachers to provide them with background resources for teaching environmental issues.

Future Directions

During the fall 2001 semester, the Environmental Action Program began collaborating with the university's First Year Experience Program (FYE) to increase student motivation outside the intended major. The idea was to have students living together in the residence halls work together as a single class on the same environmental project. Such an arrangement would support the First Year Experience Program's goal of developing social and academic support networks that make the transition to college less traumatic and improve student performance. FYE students were placed in four sections of Environmental Science and worked together with an agency as a single class. Program leaders also hoped that this arrangement would decrease faculty administrative time and increase integration of project topics into the curriculum.

From the very beginning of the semester it quickly became clear that classes with FYE students were more at ease, asked more questions, could more readily work together as a team, and had fewer attendance problems than their non-FYE counterparts. The faculty members teaching these classes and the faculty member coordinating the project were able to focus on one site instead of 20 different agencies, so logistically this approach was much more efficient. Following the fall 2001 semester, we evaluated semester outcomes to see if there were any differences in student learning between the FYE and non-FYE sections and are considering adopting this strategy for the entire program.

Communication Arts I at Samford University
Lynette M. Sandley

Integration of Service-Learning

Communication Arts I and II are interdisciplinary courses that involve communicating effectively through writing, reading, listening, and speaking. The two core curriculum courses also entail computer literacy and primary and secondary research. The Communication Arts I course now includes a service-learning component as well. Our instructors individualize their sections by choosing agencies or issues to be the focus of at least one assignment, and most instructors tie three or even all four of the major assignments to service-learning.

Through partnering with service agencies and organizations in the Birmingham community, our students are exposed to large societal issues such as homelessness, illiteracy, and palliative care for the terminally ill. This past year, they were given the opportunity to engage in real world communication through designing web pages for service agencies, writing profiles of individuals served by agencies, and tutoring children in after-school programs. These are just a few examples of the communication projects that our students were allowed to address. But the end result of the recent redesign of the Communication Arts I course to include service-learning is that consistently, we as faculty have seen far better essays and speeches than we had gotten in the previous three years. Instructors wrote reflection essays at the end of last fall's semester, and over and over, they noted that their students' writing and communication skills were better. In one such reflection, Mary Rees, one of our instructors, noted that "Service-learning provides an intersection between the personal and the public, the felt and the thought, and it is at this intersection where great writing and speaking occur." Rees went on to say that her students had hardly reached the level of Richard Rodriguez, Jonathan Kozol, Nikki Giovanni, or Barbara Ehrenreich in their first semester. But their passion for the social issues being addressed by the service agencies where they worked and their subsequent desire for communication skills to serve those agencies better resulted in their "digging in" and in careful, critical questioning within small groups. In short, they became better at the process of communicating, even if their products still needed work.

At the end of last fall's semester, we held a Celebration of Service, an evening when we heard from instructors, service organization leaders, and students regarding the partnering of the Communication Arts I classes with the Birmingham community. The Celebration of Service was a testament to the success of the inclusion of service-learning within the Communication Arts I course. Students are engaged within both their Samford academic community and the larger Birmingham metropolis, and writing and speaking are improving as a result of the new service-learning component.

Service-Learning Accomplishments From Fall 2000

Below is a list of specific projects students completed during the fall 2000 semester.
- ◆ Students composed group observation papers after serving in Church of the Advent's food ministry. Papers were later published on the church's web site.

- The public awareness brochure was redesigned for Bread and Roses Women and Children's Shelter. Students developed profiles of women served at Bread and Roses to be used by the organization in its fund-raising efforts.
- Students completed an observation assignment interview of a worker at the Birmingham Water Works facility during the 2000 Alabama drought.
- Several students completed a 13-week mentoring course with Safe Harbor, an agency that works with teens involved in gang, occult, and drug activity.
- Students compiled research notebooks to be used both by the Safe Harbor director when talking to parents of troubled teens and by women at Jessie's Place, a women's shelter, for job-readiness training.
- Students undertook cleanup projects, partnering with the Cahaba River Society and Alabama Environmental Council. One result of this service was a campus recycling effort that students will ultimately run themselves.

About the Contributors

Femi I. Ajanaku, assistant professor of sociology at LeMoyne-Owen College, holds the Bonnie Smith Professorship in the Social & Behavioral Sciences. She is also Director of the 2002-2003 SACS Self-Study and volunteer coordinator of the African & African-American women's social activism section that operates out of the College's African and African-American Studies Center. She was among the first faculty members at LeMoyne-Owen to infuse service-learning activity into core and introductory social science courses.

Sylvia Alatorre Alva is a professor of child and adolescent development and the assistant vice president for academic programs at California State University, Fullerton. Her research interests are in the areas of acculturation and ethnic identity and the educational attainment of ethnic minority and college students. She has a Ph.D. in developmental psychology from the University of California, Los Angeles.

Nora Bacon is an assistant professor of English and administrator of the first-year writing program at the University of Nebraska at Omaha. She received her doctoral degree from the University of California at Berkeley. She has taught writing courses since 1977 and has incorporated service-learning assignments since 1989 when she helped pilot the Community Service Writing program at Stanford University. Bacon has written about community-based writing for *College Composition and Communication*, the *Michigan Journal of Community Service Learning*, and the AAHE monograph *Writing the Community: Concepts and Models for Service-Learning in Composition*. She is a senior editor of *Reflections on Community-Based Writing and Learning*.

Anne Todd Bockarie is assistant professor of biology at Philadelphia University. Bockarie holds masters and doctoral degrees in reforestation and forestry extension from the University of Florida. Along with colleagues at Philadelphia, she has developed a hands-on environmental science program for 500-600 first-year students. She is the program director of the Yale-Community Resources monitoring and evaluation team, which has a five-year contract to track park restoration, volunteer programming, and environmental education activities carried out by the Fairmount Park Commission under a grant from the William Penn Foundation. Bockarie has extensive international consulting and training experience in agriculture, forestry, and parks management in Africa and the Caribbean.

Robert G. Bringle (Ph.D., social psychology, University of Massachusetts) is the Chancellor's Professor of Psychology and Philanthropic Studies and director of the Center for Service and Learning at Indiana University-Purdue University Indianapolis. As a social psychologist, he has conducted research on jealousy in close relationships and on educational programs for psychology undergraduates. More recently, his scholarship has focused on implementing and institutionalizing service-learning, the role of service in the academy, and institutional change to support community engagement. He is editor of *With Service in Mind: Concepts and Models for Service-Learning in Psychology* (with D. Duffy), and *Colleges and Universities as Citizens* (with R. Games & E. Malloy). Bringle received the Thomas Ehrlich Faculty Award for Service-Learning in 1998.

Thomas Deans is assistant professor of rhetoric and composition and director of College Writing at Haverford College. He is the author of *Writing Partnerships: Service-Learning in Composition* (NCTE, 2000) and a forthcoming textbook for both first-year and advanced composition, *Writing and Community Action: A Service-Learning Rhetoric and Reader* (Longman). He currently chairs the Service-Learning Committee for the Conference on College Composition and Communication.

Marty Duckenfield received a bachelor of arts from Bates College and a master's degree from Clemson University. A former classroom teacher, she has been at the National Dropout Prevention Center (NDPC) within the College of Health, Education and Human Development, at Clemson University for 14 years where she serves as public information director. In this role, she oversees NDPC publications, including two newsletters and several publications series. Her responsibilities including editing, writing, and production-related activities for the *Linking Learning with Life* series of service-learning booklets and videos. She has been the southern partner in a variety of national service-learning initiatives: the former National Service-Learning Clearinghouse, the National Service-Learning Exchange, and the National Service-Learning in Teacher Education Partnership. Through all these activities, she has had many opportunities to work with middle and high school students and has found that aspect of her work to be the most rewarding.

Barbara S. Frankle is dean of faculty and professor of history at LeMoyne-Owen College, where she has been a faculty member or an administrator since 1971. She holds a Ph.D. in modern comparative history from the University of Wisconsin, Madison, a master of arts in history from the same institution, and a bachelor of arts in Victorian Studies from Mount Holyoke College. A strong supporter of civic involvement, she helped develop service-learning at the College, directing the program from its inception until it became an integral part of the curriculum. She was the principal investigator for significant grants from the Ford Foundation, the Council for Independent Colleges, and the National Corporation for National Service to design, develop, and implement the service-learning program. She was also principal investigator and director of a $950,000 grant from the Lilly Endowment/UNCF HBCU Program to establish a faculty development center focused on student learning. Frankle has made numerous presentations on service learning, faculty development, and diversity issues at national meetings. In April of 2002, she was an invited participant at a Forum on Higher Education and the Public Good sponsored by the Kellogg Foundation.

Andrew Furco is director of the University of California at Berkeley's Service-Learning Research and Development Center and a member of the faculty in Berkeley's Graduate School of Education. He is a Campus Compact Engaged Scholar and currently serves on the National Review Board for the Scholarship of Engagement, the National Service-Learning Partnership Board of Directors, the American Association for Higher Education Service-Learning Consulting Corps, and the Kellogg Learning In Deed Service-Learning Research Advisory Committee. His publications have focused on a variety of issues related to service-learning in K-12 education, teacher education, and higher education and include the book, *Service-Learning: The Essence of the Pedagogy* (co-edited with Shelley H. Billig).

John N. Gardner has led an international movement to enhance the first and senior years on campuses across the country and around the world. He is senior fellow of the National Resource Center for The First-Year Experience and Students in Transition and Distinguished Professor Emeritus of Library and Information Science at the University of South Carolina. From 1974 to 1999, Gardner served as director of the nationally acclaimed University 101 program at the University of South Carolina. He founded the National Resource Center and served as its executive director until 1999. Currently, Gardner serves as executive director of the Policy Center on the First Year of College, funded by grants from The Atlantic Philanthropies and The Pew Charitable Trusts and based at Brevard College, where he is Distinguished Professor of Educational Leadership.

Shannon K. Gilmartin is a doctoral candidate at the University of California, Los Angeles. She is pursuing a doctorate in higher education and organizational change, and her interests center on undergraduate women's intimate relationships, particularly as these affect their adjustment to and development during college. Her research examines the points at which romance, friendship, sex, and schoolwork intersect in the female college student life cycle. She also has conducted research on first- to second-year persistence, survey nonresponse bias, and the wage gap between male and female faculty members. Following a two-year appointment as Project Manager for the Your First College Year (YFCY) pilot studies, she currently serves as the Institutional Review Board liaison for the project and continues to have a hand in collecting, analyzing, and reporting YFCY data.

Julie A. Hatcher (M.S., College Student Personnel Administration, Indiana University) is associate director of the Center for Service and Learning at Indiana University-Purdue University Indianapolis and adjunct instructor at Indiana University's School of Liberal Arts, Philanthropic Studies. Her published work has focused on the institutionalization of service-learning in higher education and the use of reflection activities in service-learning. She is editor of *Service Learning Workshop Curriculum Guide* and *Service Learning Tip Sheets: A Faculty Resource Guide*. She has consulted with numerous campuses on integrating service into academic study and has offered a variety of professional workshops.

Since 2000, **Elaine K. Ikeda** has served as the executive director of California Campus Compact (a statewide coalition of more than 65 college and university presidents committed to helping students develop the values and skills of civic participation through involvement in public service). After receiving her doctorate in higher education from UCLA in 1999, Elaine served as the director of the UCLA Service Learning Clearinghouse Project. She has more than 11 years cumulative experience supervising volunteers in higher education and community settings; disseminating service-learning resource materials to the field; and conducting research regarding service-learning, volunteerism, and community service. Ikeda has organized numerous conferences, dialogues, and forums addressing the civic mission of education (for higher education and K-12), service learning, and civic engagement. She holds a masters degree in public health and has worked for public and not-for-profit community health agencies.

Following two years as a research analyst on the Your First College Year (YFCY) survey at the Higher Education Research Institute (HERI) at UCLA, **Jennifer R. Keup** now serves as the Project Director for YFCY. Recently, Keup completed a major study examining the nexus among first-year students' college expectations, experiences, and adjustment, which drew from longitudinal student interviews as well as nationwide YFCY data. Her other research interests include the influence of first-year seminars on adjustment to college, examining the nature of students' transition from high school to college, and investigating the effect of institutional transformation on student outcomes of college. Jennifer earned her doctorate in higher education and organizational change from UCLA.

Richard Muthiah, (M.A., Counseling, Ball State University) is project associate with the College Student Experiences Questionnaire (CSEQ) and the National Survey of Student Engagement (NSSE), both based at Indiana University Bloomington. Before joining the CSEQ and NSSE staff, he worked at the Center for Service and Learning at Indiana University-Purdue University Indianapolis (IUPUI). Richard is a doctoral candidate in higher education at IU Bloomington, and his dissertation will focus on service-learning. Other areas of interest include out-of-class contributions to student learning, program assessment, study of campus cultures, and Christ-centered thought and practice in higher education.

Kathy O'Byrne is a licensed psychologist and executive director of UCLA's Center for Experiential Education and Service Learning (CEESL). She graduated from Vassar College, earned a master's degree from Arizona State and a doctorate in counseling psychology from the University of Southern California. She provides regular training for community partners, faculty, and students and teaches in the Community-based Research Institute. Her research interests include civic engagement among first-year college students and the assessment of service-learning courses.

Tom O'Connell is professor of political studies at Metropolitan State University and co-founder of the of the university's Center for Community-Based Learning. Tom has had extensive experience developing community-based programs and has conducted numerous seminars and training sessions on university-community partnerships and civic engagement.

Judy Patton is director of University Studies at Portland State University. Before her appointment to UNST, she was a faculty member in the dance department for 18 years, serving as chair for two years. In UNST, she taught Freshman Inquiry, Embracing Einstein's Universe: Language Culture and Relativity and Transfer Transition, Family Studies. Patton established the UNST/High School Collaboration program and taught Senior Inquiry with the Westview High School Einstein team for three years. She is a national fellow with the National Learning Communities Project housed at The Washington Center for Improving the Quality of Undergraduate Education. Patton was a member of the Kellogg Forum of Higher Education Transformation (KFHET), was the Project Director for the Quality Assurance Collaborative (a multi-institutional project with Alverno College, Babson College, Eastern New Mexico University, Mt. St. Mary's College, and Rensselaer Polytechnic Institute) and for the RUSS Project (Restructuring for Urban Student Success) with Portland State University, Temple University, and Indiana University Purdue University at Indianapolis. Her areas of interest and publication are general education, higher education reform, student learning, learning communities, community-based learning, and assessment.

John Reiff has administered, taught in, and written about programs of writing across the curriculum, peace studies, civic arts, and service-learning at the University of Michigan, the University of California at Santa Barbara, Tusculum College, and since 2000, at the University of Massachusetts at Amherst, where he directs the UMass Office of Community Service Learning (OCSL) at Commonwealth College. He teaches courses in the Citizen Scholars Program (a two-year program leading students from direct service to work toward structural change), IMPACT! (a first-year student residential learning community), and the OCSL mentoring initiative. His areas of special interest include preparing students for life-long civic engagement and moving service-learning from community placements to community partnerships. He received a Ph.D. in American Culture from the University of Michigan in 1982.

Armeda C. Reitzel is professor of communications and program leader for linguistics at Humboldt State University. Her research and teaching interests include the first-year experience, oral histories, the communication of and with people who have disabilities, intercultural communication in teacher education and in service-learning, and the rhetoric of Cesar Chavez. She is project director for two Cesar Chavez Day of Service and Learning Grants from the governor's office in the state of California. During fall 2002, Reitzel will complete her own service-learning project—as a volunteer at the New Mexico School for the Visually Impaired. The experience will be used to reshape her courses on communication development in children and on intercultural communication.

Jayne Richmond is dean of University College and Special Academic Programs at the University of Rhode Island. Located in academic affairs, the college has responsibility for all academic support programs including New Student Programs and Orientation, Learning Assistance, International Education, Internships and Experiential Education, Athletic Advising, Academic Advising, and Service Learning. Richmond is also a professor in the College Student Preparation Program. She has established learning communities for the majority of the first-year class, including a required first-year seminar and a required community service component. Her research interests include student retention, learning communities, service-learning, and academic efficacy. She received her Ph.D. from the University of Florida in 1982.

Lynette Moore Sandley is a Co-NeXus Fellow at Samford University in Birmingham, Alabama. Always an advocate of engaged learning, she has worked for the past five years to implement service-learning and problem-based learning into Samford's Communication Arts, an interdisciplinary program integrating rhetoric, critical thinking, and reflection. Sandley's other research interests include nonfiction, creative writing, persuasion, and politics. She is currently working on a FIPSE-sponsored initiative, the Transatlantic Cooperation for Problem-based Learning in the Humanities, which supports a joint problem-based learning project between Samford and Universiteit Maastricht in the Netherlands. For this project, Sandley specifically represents the service-learning initiative within Samford's Communication Arts.

Lori J. Vogelgesang is the director of the Center for Service Learning Research and Dissemination at the Higher Education Research Institute, UCLA. Her current work includes understanding how academic departments become more engaged in their communities, the relationship between service-learning and faculty at a selective research institution, the integration of diversity and service in higher education, and how institutions can use data to examine their success with underrepresented students. Past research includes a national study on how college affects the development of civic values among students of different racial groups and a national study on how service-learning affects students. Before earning her doctorate in higher education, Lori received a master's degree in college student personnel services from the University of Maryland and worked in student affairs. She has also served as an evaluation consultant for domestic and international educational programs.

Dilafruz Williams is professor of educational policies, foundations, and administrative studies at Portland State University, where she teaches courses on a wide range of topics covering philosophy, ecology, cultural diversity, school dropout, and leadership, among others. In her role as director of Community-University Partnerships, she extended the reach of community-based learning, promoting faculty development and providing leadership for community outreach. She is co-founder of the Environmental Middle School, a special-focus school in the Portland Public School District. She co-directs a USDE-FIPSE project entitled Civic Capacity Initiative. She has published on the importance of community, ecological education, and cultural diversity in her latest co-edited book (with Gregory Smith), *Ecological Education in Action: On Weaving Education, Culture and the Environment*. Her other publications and chapters have related themes: nonviolence and Gandhi's philosophy of education, community-university-school partnerships, service-learning and political involvement, inclusive education, among many others. She recently received the national Thomas Ehrlich Faculty Award for Service-Learning.

Edward Zlotkowski is founder of the Bentley College Service-Learning Center near Boston, Massachusetts. Zlotkowski is professor of English at Bentley College. He is a senior associate at the American Association for Higher Education (AAHE) and a senior faculty fellow at Campus Compact. He has also served as editor of an 18-volume series on service-learning in the academic disciplines. His book *Successful Service-Learning Programs* was published in 1998 by Anker.

Additional Titles from
the National Resource Center for The First-Year Experience &
Students in Transition

Monograph 28. *Using National Newspapers in the College Classroom: Resources to Improve Teaching and Learning.* Steven R. Knowlton and Betsy O. Barefoot, Editors. This volume includes articles written by more than 40 colleges and university faculty members in a variety of disciplines. The authors describe how national newspapers have become an essential resource in their classrooms for engaging students as critical readers of media, making connections between course content and current national/international events, enlivening instruction by adding immediacy and relevance, and engendering the habit of daily newspaper reading. 106 pages. ISBN 1-889271-29-2. $30.00. 1999.

Monograph 26. *Learning Communities: New Structures, New Partnerships for Learning.* Jodi H. Levine, Editor. Learning communities have become one of the most widely used structures for achieving both academic and social integration of new students. Chapters in this monograph, authored by experienced learning community professionals, describe various successful models, link theory with examples of good practice, and describe how learning communities can facilitate faculty development. In addition, chapter authors outline strategies for dealing with logistical concerns and provide comprehensive resource listings and recommendations for building learning community programs. 180 pages. ISBN 1-889271-27-6. $30.00. 1999.

Monograph 17. *Beyond Critical Thinking: Teaching the Thinking Skills Necessary to Academic and Professional Success.* William T. Daly, Editor-in-Chief. William T. Daly expands the familiar concepts of critical thinking to include "independent thinking," arguing that many of the mental activities required for independent thinking run counter to the way the human brain actually works. The monograph includes classroom strategies for providing students needed experience in higher order thinking skills. 29 pages. ISBN 1-889271-14-4. $20.00. 1995.

Learning Interdependence: A Case Study of the International/Intercultural Education of First-Year College Students. David J. Bachner, Laurence J. Malone, and Mary C. Snider. Challenging the notion that study abroad programs are best suited for "mature" students, faculty and administration at Hartwick College designed an intercultural, interdisciplinary course for first-year students, spanning an entire academic year. The book includes information on program development and student outcomes, with an appendix featuring syllabi from six courses based on the model. As we struggle with the meaning of education on an increasingly connected planet, this book offers a bold new way of thinking about teaching and learning in the first college year. 203 pages. ISBN 1-889271-35-7. $30.00. 2001.

Moral Action in Young Adulthood. Ralph L. Mosher, David Connor, Katherine M. Kalliel, James M. Day, Norma Yokota, Mark R. Porter, and John M. Whiteley. This book is an extension of the Sierra Project which began at the University of California, Irvine in the mid-1970's. The original Sierra Project was both a curricular development initiative for first-year college students and a longitudinal study of growth and development of character over four years of undergraduate study. In this groundbreaking follow up, the researchers have returned to the original Sierra students to measure their continuing growth in moral reasoning and to understand the nature and meaning of moral action in response to the moral dilemmas inherent in everyday life. 280 pages. ISBN 1-889271-26-8. $30.00. 1999.

Use the order form on the next page to order any of these titles from
the National Resource Center.

Use this form to order additional copies of this monograph or to order other titles from the National Resource Center for The First-Year Experience & Students in Transition.

Prices advertised in this publication are subject to change.

Item	Quantity	Price	Total
Monograph 34. *Service-Learning and the First-Year Experience*		$35.00	
Monograph 28. *Using National Newspaper*		$40.00	
Monograph 26. *Learning Communities*		$30.00	
Monograph 17. *Beyond Critical Thinking*		$20.00	
Learning Independence		$30.00	
Moral Action in Young Adulthood		$30.00	
		Shipping and Handling	
		Total	

*Call for shipping charges on this item.

Shipping Charges:	Order Amount	Shipping Cost
U.S.	$0 - $50	$ 6.50 US
	$50 - $150	$10.00 US
	over $150	$15.00 US

Customers outside the U.S. will be billed exact shipping charges plus a $5.00 processing fee. Fax or e-mail us to obtain a shipping estimate. Be sure to include a list of items you plan to purchase and to specify your preference for Air Mail or UPS delivery.

Name _____   Department _____

Institution _____   Telephone _____

Mailing Address _____

City _____ State/Province _____ Postal Code _____

E-mail Address _____

Select your option payable to the University of South Carolina:

❏ Check Enclosed   ❏ Institutional Purchase Order   Purchase Order No._____

Credit Card: ❏ *VISA*   ❏ *MasterCard*   ❏ *Discover*   Expiration Date: _____

Card No. _____

Name of Cardholder _____

Signature _____

Mail this form to: National Resource Center for The First-Year Experience & Students in Transition, University of South Carolina, 1629 Pendleton Street, Columbia, SC 29208. Phone (803) 777-6229. FAX (803) 777-4699. E-mail burtonp@gwm.sc.edu Federal ID 57-6001153.